The publisher gratefully acknowledges the generous contribution to this book provided by the S. Mark Taper Foundation.

Who Are the Jews of India?

Who Are the
Jews of India?

Nathan Katz

UNIVERSITY OF CALIFORNIA PRESS
Berkeley · *Los Angeles* · *London*

University of California Press
Berkeley and Los Angeles, California

University of California Press, Ltd.
London, England

Library of Congress Cataloging-in-Publication Data

Katz, Nathan.

   Who are the Jews of India? / Nathan Katz.

      p. cm.—(S. Mark Taper Foundation imprint
   in Jewish studies)
      Includes bibliographical references (p.) and
   index.
      ISBN 0-520-21323-8 (cloth : alk. paper)
      1. Jews—India—History.   2. Jews—India—
   Identity.   3. India—Ethnic relations.   4. Bene-
   Israel.   I. Title.

   DS135.16 K38 2000
   954'.004924—dc21

                              00-042617

Manufactured in the United States of America

09   08   07   06   05   04   03   02   01   00

10   9   8   7   6   5   4   3   2   1

for E.S.G.

Contents

List of Illustrations   ix

Acknowledgments   xiii

Introduction   1

1. A Balanced Identity: The Jews of Cochin   9
2. An Identity Transformed: The Bene Israel   90
3. An Identity Aloof: Baghdadi Jews of the Raj   126

Conclusion   161

Notes   167

Glossary   185

References   191

Index   201

Illustrations

Map of India   xi

1. Sattu Koder addressing His Highness Rava Varma, the maharajah of Cochin, 1949   16

2. The copper plates granting autonomy to Joseph Rabban, leader of the Jews of Cranganore   34

3. View from a window in the maharajah of Cochin's palace, 1986   39

4. Interior of the Cochin Synagogue, 1986   41

5. Shalom Cohen praying in the Cochin Synagogue, 1987   43

6. The eternal light (*ner tamid*) before the Holy Ark in the Cochin Synagogue, 1986   44

7. Yechezkel Rahabi, Jewish merchant-prince of Cochin   51

8. Jewish men of Cochin, early twentieth century   56

9. Prime Minister Indira Gandhi greeted in the Cochin Synagogue, 1968   58

10. Jewish funeral in Chendamangalam, circa 1940s   66

11. Yosef Hallegua sounding the shofar for Rosh Hashanah in the Cochin Synagogue, 1986   83

12. Different styles of Bene Israel male dress, Bombay, early twentieth century   92

13. Bene Israel family pressing oil in Revdanda, 1992   94

14. Malida ceremony at Khandala, 1987   104

15.   Bene Israel couple, Karachi, 1902   117
16.   *Lal Dewal* (Red Temple) Ohel David Synagogue,
      Pune, 1987   127
17.   Beth-El Synagogue, Calcutta, 1987   134
18.   Moses Elias in his home in Calcutta, 1986   137
19.   Shaikh David Sassoon   138
20.   Kenesseth Eliyahoo Synagogue, Bombay, 1987   140

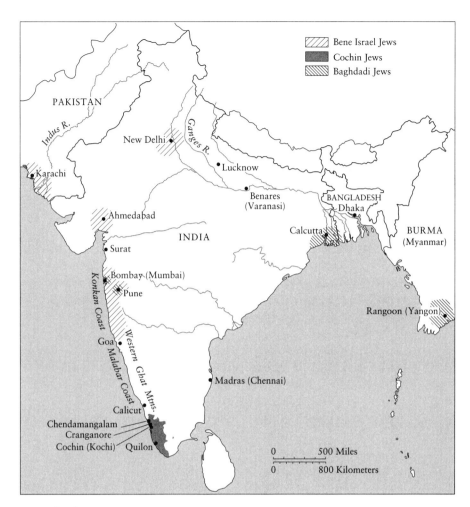

Map of India

Acknowledgments

My deepest and loving thanks to my wife, Ellen S. Goldberg, coauthor of *The Last Jews of Cochin* and coresearcher not only for that book but also for much of what is found in this one. The study of Indian Jews has led us both on an unanticipated spiritual journey into Judaism.

My thanks to those of my teachers who encouraged my interest in Indo-Judaica long before it became fashionable—the late Bibhuti S. Yadav, Maurice S. Friedman, Elie Wiesel, Daniel J. Elazar (*zichron l'baracha* [z"l], of blessed memory), and Zalman M. Schachter.

I am indebted to the Council for International Exchange of Scholars and the United States Educational Foundation in India for a senior Fulbright research grant, 1986–1987, which enabled us to visit Jewish communities in Kochi (Cochin), Mumbai (Bombay), Pune, Ahmedabad, Delhi, Calcutta, Yangon (Rangoon), and Chennai (Madras). We first visited Cochin in 1984, and again in 1997, the last time with our son, Rafael Yehiel. Friends/informants in India made this work meaningful as well as possible, and I thank Jacob (z"l) and Sarah Cohen, Sattu Koder (z"l), Gladys Koder, Sammy and Queenie Hallegua, Gamliel and Reema Salem, Raymond Salem (z"l), Jackie Cohen (z"l), I. S. Hallegua, Kenneth Salem, Pearlie Simon Hallegua, Elias Koder (z"l), P. M. Jussay, and Dr. Blossom Hallegua of Cochin; Prem Doss Yehudi of Trivandrum; Dilip Patwardhan, Ben and Sally Affif, Ralphy and Yael Jhirad, Clement Aron, Nissim Ezekiel, and Sophy Kelly of Mumbai; Ezra Kohlet (z"l),

Ezekiel Isaac Malekar, and Sharada Nayak of New Delhi; the late Ashin Dasgupta, Uma Dasgupta, and Norman Nahoum (z"l) of Calcutta; Jack Samuels of Yangon; and Ranjeet Henry of Chennai.

My sincere thanks to Douglas Abrams Arava, who first suggested writing this book, and to Reed Malcolm, who saw it through the publishing process. My thanks also to my friend and neighbor, Erica Meyer Rauzin, for copyediting, and to Danielle Sharon, Hebrew instructor at Florida International University, for checking over the romanized Hebrew.

The author is grateful to the following publishers and individuals for permission to quote from published and unpublished materials: To Sattu S. Koder for permission to quote from his many articles; to Judith Elias Cooper for permission to quote from *The Jews of Calcutta: The Autobiography of a Community, 1798–1982,* coauthored with Flower Elias; to Joan G. Roland for permission to quote from *Jews in British India: Identity in a Colonial Age;* to Esmond D. Ezra for permission to quote from *Turning Back the Pages: A Chronicle of Calcutta Jewry;* to Orient Longman Limited of Hyderabad, India, for permission to quote from Benjamin J. Israel, *The Bene Israel of India: Some Studies;* to Shalva Weil for permission to quote from "Bene Israel Jews in Lod, Israel: A Study of the Persistence of Ethnicity and Ethnic Identity"; to Oxford University Press for permission to quote from Stanley A. Wolpert, *A New History of India,* 4th edition; to the Maxwell School of Citizenship and Public Affairs of Syracuse University for permission to quote from Holly Baker Reynolds's article "The Auspicious Married Woman," in Susan S. Wadley, editor, *The Powers of Tamil Women;* to Rabbi Ezekiel N. Musleah for permission to quote from *On the Banks of the Ganga: The Sojourn of Jews in Calcutta;* to Indiana University Press for permission to quote from David Mandelbaum, "The Jewish Way of Life in Cochin," in *Jewish Social Studies* 1/4; to Shirley Berry Isenberg for permission to quote from *India's Bene Israel: A Comprehensive Inquiry and Sourcebook;* to Barbara C. Johnson for permission to quote from both her M.A. thesis and Ph.D. dissertation.

I am also most grateful to the following individuals and institutions for permission to use photographs of or by them: To Ellen S. Goldberg for permission to use her photographs, which are identified in the book; to Frederic Brenner for permission to use the photograph of Moses Elias; to the Israel Museum's ethnography department for photographs of turn-of-the-last-century Cochin Jews and of an early-twentieth-century Bene Israel family, for Joan Roth's photograph of oil pressers of the

Konkan, for the photographs of the Bene Israel couple from Karachi and of the statue of David Sassoon, all of which appeared in the catalogue *The Jews of India;* to Sattu and Gladys Koder for the photographs of himself and the maharajah of Cochin, of Mrs. Gandhi in the synagogue, and the portrait of Yechezkel Rahabi; to Tova Sofer and Reuven Sofer for the photograph of turn-of-the-last-century Cochin Jews; to P. A. Aron for the funeral photograph; and to my friends who appear in the photographs and gave permission to have them published in this book.

Introduction

My uncle was the kosher butcher in Camden, New Jersey, where I grew up. I remember so clearly how he would take me aside and, with more seriousness than his jovial personality generally allowed, tell me, "Always remember. Always remember that you are a *kohen.*"

I wasn't altogether sure what a kohen was, but I remember that at my grandfather's funeral my father, uncles, brothers, and I had to stand outside the cemetery gate as he was interred. The mourners then walked toward us and the memorial prayer was intoned. I felt pained at being excluded from the grave site but proud to be among an elite. Later, I learned that a kohen is a hereditary priest in Judaism and that *kohanim* are said to be descendants of Aharon, the brother of Moshe (Moses).

The combination of story and ritual has always fascinated me. The story of Aharon and his sons makes the rituals of the kohanim—Judaism's attenuated priesthood—real and intimate. Many generations have passed this secret of kohenite ancestry along to the next just as my uncle did. A whisper, a knowing gaze convey the sense that this is an important secret, so important that it has been safeguarded orally for three thousand years.

As I developed my critical faculties, I began to wonder whether this oral transmission could be accurate in any literal sense. Studying myths and legends, I was awed by their cognitive power, their ability to organize the inchoate data of perceptions into meaningful experiences. A myth, I was taught, was neither true nor false. Its cognitive power, instead, lay in the majestic sweep of its vision. Perhaps so, but a generation of scholars learned that myths and legends, and the rituals that enact them, are constructed to justify and perpetuate power relationships in society.

That was my orientation about fifteen years ago, when my wife and I began to study Indian Jewish communities and immediately encountered legends in the field. The Cochin Jews claim to have originated in Jerusalem, having fled the Roman invasion and destruction of the Second Temple in 70 c.e. The Bene Israel say their ancestors' sailing vessel from ancient Israel was shipwrecked off the Konkan coast. We interpreted these stories in terms of how they helped shape an Indian Jewish identity, borrowing status-generating motifs from both Indic and Judaic civilizations. While we affirm this previous analysis, I also recognize how unsatisfying it may be in the light of new data.

Recently two researchers at the University of London's Center for Genetic Anthropology announced that they had isolated a "kohen gene," or Y-chromosome to be more precise, which indicates a common paternal ancestor: presumably Aharon of the Bible.[1] Scientific research was confirming what my uncle had whispered. The issue is much greater than whether my ancestor was actually Aharon. The issue is the historical significance of traditional legends, Jewish or otherwise. The self-perceptions not only of contemporary kohanim, but of all traditional peoples, are the stakes behind the kohen gene.

As if the researchers anticipated my next question, the same study revealed genetic kinship among Jews from Yemen, Lemba tribespeople of southern Africa, and the Bene Israel. What for years had been assumed to be *merely* a myth, this DNA research suggests, has a scientific basis. If the Bene Israel are related to the Yemenite Jews, then their story of a shipwreck is credible. The study gave oral history itself unanticipated confirmation.

This book takes this intersection of myth and ritual as a basis for exploring the three major Jewish communities in India: the Cochin Jews of the Malabar Coast, the Bene Israel Jews of greater Bombay, and the "Baghdadi" Jews (the term applied in India to Jewish immigrants from the Arabic- and Persian-speaking worlds, whether actually from Baghdad or not) of India's port cities, especially Calcutta and Bombay. It focuses on questions of identity—how these three distinct communities came to their individual senses of self, how historical and social forces mediated the Jewish and Indian poles of their identity, and how this identity is established and expressed in historical legend and religious ritual.

This book attempts to get at these questions from the inside, to understand how these two great and ancient civilizations, Indic and Judaic, interact within the very being of India's Jews.

In their legends and in their synagogue life, Indian Jews developed identities that reflected and generated high status. Creating this identity was a reciprocal process involving their neighbors as well as themselves. To fit into the highly stratified Indian society, the Jews obviously needed to have their status confirmed by local high-status groups. These "reference groups," as I call them, were different for each Indian Jewish community, which in part accounts for their distinctiveness from one another.[2]

In seeking a comfortable home in exile, India's Jewish communities are very much like Jewish communities everywhere. As in most places, proximity to and emulation of high-status groups confer status. India's cultural conditions were unique, but the Jewish acculturational process resembled general patterns elsewhere in the Diaspora.

A crucial distinction between India and the rest of the Diaspora, however, is that in India acculturation is not paid for in the currency of assimilation. By *acculturation* I mean fitting comfortably into a society while retaining one's own identity, whereas by *assimilation* I mean that the loss of that identity is a perceived condition for acceptance. The study of Indian Jewish communities demonstrates that in Indian culture an immigrant group gains status precisely by maintaining its own identity. Such is the experience not only of India's Jews, but also of local Christians, Zoroastrians, and recently, Tibetan Buddhists. This striking feature of Indian civilization is reflected by each of these immigrant groups. Legends that narrate their sojourns in India begin with a local ruler's welcoming them on the condition that they preserve their unique religious and cultural traditions. Like these other foreign groups, the Jews made their places in India in part by fidelity to their own traditions, by being good Jews.

In this sense, Indian conditions differ from those in other hospitable corners of the Diaspora, such as America and China. Success for American and Chinese Jews demands mastery of Gentile learning—whether the dreaded SAT examinations in the contemporary United States, which heavily influence admissions to America's elite universities, or the Confucian-based civil service examinations of traditional China, which were decisive for admission to the Mandarinate. As a caste-bound society, India has no monolithic cultural paradigm, Ivy or Mandarin, to impose on its minorities. Instead, India demands—even legislates in its oldest law code, the *Manushastra*—that the foreigner remain true to himself, and if he and members of his community preserve their own traditions, then the group becomes elevated in esteem and social ranking.[3] In short, Indian Jews face challenges and opportunities unlike those elsewhere in the Diaspora.

Jews navigated the eddies and shoals of Indian culture very well. They never experienced anti-Semitism or discrimination at Indian hands. They contributed to Indian civilization in a variety of secular arts, in medicine, commerce and industry, cinema, politics, agriculture, and the military. They contributed to Judaic civilization by composing liturgical songs in Hebrew and folk songs in local languages, by writing rabbinical opinions as well as secular poetry and novels, and by developing creative ritual behaviors within the context of Judaic law. Generally they were pious, and piety of any variety is esteemed in India. Indian Jews lived as all Jews should have been allowed to live: free, proud, observant, creative and prosperous, self-realized, full contributors to the host community. Then, when twentieth-century conditions permitted, they returned en masse to Israel, which they had always proclaimed to be their true home despite India's hospitality.

The Indian chapter is one of the happiest of the Jewish Diaspora. Understanding how Jews made their place in three very different Indian contexts—Cochin (now Kochi), Bombay (now Mumbai), and Calcutta—casts light not only on India and its Jews, but on the Jewish Diaspora and Jewish identity as a whole. It illustrates how identity is formed, and provides analogies to the western Jewish experience. To western Jews, Indian Jews are simultaneously very familiar and very foreign, *hamische* (pleasantly homey) and exotic. Knowledge of the ways Jews maintained continuity in India indicates how American Jews might do the same. It also demonstrates something of particular relevance today: that not all Gentiles have treated Jews harshly.

Here we encounter the error of the facile equation of Jewish culture with western civilization; Jews are not western, but global. Jewish history does not begin and end in Europe. It is also richly Asian, both in origin and destiny. Thus, the Jewish experience in India modifies our understanding of Jewishness and of immigrant identity.

At the same time, learning about Indian Jews offers a fresh, enlivening perspective about India. Working from a "familiar" (Jewish) standpoint clarifies what is distinctively Indian about India. A colleague of mine developed an introductory course on Japan that illustrates the value of this perspective. This professor took baseball as a standpoint, reasoning that the familiar game would provide a perspective on a great culture. One of his textbooks was *You Gotta Have Wa*, a juxtaposition of a familiar Broadway song, "You Gotta Have Heart" from *Damn Yankees*, with an alien concept, *Wa*, which means "harmony" or perhaps "teamwork."[4] The rules of baseball are the same in America as in Japan, just as *Halachah* (Judaic law) is the same, or close enough, in America and India. But in America baseball is a sport of individual achievement, of batting averages and home run records and ERAs, and in Japan it is quintessentially a team effort. It is still baseball, the rules are the same, but the ethos of the sport is transformed by its cultural context.[5] The American adage is that the squeakiest wheel gets the grease, but Japanese youngsters are taught that the tallest blade of grass is the first to be cut down. This context is highlighted when viewed from the standpoint of the familiar. So, too, with Judaism. It is the "same" religion in America and India, with the same rules and liturgies, but its ethos is transformed in India.

Take another example: a Jewish community thrived in Middle Kingdom China during medieval times. Like the Jews of Cochin, the Jews of Kaifeng were never persecuted. They were prosperous and pious; they practiced commerce and excelled in government service, agriculture, and the military. They, too, were *Halachic* Jews, knowledgeable about Judaic law and observant. When they reconstructed their synagogue in 1488 after a flood of the Yellow River, they erected a stele as was the custom in China. On this stele they engraved their self-perception of Judaism: "Although our religion agrees in many respects with the religion of the literati [Confucianism], from which it differs in a slight degree, yet the main design of it is nothing more than reverence for Heaven and veneration for ancestors, fidelity to the prince, and obedience to parents."[6] Even the metaphor they used for God, "Heaven," was apt. Both cultures use it as a metaphor for God, expressed in Chinese as *T'ien* and in Hebrew as *Shamayim*.

This is how the Kaifeng Jews put their Judaism in a nutshell. Nothing about it is alien to Judaism, but these are not the elements of the religion an American Jew would be likely to single out as the essence of Judaism. Or an Indian Jew for that matter. But for the Chinese Jews, it was natural to highlight those motifs from their religion which were most consonant with the Confucian host culture. Doing so, they illuminate the core values of China's Middle Kingdom during the late fifteenth century. In a similar vein, an American Jew might highlight monotheism and social ethics as quintessential Judaic values, and as we shall learn from the

Cochin Jews, in India the bedrock Judaic issues are purity and displays of royal pageantry. These are all Judaic values, but those that immigrant communities emphasize are those most resonant with the hospitable host culture. Baseball may be baseball, but Yokohama isn't San Francisco.

The period from 1985 to 1995 was a groundbreaking era for the study of Indian Jewish communities and offers interested readers several other sources to pursue. The last half of the 1980s saw the publication of three important books: *Jews in India,* a volume of studies edited by Thomas A. Timberg; *Jews in British India: Identity in a Colonial Age,* Joan G. Roland's insightful analysis of the tortured relationship between the Bene Israel and Baghdadi Jews in Bombay; and *India's Bene Israel: A Comprehensive Inquiry and Sourcebook,* Shirley Berry Isenberg's encyclopedic study. In the 1990s my wife, Ellen S. Goldberg, and I wrote *The Last Jews of Cochin: Jewish Identity in Hindu India,* an analytical study of the Cochin Jews' history and religious life, and J. B. Segal authored *A History of the Jews of Cochin.* Four memoirs of the Calcutta community were published: Rabbi Ezekiel N. Musleah's *On the Banks of the Ganga: The Sojourn of Jews in Calcutta,* Esmond D. Ezra's *Turning Back the Pages: A Chronicle of Calcutta Jewry,* Mavis Hyman's *Jews of the Raj,* and Solly Solomon's *Hooghly Tales: Stories of Growing Up in Calcutta under the Raj.* Ruby Daniel wrote a book of reminiscences about Cochin with Barbara C. Johnson, *Ruby of Cochin: An Indian Jewish Woman Remembers.* Indian Jews were featured in a number of novels as well, including Anita Desai's *Baumgartner's Bombay,* a story about a German Jewish refugee; Gay Courter's *Flowers in the Blood,* a romance about the opium trade; Amitav Ghosh's acclaimed postmodern novel, *In an Antique Land;* Salman Rushdie's *The Moor's Last Sigh;* and Esther David's *The Walled City,* heralded as India's first Jewish novel. In 1995 Jerusalem's Israel Museum held a major exhibition about Indian Jewry and published an attractive catalogue, *The Jews of India,* edited by Orpa Slapak.

Late-twentieth-century studies were distinguished from earlier work in the field by the emergence of an intellectual context for the study of Indian Jewish communities. Once relegated to the "exotic" nooks and crannies of Jewish studies, the study of Indian Jewry has become central to the field of Indo-Judaic studies, which offers a new way of looking at both worlds.

The very marginality of Jews as India's tiniest minority, and simultaneously the marginality of India as home to one of the smallest Jewish communities in the world, has tremendous cognitive powers. Once one considers the experience of India's Jews seriously—which is to say, as soon as one ceases to trivialize them as an exotic curiosity—both India and Judaism are forever changed. Both civilizations reconfigure themselves. What may be accidental to Judaism in America becomes central in India. What might be an Indian cultural afterthought, if only the usual religions of Hinduism and Buddhism are considered, becomes highlighted when a Jewish perspective is included. Indeed, all of India's extrinsic religions (Judaism, Christianity, Islam, and Zoroastrianism) force us to look at India in a new way, but by virtue of its microscopic size, the Jewish experience can be the proverbial fly on the wall in India's cultural palaces.[7]

ONE

A Balanced Identity

The Jews of Cochin

Crows caw, fans whirl, and bats flutter in the Cochin Synagogue. The blue-willow-pattern floor tiles cool the bare feet of the men who gently sway from side to side as they chant the haunting melodies of the unique Cochini prayer service. On this sultry Saturday in March 1984, in the women's section upstairs, Sarah Cohen says to my wife, "Listen. There's something going on at the Hindu temple next door." She closes her eyes and adds, "We can hear their prayers, and they can hear us, too," her smile expressing the belief that the commingling of Hebrew and Sanskrit prayers is more a harmony than a cacophony. For at least a thousand years and perhaps twice as long, a small number of Jews have made their home along the tropical Malabar Coast of southwestern India. Pious and faithful to the traditions of their people, they have creatively interacted with the tolerant host culture in their social, commercial, and religious lives.

When people learn that my wife and I spent a year with the Jews of Cochin, they inevitably ask, "Are they Jewish *or* are they Indian?" The question appears innocent enough, but it reveals manifold inappropriate assumptions about Judaism, identity, and history. The identity of the Jews of Cochin is seamless: they are simultaneously fully Indian and fully Jewish. Their experience eschews the facile dichotomy between East and West, as they are firmly rooted in two great civilizations, Indic and Judaic. Thus, the Cochin Jews exemplify a successfully acculturated identity. They have neither submerged their Jewishness by assimilating into their host culture nor used their Jewishness as a refuge from a hostile Gentile host society. The Cochin Jews have cultivated their finely balanced identity in the affectionate cultural embrace of their Hindu, Christian, and Muslim neighbors. Sarah Cohen's comment provides an apt metaphor for the Cochin Jews' place in the Hindu society of Kerala, the modern name of their state: side-by-side but not submerged, acculturated but not assimilated.

Their experience shows how a microscopically small minority can preserve its religious and cultural identity without either rejecting or being overwhelmed by the larger society. This achievement owes much to the tolerance of the Hindu culture of Kerala and to the resourcefulness and creativity of the Cochin Jews. Three mechanisms are of note:

First, the Jews of Cochin articulated a narrative about themselves, a legend filled with motifs that generate status in both the Judaic and the Indic worlds.

Second, they emulated and thereby affirmed the social hierarchy of Kerala.

Third, they judiciously borrowed symbolic and ritual motifs from the local Hindu culture and enacted them in their own ritual life, within the framework of Judaic law (*Halachah*).

These mechanisms correlate with features of Indic civilization, mirroring an Indic sense of place and history, India's underlying hierarchical social structure, and the twin poles of its ritually generated status: the ascetic and the royal. Specifically, the Jews adapted the religious behaviors and symbol complexes of two significant Hindu reference groups: the dominant Nayar caste (particularly the local royal family) and, from a distance, the Nambudiris, the highest brahmin caste of Kerala.

LEGENDS, RIVALRY, AND RITUAL

Who one *is* depends upon who one *has been*. People know themselves as members of a community, and a community understands itself in relation to the larger society. To achieve a place in the Hindu-dominated yet cosmopolitan world of Kerala, the Jews constructed a sentimental narrative of their past, creating legends to explain their self-understanding. For this socially well-positioned yet tiny Jewish community in venerable

India, history became a matter of prestige, in both Jewish and Hindu terms. The Cochin Jews' legends articulate a twofold *yichus* (lineage), emphasizing continuity with two sacred places, ancient Israel and their local ancestral home of Cranganore, or as it is known in medieval Jewish geography, Shingly.

This tale of antique origins and long-standing honor emerges in their folk songs in the Malayalam language, in their unique Hebrew songs, or *shirot,* in their relatively recent autohistorical (*toldot*) writings, in ten paintings commissioned for the synagogue's quatercentenary celebrations in 1968, in conversations, in tourist guidebooks, and mostly in memories and legends.[1] This selective narrative emphasizes both Jewish and Indian status. The paintings encapsulate numerous complex events in ten serial images. Most of the legend cannot be corroborated or disproved by what little we know of ancient and medieval Kerala history. It tantalizingly weaves plausibility upon plausibility, so that it cannot be dismissed as legend or fiction. Like all myths, its power lies not in its historic facts, but in its sweep of vision. It conveys a basic metaphor of identity, a structure through which the data of history are organized to achieve meaning, thus revealing much of whom the Cochin Jews understand themselves to be, and therefore of whom they actually are.

As individual narrative constructions of self order their past experiences, so the Cochin Jews constructed a balanced, Indian-Jewish identity in part by narrating a story that interwove Jerusalem with Cranganore and that emphasized their high status and proximity to the maharajahs. They created a charming tale of honor and affection, of spices and piety.

There is a complex relationship between the artifacts of the Cochin Jews' history and their narration, which partially depends upon those artifacts. While the data can be used to justify their narration, they could justify other narratives as well. Indeed, Cochin Jews have offered varying narratives in varying circumstances. To tell their story, therefore, is to interweave artifacts and narrative. One is warp, the other woof, in a tapestry of meaning, a myth that creates identity.

In this chapter we begin with the most recent, most "standard," of the community's stories and compare it with the stories of Kerala's Christians, Muslims, and Hindus in order to discern patterns of narrative meaning specific to Kerala. Those other local religious communities were important for the Jews, who looked upon the higher castes as role models. We will also examine briefly the deep background of the artifacts of history and describe the relevant ancient connections between India and

West Asia as revealed through archaeology and assorted texts. Then we will consider how Cochin's Jews organized these artifacts.

This brings us to the one aspect of culture in which the Cochin Jews willfully violated Judaic norms in favor of Hindu sensibilities. In straining to emulate Hindu social organization, Cochin's Jews practiced a form of discrimination against one another, the infamous "Jewish Apartheid." As legend is the first way Cochin Jews created identity, this rivalry between the so-called black Jew and white Jew factions is the second, and their ritual life is the third. Certain unique Cochini ritual customs, especially their observances of Simchat Torah, weddings, and Passover, bear an unmistakable Hindu stamp;[2] however, the Cochin Jews were knowledgeable enough to incorporate these borrowings from Hinduism within a strict Judaic framework.

These three strategies articulated and celebrated the Cochin Jews' Indian-Jewish identity: the narration of an appropriate historical legend, the reflection of Hindu social hierarchy that set Jew against Jew, and the adaptation of Hindu temple behaviors and symbols into synagogue life.

LEGENDARY ORIGINS: HISTORY IN TEN IMAGES

The celebrations commemorating the quatercentenary of the Cochin Synagogue in 1968 were a watershed event in the community.[3] They brought newspaper reporters from around India and the world and scholars from universities in Kerala, as well as from London, New York, and Berkeley. Prime Minister Indira Gandhi came from New Delhi to wish the community a *mazal tov*.[4] At the very moment the seeds of the community's demise were planted, it held a celebration of unprecedented proportions, reveling in the past just as the future became most ominous. The lure of Israel was too great, just as the pressures of life in newly independent India were too strenuous. The celebrations of 1968 were but a lull between waves of immigration to Israel.

Local artist S. S. Krishna emblazoned the community's history onto ten large canvases, a focal point for the exhibition and seminar planned for the anniversary. These paintings crystallized the community's identity before the world.[5] Today, they hang in a storeroom of the synagogue, soon to be forgotten—like the moment more than thirty years ago when they were proudly displayed for all the world to see.

The first painting shows a bazaar filled with spices and ivory, a shipping entrepôt of the ancient world. It is Shingly, the Jews' ancestral home, known in Malayalam as Kodungallur, in Anglo-Indian as Cranganore, and to the Romans as Muziris. The caption reads, "There was trade between King Solomon's Palestine (992–952 B.C.) and Malabar coast. The Biblical name for India was 'Odhu' [Hodu]. Teak, ivory, spice and peacocks were exported to Palestine." This establishes a linkage between India and Israel long before the birth of the Cochin community, grafting the entire history of the community onto yet earlier traditions and making the splendor of Solomon's reign the taproot of glory for the Jewish princes of Shingly.

The second painting depicts Herod's Temple ablaze, Jews fleeing in all directions. In the lower right of the painting a ship sails east, to Shingly. The moment of the birth of the Diaspora is also the moment of the birth of Indian Jewry. "Destruction of the Second Temple in 70 A.D. by the Romans," the caption reads, "and the consequent dispersal of the Jews to the four corners of the earth from Palestine."

In the third painting, a ship full of biblical-looking Jews is about to land on a verdant, hospitable coast. Lest there be any doubt, the lower right corner displays a map of India, an arrow pointing toward Shingly: "Landing of the Jews at Shingly (Cranganore) in 72 A.D." A fourth canvas depicts a king greeting the Jews amid graceful palm tress. He is attired like an idealized Nayar maharajah, his retinue holding the royal parasol and beating royal drums. "The raja of Cranganore receives the Jews," the caption simply states.

The fifth painting embellishes the theme of the Jews' hospitable reception in India. A Jew—their leader, Joseph Rabban—is in the audience hall of the maharajah, a room whose murals bring to mind the neighboring Mattancheri Palace of the maharajah of Cochin, the patron of the Jews. The caption states, "Joseph Rabban, leader of the Jews, receiving the copper plates from Cheramperumal. He was made prince of Anjuvannam and thus a Jewish kingdom was established at Cranganore in 379 A.D." The date may be less than accurate, the term *kingdom* may be an exaggeration, and the name *Cheraman Perumal* refers to the Chera dynasty and not an individual ruler (today's state of Kerala takes its name from the first two syllables of this dynasty's name), but the basic idea is accurate. Like other immigrant groups, the Christians and Muslims, Jews were accorded autonomy and respect by the rulers of ancient and medieval Kerala. The copper plates, which are more likely from the tenth or eleventh century, remain in the Ark of the Cochin Synagogue.[6] To the Jews, Cheraman Perumal was the idealized Kerala king, the model for the beloved Cochin maharajahs. So, too, Joseph Rabban became the ideal Jewish leader, the model for a succession of Jewish "merchant princes" in service to the maharajahs and the Dutch colonial rulers, as well as for every Jewish bridegroom. Together, Cheraman Perumal and Joseph Rabban became archetypes of the relationship between Hindus and Jews in Kerala, an important motif in the Cochin Jews' self-understanding.[7]

The sixth painting depicts discord, the loss of the paradisiacal Shingly. At the same time, it continues the theme of establishing the Cochin Jews' connections with the royalty of ancient Israel in the days of the Temple. "Two of the original silver trumpets, used in the Second Temple at Jerusalem, with the ineffable name carved on them, were brought to Cranganore and were blown by Levites on the eve of the Sabbath. Once the Levites were late and the laity (non-Levites) usurped their privilege and in the resulting quarrel, the trumpets were unfortunately destroyed." To say that the trumpets of the Temple were brought to Cranganore obviously connects Shingly with Jerusalem; indeed, even today the Cochin of "the good old days" before mass emigration to Israel is referred to as Little Jerusalem. We do not know what history lies behind this legend of a quarrel between the Levites and the "laity," although it could be alluding either to the struggle between the Malabaris (the original Jewish settlers) and the Paradesis (the "foreign" or Sephardic Jews who arrived during the sixteenth century) or to the struggle between the "Jews with lineage" (*meyuchasim*) and "those with writs of manumission" (*meshuchrarim*). The destruction of the trumpets may be an allegory for the destruction of Shingly.

The seventh and eighth paintings are out of chronology, and in any case the eighth has been so badly eaten by white ants that it is no longer displayed. Like the sixth, both paintings depict the abandonment of Shingly, the maharajah of Cochin's welcoming the Jews, and the reestablishment of the community there. Six paintings, then, touch upon the Jews' being welcomed by Hindu kings—first of Shingly and later of Cochin. This theme of welcome, royal patronage, and hospitality is the guiding metaphor for Hindu-Jewish symbiosis in Kerala.[8]

The seventh caption reads, "Construction of the Cochin Synagogue next to the Maharajah's palace and temple in 1568." The Cochin Synagogue was built in 1568 next door to the maharajah of Cochin's "Dutch" Palace in Mattancheri (which was actually built for him by the Portuguese) and to his private Krishna temple. The eighth painting depicts the sack of Shingly in 1524: "Destruction of Cranganore by the Moors and Portuguese in 1524. Joseph Azar, the last Jewish prince, swam to Cochin with his wife on his shoulders. The Jews placed themselves under the protection of the Maharajah of Cochin." Joseph Azar was the last in the line of Joseph Rabban. He bears the same family name as the last Jewish kings of Himyar in Yemen, which may be more than a coincidence, because of the sustained maritime traffic and religious interchange between Yemen and Cochin.[9]

The ninth and tenth paintings continue the theme of the Jews' special relationship with the maharajah. Both are set inside the Cochin Synagogue. The ninth shows the Cochin Jews in Middle Eastern dress. With them is a stylized maharajah. The Torah scrolls are prominent in the open Ark. The painting bears the caption, "The Maharajah of Travancore presenting a gold crown for the Torah in 1805." Travancore, the neighboring princely state, had a Jewish community in North Parur. The gift, a twenty-two-carat, jewel-encrusted *Keter Torah,* is a very tangible symbol of Hindu-Jewish amity.

The final painting is poignant. Jews in western dress, many of them identifiable individuals, meet in the synagogue with the maharajah of Cochin. The Torah scrolls are again prominent in the open Ark. "The last reigning Maharajah of Cochin addressing Jewish subjects in the synagogue before relinquishing his throne in 1949," the caption reads. Cochin was not properly part of British India and enjoyed at least nominal sovereignty until Cochin's and neighboring Travancore's amalgamation into the Union of India shortly after independence. Although they were patriotic citizens of India, the Jews realized that their position in Indian society was bound to deteriorate if for no reason other than demographics. A few thousand Jews in a small, princely state could exert considerable influence. But in a republic of 350 million, their number would be too infinitesimal to maintain their high position. The maharajah appreciated the situation, as seen in his farewell address to the community, well remembered by all elderly Jews. On March 24, 1949, he congratulated his loyal subjects on Israel's recent independence from Great Britain and wished them well in their newly regained homeland (see figure 1).[10]

At the time, not all of the Jews realized the significance of the maharajah's words, although Sattu Koder wrote of the occasion, "The establishment of the State of Israel has created a general stir in the community. Hundreds have already left to build the Land of their forefathers and many more are waiting their turn, and it may be that after a few years

Figure 1.   Sattu Koder addressing His Highness Rava Varma, the maharajah
of Cochin, in the Cochin Synagogue in 1949. This was the maharajah's last
visit to the synagogue before retiring to private life. (Photograph courtesy of
the late Sattu S. Koder)

the story of the Jews of Cochin . . . will come to an end." [11] Koder and
the maharajah were prophetic. If a Cheraman Perumal chartered the
Jewish community's establishment by giving it the copper plates, then
the maharajah of Cochin chartered its demise in his 1949 address.

    Other versions of the Cochin Jews' historical legends exist, but these
ten images crystallize their contemporary view of their long sojourn in
India. During their quatercentenary celebrations, with media attention
focused on the tiny community and distinguished visitors coming from
around the world, they chose to emphasize their long-standing residency
in India, an antiquity that confers the prestige of lineage, or *yichus,* both
from Jerusalem and Shingly; their close connections with the Nayar rulers of Cochin, whether the Cheraman Perumals or the maharajahs of
Cochin; and the affection and respect they always enjoyed from their
neighbors in India. "Anti-Semitism doesn't exist in our Indian dictionary," Cochin Jews like to remind visitors. Their high position in Kerala
society, along with their origins in ancient Israel, constitutes the core of
the community's pride.

THE CONTEXT OF THE LEGEND

To understand the Cochin Jews' story, view it in two contexts. First, look at it in the context of their neighbors' legends, the narrations of Kerala's Christians, Muslims, and Hindus. This clearly shows how the Jews' narrative functions to claim a social place among Kerala's myriad, hierarchically ranked castes; at the same time, it responds to the Jewish world outside of India. This intertwining of Cranganore with Jerusalem exemplifies the Jews' story and, therefore, their sense of identity. Second, examine it against the background of history. Nothing historically known about Cochin's Jews or their neighbors contradicts their legend, but by the same token the legend cannot be taken at face value. Since our central concern is how their mythic narrative structures their sense of self, we must explore those historical trends and episodes that bear on the question of identity.[12]

THE CHRISTIANS' STORY

The self-understanding of Kerala's Christians, who comprise roughly 20 percent of the population, is based on the *Acts of Thomas,* a curious second- to fourth-century compilation from various sources that are part gospel and part *midrash* (stories that embellish the Torah's narratives).[13]

The First Act contains the relevant passages. It begins in Jerusalem, where Jesus and his apostles "divided the regions of the world, that every one of us should go unto the region that fell to him and unto the nations whereunto the Lord sent him." They drew lots, and India "fell unto Judas Thomas," much to his dismay.[14] Just then, Abbanes, an Indian merchant and emissary of the Indian king Gundaphorus—judging from his name, a Greco-Indian ruler of Bactria, in northwest India—arrived. In a story that remains popular in Kerala Christian wedding folk songs, the merchant wished to purchase a carpenter slave on behalf of the king, who wanted to construct a temple as magnificent as Solomon's had been. Jesus then sold Thomas to Abbanes, and Thomas had no choice but to acquiesce. The two set sail for the city of Andrapolis in India, which local Christians identify as Cranganore.[15]

They arrived at Andrapolis on the wedding day of the king's daughter. Amid food and drink, a girl flute player, "by race a Hebrew," happened to pass by. Thomas began reciting mystical poems in Hebrew understood only by the girl, who fell in love with him. The apostle rebuked her with discourses about the virtue of chastity, leading to her conversion and that of the king's daughter, who decided to eschew sexual relations with her new husband.[16]

This is the basic origin legend of Kerala's Christians: their community originated with the Apostle Thomas, whom Jesus had sent to India, and who began his mission by converting a Jew already there. It has led many of the "Saint Thomas Christians"—one of the names by which they are known—to claim Indian Jewish heritage. According to them, they are close kin to the Jews, having originated from the original "Jewish-Christians." Thus they are often known in Malayalam as *Nazaranee Māpillas,* from the Hebrew *nazar,* by which Jews had originally designated the primitive Christians. *Māpilla* is an honorific signifying "prince" or "royal son" in Tamil. Muslims are known as Jonaka Māpillas to distinguish them from the Christian Nazaranee Māpillas.[17]

The oldest group of Christians are also known as Knani, or Canaanite, Christians, named for a fourth-century merchant. According to their narrative, Knayi Thomen came to India and encountered "people wearing wooden crosses, Christians they claimed but steeped in idolatry. Thomas concluded that these people were the remaining descendants of those natives whom St. Thomas the Apostle to the East had converted centuries before."[18] Returning to his native Edessa, Syria, Thomas organized Christians from there, Jerusalem, and Baghdad into a colonizing mission to purify Christianity in Malabar. Some seventy-two families, four hundred persons all told, set sail aboard seven ships. "Before leaving they burned all their houses and personal belongings, carrying only some ashes as mementos. Before leaving all swore to maintain their racial purity, teach the true religion and stay loyal to the Patriarch."[19] The narrative continues with a royal welcome from "Cheraman Perumal," the bestowal of a copper plate grant of sovereignty at Mahadeva-pattanam, "the city of the Great God," in Cranganore, and rights to the seventy-two privileges of royalty. They prospered there until military losses to the Muslims of north Malabar forced them to move south to Cochin and Travancore.[20]

The Knani Christians share the Jews' high-caste status as well as many customs, including taboos about women in their menses and a hereditary priesthood.[21] The latter may well reflect their purported Hindu brahmin pedigree or Jewish kohenite (priestly) origin and has been used as evidence for both.[22] The Christians marry under a canopy, or *pantal,* analogous to the Jewish *chuppah.* Prior to the wedding, the bride immerses herself in a *kuli,* similar to the Jewish *miqveh* (ritual bath). The Christians sing folk songs very similar to those of the Jews, describing their arrival in India and referring to such observances as Yom Kippur.[23] Virtually all of their home observances are preceded by the ceremonial lighting of a lamp, *vilakku,* and they eat unleavened bread at a special ritual meal held after nightfall on Maundy Thursday, during which the father ceremonially washes his hands twice, as is done at a Passover Seder.[24] They also eschew any efforts at converting others to their religion, the apostle's original evangelical mission notwithstanding. Israeli sociologist Shalva Weil, who studied Christian-Jewish parallels in Kerala, cited several other similar customs, including "the position of the bride standing on the right of the bridegroom . . . , the bridal veil . . . , burial of the dead to face . . . Jerusalem . . . , the priests' black velvet cap which is supposed to be similar to the Jews' head gear . . . , and the 'Kiss of Peace' ceremony . . . which . . . was copied from the Jews . . . , the ululatory sounds uttered by Knani women known as *kurava,* the unique Knani betrothal ceremony, and the symbolic six-pointed star which appears on the sleeve of the bridegroom's long velvet coat."[25] On their deathbed, these Christians bless their children and grandchildren:

> God gave His blessing to Abraham,
> Abraham gave that blessing to Isaac,
> Isaac gave that blessing to Jacob,
> Jacob gave that blessing to my fore-fathers,
> My fore-fathers gave that blessing to my parents,
> And my parents gave that blessing to me.
> Now, dear son (daughter), I give that blessing to you.[26]

Beyond these ritualistic parallels, there are similarities in legends, Malayalam folk songs, geographic patterns of settlements, and a common sense of origin and history.[27] The Christians also share with Jews the tradition of having received a royal charter, an *âcâram* or *sthânam,* engraved on copper plates, from the idealized Hindu emperor, Cheraman Perumal.

The events described in the *Acts of Thomas* were relocated explicitly to Kerala by Maliekel Thômâ Rambâm in the 1601 Malayalam epic poem *Thômâ Parvam,* which holds that he "converted the people of all castes among whom were the Nambudiris [brahmins] of thirty-two families. . . . Of these, the [Sankarapuri and Pâlamattam] . . . families were ordained and set apart for sacred orders and bishops. The priesthood has been practically hereditary in the two families . . . for several centuries with inheritance in the female line." Thomas is believed to have built seven churches in Kerala, the oldest at Parur. All are located near Jewish settlements.[28]

THE MUSLIMS' LEGEND

Like Christians, Muslims make up about 20 percent of Kerala's population. They were preceded by their ethnic, if not religious, ancestors, the Arabs, who had traded between Kerala and the Middle East since prehistory. Some hold that Arab trading settlements have been in Kerala ever since the second century.[29]

Archaeological evidence from northwest India indicates trade between the prehistoric Indus Valley Civilization of India and Sumer between the twenty-fifth and nineteenth centuries B.C.E.[30] As early as 25 B.C.E., Hellenized Jews, in alliance with the Romans, led an expedition that wrested the spice trade monopolies from the Arabs. Alexandria, with its large Jewish population, became the chief western center for the spice trade.[31] For centuries before the rise of Islam, Arabs traded with China and India, pursuing both the overland silk route and the monsoon-driven sea lanes from Aden to various west Indian ports, including Cranganore.

Hindu-Muslim strife was virtually unknown in Kerala. While the north was besieged, embattled, and subjected to an unwelcome rule, "Islam, like Judaism and Syrian Christianity in earlier centuries, came into Kerala not like a conqueror but as an honoured guest in the house."[32]

A sign in Cranganore's Cheraman Juma Masjid proudly proclaims it to be India's oldest mosque, dating to 621. There can be no vouching for the sign's historical accuracy, but this would date the mosque from the lifetime of the Prophet himself, connecting Kerala's community directly with Muslim sacred time, in accord with local legend.

Our best source for the idealized history of the Muslims of Kerala is the *Tohfut-ul-Mujahideen,* an Arabic history by Shaikh al-Mabari Zain al-Din, written in the sixteenth century.[33] This intriguing text was written to encourage the Muslims to resist "*al-Afrunj,*" the Portuguese, who had made important inroads into Muslim- and Jewish-dominated trade monopolies. Al-Din's assumption that amity, not strife, marked the Muslims' arrival in Malabar is an important part of the local Muslims' self-understanding. Wrote al-Din, " . . . the Lord most high hath willed that the faith of Islamism should flourish throughout the chief of the inhabited regions of the earth; in some countries making the sword and compulsion the means of its dissemination, in others preaching and exhortation. But he mercifully ordained, that the people of Malabar, beyond the other nations of India, should evince a ready and willing acceptance of this holy creed."[34] The text holds that Muslims arrived in Kerala in the year 710, when a company of three poor, pious Muslim pilgrims heading to Adam's Peak in Sri Lanka from Arabia, "under the spiritual guidance of a Sheikh," stopped at Cranganore. The king received them warmly. The sheikh (a term used in Sufism to indicate a spiritual teacher; in exoteric Islam, a secular leader) told the king about the Prophet Muhammad. The king, intrigued, commanded the sheikh to return to Cranganore after making pilgrimage. When the sheikh came back, the king secretly accompanied the pilgrims back to Arabia, where he converted to Islam.

Local Hindus share the narrative. The nineteenth-century, quasi-historical Malayalam text, the *Keralolpatti,* records that the last Cheraman Perumal king went to Makkah, converted to Islam, and became known as Makkattupoya Perumal, "the emperor who went to Makkah."[35] As ritual recompense for this familial apostasy, the maharajahs of Travancore used to recite, when they received swords of office at their coronation, "I will keep this sword until the uncle who has gone to Mecca [Makkah] returns."[36] The text and the custom reveal a basic familial structure for interreligious relationships in South India. The apostate king remains the "uncle" of succeeding generations of maharajahs.

After the demise of Cheraman Perumal's dynasty in the twelfth century, political supremacy in Malabar was divided between the zamorin of Calicut in the north and the maharajah of Cochin in the south, with many tributary states in between. Although himself a Hindu, the zamorin was patron to the Muslims, and under his leadership Calicut became a major trading center. The maharajah of Cochin favored the Jews and formed alliances first with the Portuguese and later with the Dutch. Like Calicut, Cochin developed into a major port. The twin centers dominated trade with China to the east and Egypt to the west during medieval times.

The great Cheraman Perumal kings made grants to various foreign religious communities. Most famous is the copper plate grant that King Bhaskara Ravi Varman gave to the Jewish community at Cranganore, led by Joseph Rabban, probably during the early eleventh century. King Sthanu Ravi gave a similar copper plate grant, believed to date from the ninth century, to the Christian community at Kollan, led by Mar Sapir Iso. Modeling himself after the Cheraman Perumals, a zamorin of Calicut left a stone inscription at the Muccunti mosque of Calicut establishing a rice grant for the maintenance of the mosque.[37]

Kerala's Muslims adopted the local Nayar's system of matrilineal inheritance.[38] They also proliferated subcastes, dividing "native" Muslims, Māpillas, from those of Arabian origin, mirroring similar schisms among Jews and Christians.

SIMILARITIES IN THE LEGENDS

The three Abrahamic religious communities in Kerala—the Jews, Christians, and Muslims—each developed legendary accounts of their origins and sojourns in southwestern India. These legends are not fixed; they are periodically reconstructed to reflect the conditions of the time. Nevertheless, striking similarities on several points among the three sets of legends shed light on the unique and salient features of Kerala civilization:

1. *Each community traces its origin to a sacred time and sacred place.* The Jews' story begins with the destruction of the Second Temple and the Diaspora to "the four corners of the earth." Thus the sacred city of Jerusalem was connected with Kerala and replicated in the local traditions of Shingly. The Christians' tradition credits their origin to Jesus himself when he commissioned Thomas to voyage to India. The Muslims' legend connected their community to Makkah and the time of the Prophet.

2. *All three communities' legends refer explicitly to sea travel.* Land travel was possible at the time, but given the dependence of each community on maritime trade, arrival by the sea routes would be an obvious choice. Each legend embellishes this point with references to continuing contact by sea with the site of origin.

3. *The prevailing theme in each legend is the hospitable welcome received from the Cheraman Perumal.* This theme dominates six of the ten paintings the Jews selected to present themselves to the outside world. The Thomas legend recounts his reception at a royal wedding feast, the song of the Jewish flute-player girl, and the conversion of brahmin families. Thus, three extant, high-caste communities—the rulers, the Jews, and the brahmins—all participated in receiving Thomas. The Muslim legend recounts the Cheraman Perumal king's invitation to the pilgrims to return after visiting Adam's Peak. In one version, he accompanies them back to Makkah and converts to Islam.

4. *Each community received a royal charter granting high privileges and a degree of autonomy.* These charters, two on copper plates and one a stone inscription, are often associated with the erection of synagogues,

churches, or mosques. Similarly, each group attained high-caste status in Kerala and generally eschewed missionizing on any large scale. Each group's adaptation to Kerala social structures was reflected in Hindu accretions in their religious and ritual traditions and in a proliferation of subcastes, the higher-status subgroup claiming antique origins in Israel or Arabia, the lower-status group considered native.

5. *In exchange for royal patronage, each group contributed to the prosperity of Kerala.* They did so by serving as windows to the outside world and as large-scale cultivators, government officials, and soldiers. University of Calicut historian M. G. S. Narayanan aptly calls this unique set of arrangements between Hindu kings on the one hand, and Jewish, Christian, and Muslim settlers on the other, cultural symbiosis.[39] The paradisiacal accounts of these foreign settlements in Kerala also focus on prosperity.

All these themes have mirror images or counterparts—albeit imperfect —in the historical traditions of Kerala's Hindus, now about 60 percent of the population.

THE HINDUS' LEGEND

Consideration of Hindu legends completes the background of other religious communities' narratives as they influenced the Jews' self-understanding. Significant Hindu stories emphasize Kerala's unique geography and also stress the presence and legitimacy of foreign elements within the local population.

Hindu legends about Kerala's origins reflect the region's topography. Bounded on the east by the densely forested Western Ghat mountains and on the west by the Arabian Sea, this thin littoral land is cut off from the rest of India but open to the West. Arab and Jewish traders called the region Malabar, deriving from *mala,* old Tamil for "hill," and *barr,* Arabic for "country." Appropriately, the very name of the country reflects a symbiosis of Hindu and Middle Eastern language and, therefore, culture.[40] Its alternate name, Kerala, shares a root with the ancient dynasty of Chera kings, the Cheraman Perumals. Several etymological possibilities account for that term; one derives from *chernta,* "added," so Cheralam (Kerala) would mean "the land that was added on (to the already existing mountainous or hilly country)."[41]

Both names square with geology and legend. The land was once under water and emerged from the Arabian Sea bordering the Western

Ghats. Volcanic or seismological forces elevated the coastal planes, creating Kerala's numerous rivers and backwater lagoons.[42] Legend likewise has it that the land was "added on," but by divine rather than natural forces. Parashurama, "Rama Who Wields the Battle-Ax," the sixth of the ten incarnations (*avatara*) of Vishnu, "the most violent character in Sanskrit literature" is among the most popular gods of the region.[43] He is a paradoxical god, a brahmin-warrior who fought against the local nobility (*kshatriyas*) to establish the supremacy of newly arrived brahmins. In a legend of brahmin ascendancy in Kerala, "Parasurama threw his *parasu* or ax across the sea from Gokarnam [in Karnataka] to Kanyakumari [at the southern tip of India] . . . and water receded up to the spot where it fell. The tract of territory so thrown up is said to have constituted the land of Kerala."[44]

As Rama was to become associated with Vishnu, these legends also indicate the ascendancy of the worship of Vishnu in Kerala, especially among the ruling class, who in Kerala were artisans (*shudras*) and not nobility (*kshatriyas*). Thus, the rise of the Nayars and the rise of Vishnu and his religion, Bhagavatism, were connected. Parashurama the brahmin became the champion of the Nayars because he aligned with them to challenge the kshatriyas' claim to divinely ordained leadership of society. The divine defeat of the kshatriyas was necessary to legitimize the Cheras' shudra rule. Since Bhagavatism is open to all castes, its adoption by Kerala's ruling Nayar families served to legitimize their "unnatural" rule.[45]

The *Keralolpatti* discusses the establishment of various villages and social institutions and the absorption of foreigners into the fabric of Keralan society with the approval of the ruler and highest-ranking citizens. The Cheraman Perumal himself apparently invited these foreign merchants to settle in his country.[46] A combination of factors led to the Hindu kings' unique hospitality to foreign traders:

1.   "The Brahmin-Kshatriya prejudice against trade and navigation . . . induced them to leave such 'vulgar' affairs in the hands of the foreigners."[47]

2.   The geography of Kerala tends to seal it off from the rest of India and open it to the Arabian Sea.

3.   The foreigners possessed precisely the skills needed to assure the prosperity of the kingdom.

4.   Finally, Hinduism is well known for its tolerance of other faiths.

Narayanan cogently wrote, "What lay behind such tolerance? Was it the expression of the nation's innate generosity or a cosmopolitan philosophy? There is another, more significant, explanation. It is a fact that the early Jews and Christians came to this undeveloped semi-tribal Dravidian society, devoid of naval power and coinage, with shiploads of gold and the promise of trade. The interests of trade must have induced harmony in spite of religious and racial differences. . . . Thus it was probably the wealth of Joseph Rabban, the Jew, which endeared him to the Cera king Bhaskara Ravi. . . . In other words, charity began at the market place."[48] The arrival of Jewish, Christian, and Muslim traders filled a void in Kerala's economic life.[49] Ancient Kerala's reliance on the sea for its riches is reflected in one of the oldest known Tamil works, a second-century epic that recounts, "The riches of the Puhâr [*Kaveripumpattinam*] ship owners made the kings of faraway lands envious. The most costly merchandise, the rarest foreign produce, reached the city by sea and caravans."[50]

HISTORY AND MEMORY

Seafaring trade is just one of the common bases revealed when the Jews' narrative is compared to their neighbors' sagas. Such memories tantalize because, for the most part, they are plausible. Nothing in our evidence— whether archaeological, epigraphic, or numismatic; whether letters of medieval Jewish merchants, diaries of Christian or Muslim travelers, or Hindu historical texts; whether folk songs or our best attempts at inference—explicitly contradicts the Jews' narrative of their long sojourn in India. At the same time, no evidence can confirm the narrative either, especially as regards premedieval times. Part of the problem is that Portuguese invaders burned vital Jewish historical texts, along with Torah scrolls and prayer books, in the sixteenth century. Yet even this relatively recent book-burning incident has been questioned by modern scholars who hold it to be a fabrication to conceal precisely the absence of such documentation.[51]

Written proof is only part of the equation; a people's historical self-understanding shapes its identity more than mere history, though history may be demonstrable and legend is not. Mere facts are mute. They are almost irrelevant to the identity-generating narrative process. The French Jewish anthropologist Claude Lévi-Strauss labeled the "double structure" of myths "altogether historical and anhistorical." The legends of the Cochin Jews are historical in the sense that they claim to describe past events; they are ahistorical in that their "meaning" is not to be found simply in recounting the past. As Lévi-Strauss wrote about the meaning of a myth, "[W]hat gives the myth an operative value is that the specific pattern described is everlasting; it explains the present and the past as well as the future."[52]

FROM LEGEND TO HISTORY

Given this background in the legends of Kerala's communities and a caution about how the vast and chaotic bits of historical evidence mesh with the conflicting legends and myths, we can now grapple with Cochin Jewish history in four distinct periods: ancient, precolonial, colonial, and postcolonial.

During ancient times considerable commerce existed between South Asia and West Asia. Evidence of the oldest strata of this trade is found in archaeological reconstruction of prehistoric times. Other sources include the Hebrew Bible, Josephus's histories, the Talmud, and Greek, Roman, and early Christian documents. Out of these fragments the Jews' origin story was constructed.

In India's precolonial era, Jewish communities enter history proper, yet we know very little about this formative period in Shingly. A few pieces of relevant epigraphic evidence and some letters are available but little else, so we rely primarily on legends, folk songs, and observations first by Muslim, later Jewish, and finally Christian travelers. Cochin's earliest synagogues date from this period.

Jewish life during the colonial period had its glories and its tragedies. When the Portuguese arrived in 1498, they brought a spirit of intolerance utterly alien to India. They soon established an Office of the Inquisition at Goa, and at their hands Indian Jews experienced the only instance of anti-Semitism ever to occur on Indian soil. Dutch rule, from 1663 to 1795, heralded a second "Indian golden age," and Jews profited greatly from their close connections with both Dutch colonial merchants and the Cochin royal family. Cochin Jews were refreshed by contact with Jewish communities in other parts of the Dutch commercial empire, from Amsterdam to New Amsterdam to Indonesia. The community's decline came with the British, who ruled India from 1797 to 1948. Because it was not officially part of British India, Cochin's economic importance diminished simultaneously with the rise of Bombay and Calcutta.

The postindependence era began with a fervor of both Indian and Jewish nationalism. Cochin Jews strongly supported both movements, Indian *Swaraj* (literally, "self-rule") and Zionism. But as political, demographic, and economic realities in Cochin changed rapidly, life became increasingly precarious for the relatively prosperous, minuscule minority. This period, which began with the greatest enthusiasm and the highest hopes, reversed itself and witnessed the dissolution and, ultimately, the death of this proud outpost of the Diaspora.

INDIA AND ISRAEL IN THE ANCIENT WORLD

When we scrutinize what is known of South and West Asia during ancient times, the Cochin Jews' claim to a first-century arrival in India seems entirely plausible. Commerce between the two regions dated from the days of Mesopotamia in West Asia and the Indus Valley Civilization in South Asia, between the mid-third and fifth millennia B.C.E.[53] Ancient tablets discovered at Ur, the city of Abraham, describe ongoing trade with Dilmun/Telmun, an entrepôt for trade between Mesopotamia and the inner reaches of the Indus Valley. Seafaring traders, known in Sumerian as alik-Telmun, brought silver, gold, and garnets to trade for pearls, ivory-inlaid tables and combs, beads, and especially copper.[54] The Hebrew Bible, which contains Sanskrit and Tamil words, suggests and describes trade between Solomon's kingdom and India. The First Book of Kings 10:22 describes the opulence of the court of King Solomon, an opulence that the Bible suggests derived from the India trade. Israeli philologist Chaim Rabin found evidence in the Book of Exodus of trade between ancient Israel and India, direct or indirect, in no less than four Hebrew words of Indic origin, the terms for cinnamon, emerald, sapphire, and topaz.[55]

The Buddhist *Bâveru Jâtaka* also refers to the ancient trade between India and Babylon, *Bâveru* in Sanskrit.[56] The text cites "Indian merchants who took periodic voyages to the land of Bâveru." Similarly, in the *Kevaddhu Sutta*, a sacred text that tradition holds was spoken by the Buddha himself during the sixth century B.C.E., and that was first written down during the first century B.C.E., "we read of how *long ago* merchants sailed far out of sight of the coast, taking 'shore-sighting' birds, which were released from time to time, in order that they might guide the mariners to land." [57] Not only is this verse reminiscent of the Noah story, but these Buddhist texts indicate a much earlier use of Indian Ocean sea lanes than is commonly believed.

One more connection to King Solomon can be found in Buddhist literature. In the *Mahoshadha Jâtaka,* the Buddha adjudicates a dispute between two women, each claiming to be the mother of the same baby. The Buddha orders the two to pull at the infant and one of them demurs. "But soon as they pulled at him, the mother, seeing how he suffered, grieved as if her heart would break. And letting him go, she stood there weeping. Then the future Buddha asked the bystanders, 'Whose hearts are tender to babes? those who have borne children, or those who have not?' And they answered, 'O Sire! the hearts of mothers are tender.' Then he said, 'Whom do you think is the mother? she who has the child in her arms, or she who has let go?' And they answered, 'She who has let go is the mother.'" [58] This legend of the Buddha is strikingly similar to the tale of King Solomon's judgment (I Kings 3 : 16 – 28). It impossible to say who is borrowing from whom, or whether both Jews and Buddhists were borrowing from a yet older common source, or whether this striking similarity is simply coincidental.

The Talmud contains several references to India. For example, *Pirqei Avot* first uses the term *pilpul,* meaning "sharpening of the wits through debate," characteristic of vociferous yeshiva education to this day.[59] The term derives from the Hebrew for pepper, *pilpeil,* which is cognate with the Sanskrit and the Tamil *pippali.* Pepper was India's most prized product during the Greek and Roman Empires. Other rabbinic references to India come from Saadia Gaon (882–942) and Rashi (1040–1105).[60]

The earliest Greek document pertaining to India is by the Greco-Cairene Skylax, commissioned in 519 B.C.E. by Cyrus, emperor of Persia, to chart the maritime route between the Indus and Egypt. According to the great classical historian Herodotus, Skylax sailed from the mouth of the Indus to the Gulf of Aden, finally reaching the Red Sea and the Gulf of Suez. The voyage took thirty months—such a long time that Skylax was obviously unaware of the monsoon winds that would have speeded his travels.[61]

Greece's next encounter with India, and perhaps its most significant, was forged by the armies of Alexander of Macedon, who campaigned in India from 331 to 324 B.C.E. Alexander (known in India as Iksander) was followed by more than soldiers: some ten thousand craftsmen, philosophers, artists, historians, merchants, and writers all traveled with him, so cultural and mercantile exchanges were both broad and deep.

The rise of Rome meant Roman domination of the India trade, especially the lucrative spice trade, which had been firmly in Arab hands since the breakdown of the Persian empire. In 25 B.C.E. a Roman expeditionary force, which included many Jews, Egyptians, and Nabatean Arabs, set sail from Suez to wrest trade routes from the Himyarite and Sabean Arab monopolies.[62]

The "epoch-making" event that greatly expanded maritime trade with India, however, was the discovery of the monsoon winds by Hippalus, sometime around 45 C.E.[63] Thereafter, these regular winds carried ships from the Middle East to India each spring and propelled their return journey each autumn; travel time was reduced from Skylax's thirty months to just forty days.[64] Hippalus's discovery revolutionized trade and commerce.

Having secured the sea lanes of the spice trade and the overland silk route, the Romans established their first permanent colony in India at Muziris, "the nearest mart in India."[65] Muziris, known in the Jewish world as Shingly, was also the earliest Jewish settlement in India. Muziris was the greatest center of the spice trade, about twenty miles north of today's Cochin. Around 60 C.E., the *Periplus of the Erythrean Sea,* a mariner's guide to the Indian Ocean, noted, "Muziris . . . abounds in ships sent there with cargoes from Arabia, and by the Greeks. . . . [Kings] send large ships to these market towns on account of the great quantity and bulk of pepper."[66] The depiction of Muziris in the Peutingerian Tables—fresco maps dating from 226 C.E.—proves its importance to Europe. In the fresco, the port city includes a temple dedicated to Augustus Caesar.[67] "Thousands of Roman coins from the first century C.E. . . . found at twenty-nine archaeological sites in South India" also suggest a very brisk pepper business.[68] Logically, the Cochin Jews believe their settlement at Muziris began during this century of rapidly expanding trade, especially in pepper and the other spices growing luxuriantly in Malabar's tropical climate.

In addition to commerce, art, and conquest, the Greeks valued philosophy. In the historian Megasthenes's view, the philosophers are to Greece as the brahmins are to India and as the Jews are to the Middle East. According to the philosopher Clearchus, Aristotle taught that the Jews are descended from India's brahmins, making them "the heirs and torch-bearers of the Indian sages, whose disciples they were."[69]

The greatest Jewish historian of ancient times, Josephus, shared the Greeks' high opinion of Indian philosophers. In his account of the martyrdom at Masada, the Jews' leader, Eleazar, lauds Indian philosophers for their bravery in the face of death, thereby convincing the Jews to commit suicide rather than be conquered.[70] Clearly, Jews of the late Second Temple period were aware of Indian spirituality and regarded it highly. Not only Josephus, but the other monumental Hellenized Jewish author of the period, Philo of Alexandria, idealized Indian philosophers, or *gymnosophists*, depicting the renunciate Calanus as a paradigm of love of freedom and courage in the face of assimilationist demands from none other than Alexander himself.[71]

Four well-established first-century events thus coalesce to make the Cochin Jews' version of their history entirely plausible:

1. Jewish participation in Greco-Egyptian and/or Roman expeditions to usurp Arab trade monopolies;

2. Hippalus's discovery in 45 C.E. of the monsoon winds, which greatly facilitated travel;

3. Roman establishment of a settlement at Muziris (also called Shingly, Cranganore, or Kudungallur), which was known in the western world; and

4. Israel's defeat by the Romans and the destruction of Jerusalem in 70 C.E.

TRAVELING THE PAPER TRAIL: TRACKING KERALA'S JEWS IN PRECOLONIAL TIMES

Information about the transition from ancient times to the Middle Ages in Kerala is sketchy at best. No external documentation proves Jews lived there between the fourth and ninth centuries. The decline of the Roman Empire led to Arab ascendancy in the spice trade, and when Arab trading expertise was blended with the religious fervor of Islam in the seventh century, commerce exploded and settlements multiplied as far off as India.

As Arab trade increased, Arabic travelers' diaries proliferated. They refer to the Jews of Kerala as early as the mid-ninth century, when Jewish merchants known as the Radanites reached the apex of their wealth and influence. By one account, their trading routes stretched from France as far as India.[72] The Muslim caliph As-Saffah sent the first Jewish emissary to India between 750 and 755 C.E. Five centuries later, the well-known scholar Abraham Meir ibn Ezra said this anonymous Jew had wanted to learn Hindu mathematics.[73]

The first extensive Jewish account of the Malabar was left by Benjamin of Tudela, "the greatest medieval Jewish traveller," who visited most of the known world between 1159 and 1173.[74] Benjamin knew Malabar by the name of Chulam, the Quilon of today, a city one hundred miles south of Cochin. He traveled as a merchant, but his personal agenda was "for the express purpose of ascertaining the situation of the dispersed tribes." [75] His valuable, firsthand accounts of Jews in Europe, North Africa, the Middle East, Israel, Baghdad, and Persia reconstruct Jewish life in the early Middle Ages. Yet his tales of the Jews of South and East Asia—in India, Ceylon, Tibet, and China—are much less reliable, because he based them on oral and written materials from other contemporary travelers and scholars. He was famous among the Jews of twelfth-century Spain for his accounts of settlements that were unknown in Europe.[76]

Benjamin described Chulam at considerable length. He found the people notably trustworthy. The numerous foreign merchants, he said, "may even leave [their goods] in the open fields without any guard." He discussed the cultivation of pepper, "cinnamon, ginger and many other kinds of spices." [77] Like virtually every traveler who ever visited the country, he commented on Kerala's ferocious heat.[78]

Benjamin also described the Jews in twelfth-century Malabar. "All the cities and countries inhabited by these people contain only about one hundred Jews, who are of black colour as well as the other inhabitants. The Jews are good men, observers of the law and possess the Pentateuch, the Prophets and some little knowledge of the Thalmud and its decisions." [79]

Benjamin noted Aden's role in the India trade. "Some rich merchants reside here," he wrote, "and vessels from India occasionally arrive." [80] Yemen and Aden played a pivotal role in the India trade. "One must remember that trade with India prospered for a long time and often resulted in permanent settlements. Aden was the beginning point. There, in Aden, were the main stores, and from there, the merchants continued their journey to Ceylon and Malabar." [81]

Soon after Benjamin's travels, Rabbi Moshe ben Maimon (1135–1204), one of medieval Jewry's greatest scholars and alternately known as Maimonides or the Rambam, referred to Jews in India in a famous letter. He wrote, "the *Mishneh Torah* . . . has enlightened Jews as far as India. They have nothing of religion except that they rest on Sabbath and perform circumcision on the eighth day." [82] The *Mishneh Torah* is the Rambam's encyclopedic code of Talmudic legal and religious decisions.

Among observant Jews, when books and documents bearing God's name must be discarded, they are placed in a *geniza*. Such a repository used in medieval Cairo now provides a rich source of information about medieval Indian Jewry. The Cairo geniza documents include medieval merchants' letters composed in a vernacular Arabic with Hebrew letters known as Judaeo-Arabic. The late Solomon D. Goitein, who devoted much of his life to the study and translation of the letters, published eighty of them in 1973 as *Letters of Medieval Jewish Traders.* At the time of his death he was working on the *India Book*, a study of those letters about the India trade.

For the most part, Christians began visiting Malabar only after the Portuguese had established colonies there at the very end of the fifteenth century, so two earlier travelers stand out. During the Middle Ages, the greatest Christian traveler was Marco Polo of Venice (twelfth to thirteenth centuries), who mentioned Jewish sovereignty in Malabar.[83] Friar Odoric of Pordenone mentioned conflicts between the Jews and their neighbors in 1322, foreshadowing the demise of paradisiacal Shingly a few years later.[84]

In the fourteenth century, Rabbi Nissim ben Reuben (1310?–1375?) of Spain not only made his way to Shingly, but composed a song to commemorate his visit. The song has been preserved in Cochin song books, and is chanted on the second day of Shavu'oth:

> I traveled from Spain.
> I had heard of the city of Shingly.
> I longed to see an Israeli king.
> Him, I saw with my own eyes.[85]

The great Muslim travelogue writer Ibn Battúta (1325–1354) mentioned not only Jewish settlements in the Malabar, but Jewish sovereignty at Chendamangalam, near Cranganore.[86]

Several late-fifteenth- and sixteenth-century sources mention the Malabar Jews. Three recently discovered documents from 1494, 1503, and 1503/4 provide the only reliable firsthand accounts of Jewish life in Shingly. Taken together, these documents confirm the ritual continuity between Shingly and Cochin, especially as regards Simchat Torah (see below), confirm the tradition that Jews enjoyed a remarkable degree of independence in Shingly, and present an origin legend more in accord with Malabari than Paradesi versions.[87] In 1520 Rabbi David ben Solomon ibn Zimra of Cairo wrote a well-known *responsa* citing halachic grounds (see page 61) for criticizing the caste-like divisions of the Jewish community. In 1524 David Reubeni, the Qabbalist of Rome and Lisbon, wrote in his diary of "very many Jews in Singoli [Shingly], ten days from Calicut." [88] A letter sent from Tsfat, in Israel, to Italy by one David del Rossi in 1535 reads, "This [Shingly] is a big town exclusively inhabited by Jews. They sold to the king of Portugal 40,000 loads of pepper a year. They only recognize the Code of Maimonides and possess no other authorities or traditional law." [89]

PHYSICAL EVIDENCE

Precious little physical evidence remains of precolonial Jewish life in the Malabar, but those few remnants are exquisite and compelling. Ancient power shifts are made real by the first, a copper plate grant from 849 C.E. In this remarkable decree, King Sthanu Ravi of Kollam grants certain ceremonial and trading privileges to Mar Sapir Iso, founder of the city's Syrian Christian community, who arrived at Cranganore in 823.[90] In this document, witnessed by four Jews named Hassan, Ali, Isaac ben Michael, and Abraham, the king grants Jews and Christians seventy-two royal privileges, including adjudicating all disputes in the area, and he charges both groups with protecting the city's church.[91] Perhaps only in Hindu India could Jews receive such honors and concessions and be officially charged with protecting their neighboring Christians, along with their church! As the antimissionary Indian civil servant A. C. Burnell commented more than a thousand years later in 1874, "The Israelite colony is associated in trusteeship of the endowment; a strange rebuke to the fanaticism of modern times, and to the reckless attempts at proselytism which have long since destroyed all good feeling between the different sects in India." [92]

The most significant medieval physical evidence of the Jews' presence in medieval Malabar is kept to this day in the Holy Ark of the Cochin Synagogue—two small, rectangular copper plates. Engraved on two sides of one but only one side of the other, in old Malayalam, is the pedigree, the proof of long-standing Indian lineage, the *yichus* of the Cochin Jews (see figure 2). The plates' narratives declare that they were given to the leader of the Jews, Joseph Rabban, by "King Cheramanperumal" in 379 C.E. The date is debatable. As recently as 1925, the traditions of the Jews of Parur dated the plates to the Jewish year 4830, or 1069 C.E., a date much closer to contemporary scholarly assessment.[93]

According to local traditions, the plates chartered an independent Jewish principality at Anjuvannam, believed to have been a section of Cranganore. The privileges this king gave to Rabban follow the pattern of "overlord/little king" relationships that evolved historically between South Indian maharajahs and leaders of extrinsic religious communi-

Figure 2.   The copper plates granting autonomy to Joseph Rabban, leader of
the Jews of Cranganore, issued by King Cheraman Perumal, circa 1001 C.E.
(Photograph by Ellen S. Goldberg)

ties.[94] Usually only kings used elephants and parasols, but here Rabban
received the right to display these and other symbols of aristocratic rank,
along with the powerful and lucrative authority to levy duties and tolls.
    The Cochin plates read:

> Hail Prosperity! This is the gift that His Majesty, King of Kings, Sri Bhas-
> kara Ravi Varman, who is to wield sceptre for several thousand years,
> was pleased to make during the thirty sixth year opposite to the second
> year of his reign [according to Narayanan, 1000 C.E.], on the day when he
> was pleased to reside at Muyirkkode. We have granted to Joseph Rabban,
> Ancuvannam, tolls by the boat and by carts, Ancuvannam dues, the right
> to employ day lamp, decorative cloth, palanquin, umbrella, kettledrum,
> trumpet, gateway, arch, arched roof, weapon and the rest of the seventy

two privileges. We have remitted duty and weighing fee. Moreover, according to this copper-plate grant given to him, he shall be exempted from payments made by other settlers in the town to the king, but he shall enjoy what they enjoy. To Joseph Rabban, proprietor of Ancuvannam, his male and female issues, nephews, and sons-in-law, Ancuvannam shall belong by hereditary succession. Ancuvannam shall belong to them by hereditary succession as long as the world, sun and moon endure. Prosperity![95]

Kerala's aristocracy had enjoyed these privileges since ancient times. The *Shilappadikaram* describes a king "accompanied by the five estates of his ministers," who employed the same symbols of royalty granted to Joseph Rabban, many of which are reenacted in Indian Jewish weddings to this day.[96] The terms used on the copper plates for family relationships indicate that the Jews of Shingly had, to some extent, adopted Kerala's matrilineal system of inheritance.[97]

More significant than the details of the plates—whether from the fourth or tenth century, whether granting a principality or a guild, and so on—is their *meaning* for the Cochin Jews. The plates confer both the yichus of long-standing residence in India and the power of a special relationship with Kerala's Nayar ruler, factors of inestimable status-generating value to a foreign religio-ethnic group in Kerala's society. The plates express the relationship between the leader of the Jews, Joseph Rabban, and the Cheraman Perumal kings, in this case Bhaskara Ravi Varman I. As they symbolized Jewish-Hindu relationships in general, they also modeled the advisor-patron structure that dominated until independence in 1947. Ritually and symbolically, all Jewish leaders are Joseph Rabban, and all Nayar rulers are "Cheramanperumal." This amicable, honored system of relationships between Jews and the ruling family—unique in Diaspora history—is reinforced through women's folk songs in the Malayalam language.

One such folk song celebrates these plates:

In world famous Vañchi [Cranganore], from the exalted monarch,
He [Joseph Rabban] received favours such as the crown, the daytime lamp, and walking cloth [like our "red carpet," a cloth a greatly honored individual would walk upon].
He filled the city with money gladly scattered under head and foot.
He, the chief subject of the crowned king.
Sprinkle 3,600 grains of rice!
In the year *yarivitaré* [reckoned an acrostic for 1246 C.E.], from him according to everybody's desire,
He got the copper plate beautifully engraved.

You shall have an elephant if you describe the coming of Sri Anandan
   ["Blissful Lord," an honorific for Joseph Rabban].
See the royal Sri Anandan come riding on the back of an elephant;
See the virtuous Sri Anandan come riding on horseback.
Under a green umbrella, behold!
Women received him and he entered the synagogue.[98]

Rich in local color, these songs were sung by Jewish women on a variety of occasions: for festivals, weddings, and circumcisions, using the
miqveh, and baking *matsah* for Passover. They are in the uniquely Jewish Malayalam dialect, "a sort of Malabar Yiddish," injecting Hebrew,
Tamil, Spanish, Dutch, and English vocabulary into Malayalam.[99] The
songs were passed from generation to generation, and some were written down in notebooks preserved by the women. The idealized status of
the Jews in Hindu Kerala is a recurrent theme:

> When he arrives on elephant back with ornamental fans decorated with a
>   thousand peacock plumes, he lavishly throws money into every lap, the
>   jewel of a hero, the Syrian [Joseph Rabban].
> Let the Jewish synagogue prosper for hundreds of years!
> Let us proclaim that Jews live here!
> Let us bow down at the Jewish synagogue!
> Let it flourish for hundreds of years![100]

Joseph Rabban is a hero due to his investiture, portrayed in the Cochin
Synagogue paintings and expressed in the copper plates. The last lines,
summoning the listeners to "proclaim that Jews live here," are startling.
Such Jewish pride and self-confidence, due in no small way to the love
and esteem of the Hindu nobility, is virtually unknown elsewhere in the
Diaspora.

Several charming wedding songs convey the sense that "every bride-
groom is Joseph Rabban," as Jacob Cohen explained. Like Hindus, Cochin Jewish bridegrooms affect the symbols and trappings of royalty, including sitting upon a throne as the women sing a song blessing the
groom:

> May Shaddai the Almighty bless you and make you great.
> May you be the greatest among the great.
> So says God, who blessed Abraham.
> The land that is promised, from where you were dispersed—
> May you inherit it, and all blessings will be yours.
> May you be the leader, like Joseph [Rabban].[101]

To the Cochini imagination, the only other place where Jews might
enjoy the many blessings they found in India would be in redeemed Is-

rael, where they would rule like Joseph Rabban in Cranganore. Having lost the paradise of sovereignty twice (with the exile from Jerusalem, followed by the exile from Shingly), they would find it again in the days of the Messiah.

The copper plates tell us that the Jews were a respected and privileged community in Shingly, close to the king and given complete religious liberty. They apparently formed a sizable minority among the multireligious population. They built their synagogues and composed religious songs in Hebrew and in Malayalam. They evolved a unique *minhag* (local customs of religious observances), which evidences waves of immigration from Yemen, Babylonia, Persia, Spain, and even eastern Europe, as well as indicating their Indian Hindu context.

We do not know exactly what led the Jews away from Shingly, but it must have been traumatic, because to this day tradition dictates that no Jew may spend a night in Cranganore.[102] We do know, however, of several events between 1341 and 1505 that led to the destruction of the Jewish community at Shingly. In 1341, a great flood silted up Shingly's fine natural harbor, serendipitously creating the harbor at Cochin but ending Shingly's role in shipping. Internal fighting, including a quarrel over the succession from Joseph Rabban, during those years decimated Shingly's Jewish community. Too, the Jews and their patron, the maharajah of Cochin, suffered extensive military losses to Muslims allied with the maharajah's rival, the Zamorin of Calicut. Finally the arrival of the Portuguese, who captured Cranganore in 1505, forever changed the community that had welcomed Jews since ancient times.

At Shingly, Jews were spice merchants, petty traders, government officials, agriculturists, and military personnel. As late as 1550, "the Raja of Cochin refused to fight a battle on Saturday because on that day his Jewish soldiers would not fight; and they were the best warriors he had raised."[103] Probably India is the only country on earth so civilized that in war, out of deference to its esteemed Jewish soldiers, no battles were fought on the Sabbath.

The last piece of physical evidence of precolonial Jewish life in the Malabar is poignant. The 1269 tombstone of Sarah bat-Israel still stands outside the abandoned Chendamangalam Synagogue. Her grave was probably relocated to Chendamangalam from Shingly when a group of Jews fled the struggles over the succession of the line of Joseph Rabban. These refugees established a Jewish presence at Parur, Mala, Mattancheri, and Chendamangalam. Perhaps Sarah bat-Israel was among them.

THE COLONIAL PERIOD

Whatever battles the Jews may have had with their Muslim, Christian, and even Hindu neighbors in India, their greatest tormentors were, without doubt, the Portuguese. As the Dutch governor Adriaan Moens wrote in 1781, "This nation [Portugal] was no friend of the Jews and compelled many of them, by contemptuous treatment and arbitrary taxes, but specially by their religious intolerance, to leave Cranganore, and to beseech the protection of the king of Cochin." [104]

Although the Jews suffered many persecutions during the Portuguese era (1498–1663), they also achieved a great deal. Under Portuguese rule the Jews managed to establish themselves at Cochin, where they built their beautiful synagogue in 1568. They flourished in new houses of worship in several of Cochin's and Travancore's towns, and they began the novel *mudaliar* system of self-government. After the tolerant, commercially minded Dutch replaced the Portuguese in 1663, European Jews visited and corresponded with their coreligionists in Cochin. In part on the basis of their contacts abroad, Cochin's great houses of Jewish merchant-princes reached their zenith in business and diplomacy. During this era Cochin's cultural life, replete with poets and mystics, reached its greatest heights.

Jews from Shingly arrived at Cochangadi, a village now part of Cochin, soon after the 1341 Periyar River flood. In fact, the name *Cochangadi* may mean "Jews' market" in Malayalam.[105] Joseph Azar is said to have built Cochin's first synagogue there in 1344. By the time Vasco da Gama arrived in 1498, Cochin's Jewish community was already well established. Soon thereafter, in 1506, a German traveler named Balthazar Springer called the Jews "a foreign element among the pagan population of the city of Cochin." [106] This "foreign element" was made up of Sephardic Jews who came to Cochin by various routes, originating in the Iberian Peninsula. As in the Balkans, for example, when the Spanish exiles grafted themselves onto an older, indigenous Jewish community, the result was the imposition of Sephardic halachic and liturgical norms onto the older, indigenous community.[107] This happened in Cochin as well. The expulsions from Spain in 1492 and Portugal in 1497 revitalized the community, and Sephardic and local traditions blended to produce an especially rich, synthetic minhag.

Some Spanish and Portuguese Jews made their way to Cochin in 1511, traveling via Turkey and Syria. These foreign Sephardic Jews merged with some of the leading families who had moved to Cochin from Shingly—

Figure 3.   View from a window in the maharajah of Cochin's palace, 1986.
His formerly private Hindu temple is in the foreground, the Cochin Syna-
gogue's clock tower and sanctuary in the background. (Photograph by
Ellen S. Goldberg)

the Joseph Azar family, the Zakkais, and the Aarons—and gradually
formed the subcaste known as the white Jews or the "Paradesi (foreign)
Jews." The Jews who fled Shingly had lost most of their wealth, and the
infusion of the "foreign" Jews greatly enhanced the economic life of the
community as a whole.

The Perumpadappu Swarupam had been Cochin's royal family since
1405.[108] They built their palace at Mattancheri, and the most celebrated
maharajah of the era, Kesava Rama Varma (1565–1601), granted the
Jews a tract of land adjoining the royal palace and temple, inviting them
to build their synagogue and settlement under his protection (see figure 3). Like his ancestors, the Cheraman Perumal emperors, the maharajah served his economic interest by inviting the Jews to settle beside his
palace: "The fact no doubt was that the Cochin Raja hoped, with the
assistance of the foreigners, to regain some of the power and independence of which the Zamorin, with Muhammadan assistance, had robbed
him." [109] Indeed, Kerala's rulers traditionally asserted their authority
over vassal groups by patronizing their temples and shrines, a way of appropriating a portion of the power of the vassal's deity.[110] The Jewish
point of view, however, placed greater emphasis on the monarch's com-

passion. "The king of Cochin received them, the most compassionate king in the world, with beautiful kindness, and he gave them a place to build houses and a synagogue near his palace, to be a help to them in their days of distress."[111]

Jew Town was born from this land grant. Today it consists of one long, north-south street called Synagogue Lane—the street once boasted three flourishing synagogues—reaching a cul-de-sac at the Cochin Synagogue (formerly called Paradesi, or Foreigners, Synagogue) at the lane's northern end. The synagogue abuts and shares a courtyard wall with the maharajah's private Pazhayannur Sri Krishna Temple. Now the palace is a historical museum open to the public, and the temple is open to all Hindus. To this day, liturgies emanating from the Hindu temple and the synagogue fuse and can be heard in both houses of worship.

The famous Paradesi Synagogue was built in 1568, making it the oldest synagogue in the British Commonwealth (see figure 4). Today, it is one of Cochin's most popular tourist sites. During the peak winter season, as many as one thousand tourists, mostly from within India, visit the site each day. Visitors to Cochin are often struck by the serene charm of the synagogue, one of the most beautiful in all the world. Even Beth Hatefusoth, the Museum of the Diaspora in Tel Aviv, displays a model of the synagogue.

All the synagogues of Kerala are striking, bearing distinctive features unique in the Jewish world. A sloping red tile roof covers each synagogue's whitewashed, two-story building. Uniformly, the entrance is a plain wooden door through an exterior wall as high as the synagogue's first story. Inside the wall, which ensures privacy, a treeless courtyard completely surrounds the building (except in North Parur, where the courtyard bounds only three sides). The wall-and-courtyard layout closely resembles the design of Kerala's Hindu temples. The courtyard is used for a unique element in the Malabar minhag, the afternoon Simchat Torah processions (*haqafot,* circumambulations around the tevah with the Torah scrolls), much as Hindu temple courtyards are used for their annual deity processions.

Passing through the external door on the southeastern side of the building, one enters a small anteroom known as a *talam.* To the left, a stairway leads to the women's section (*ezrat nashim*), and directly ahead a second doorway leads into the courtyard and the entrance to the synagogue proper. In Cochin, a room to the right of the anteroom houses the ten paintings that symbolize the Paradesis' history. A sign at the Cochin

Figure 4.   Interior of the Cochin Synagogue, 1986. (Photograph by Ellen S. Goldberg)

Synagogue reads, "Visitors are requested to remove footwear before entering the synagogue"; this is the practice in all Kerala synagogues. It probably was borrowed from Hindus and Muslims, both of whom pray barefooted, although Cochinim say it is done to protect the floor's valuable tiles.

Inside the vestibule (*azarah*) are charity (*tsedaqah*) boxes as well as a large, brass laver, used by the hereditary priests (*kohanim*) to rinse their hands before reciting the priestly benediction on festivals and most Shabbatot. The walls of the synagogue are thick, and each shuttered window has a wide, comfortable window seat (see figure 5).

The sanctuary itself is decorated with chandeliers of silver and brass and oil lamps of every description. Some were brought from Belgium or Holland, and many are brightly colored. The ceiling is of carved wood. The *bimah* (called *tevah* by Sephardim) in the center of the room, from which weekday prayers are led and psalms are chanted, is surrounded by two dozen gleaming brass posts supporting a rail. Prayer books (*siddurim*), prayer shawls (*tallitot*), and volumes of the five books of Moses (*Chumashim*) are propped between the posts.

Three of the interior walls are lined with wooden benches, many marred from being struck with mallets to obliterate the cursed name of Haman when the Scroll of Esther is read every Purim. There are coir settees in the middle and toward the back; some bear small brass nameplates for the elders of the congregation. A finely crafted brass Chanukkah lamp (*chanukiyah*) hangs on the southern wall. Hand-painted Chinese willow-pattern tiles cover the ground floor. The tiles, brought to Cochin in 1762, are striking in their cool, blue-and-white beauty.

The eternal light (*ner tamid*) in Cochin is especially beautiful, made of graceful, curved glass tubes containing coconut oil to burn before the Holy Ark (see figure 6). At the conclusion of Shabbat, a taper is lit from the ner tamid, and the flame is carried to each household. One can still see an oil lamp beside each home's entryway, a custom shared with Kerala's Nambudiris. These lamps were lit to proclaim festivals.

At Cochin, three tiled steps lead to the teakwood Holy Ark on the northwest wall, an exceptional example of Kerala wood carving, painted red with gold decoration. A beautiful curtain (*parochet*), made from a woman's ceremonial sarong (*mundu*), hangs before the Ark.

In Malabar, the mundu is the everyday dress for both women and men, but for festive occasions women don elaborately embroidered mundus, often of silk worked with gold or silver thread. Typically, a woman

Figure 5. Sitting by the window, Shalom Cohen prays in the Cochin Synagogue, 1987. (Photograph by Ellen S. Goldberg)

Figure 6. The eternal light (*ner tamid*) before the Holy Ark in the Cochin Synagogue, 1986. (Photograph by Ellen S. Goldberg)

prepares such a mundu for her wedding, and again for the occasion of her son's first reading of a *Haftarah* (prophetic reading included in services on Shabbat and festivals), usually at the age of five or six. When a woman dies, her favorite mundu is draped upon her coffin. The mundu is then sewn onto a backing embroidered with verses from Psalms, and used as a parochet; thus she lives on through the synagogue. The custom symbolizes the power of women within the family and community. For the elaborate Cochini Simchat Torah celebrations, all of these parochets are hung around the upper part of the synagogue's walls in a vivid plethora of colors and memories.

At the beautiful red and gold *Aron Hakodesh* (Holy Ark), the parochet may be drawn aside to reveal the seven magnificent Torah scrolls. As is Sephardic custom, each parchment scroll is housed in a rounded wooden case that is often covered with beaten silver. Several of the crowns are twenty-two-carat gold, studded with rubies, sapphires, and emeralds; one of them was donated to the synagogue in 1805 by the Hindu maharajah of Travancore. Ritual objects are also stored in the Ark: two ceremonial horns (*shofarot*) of prodigious proportions in the Yemeni style are proudly kept there, as is a twenty-two-carat *kiddush* cup, which has been used in every Cochini wedding for centuries. The Ark also holds Cochin's famous copper plates, as well as a treasured guest book signed by Lord Mountbatten, Indira Gandhi, the Dalai Lama of Tibet, and Israeli president Ezer Weizman, among other notables.

On festivals and certain Shabbatot, a beautiful carpet is laid before the Aron Hakodesh. The carpet was the gift of Ethiopian emperor Haile Selaisse, known as the Lion of Judah, who explained to Sattu Koder, chief warden of the synagogue, "Our tradition is that we also consider ourselves Jews."[112]

To the north of the Ark is the Chair of Elijah, another fine example of Kerala wood carving. "On the eve before the circumcision [*milah*]," Israeli official Naphtali Bar-Giora explained, "they place . . . [the chair] near the front wall of the hall on the northern side of the Holy Ark. . . . They drape this chair with a multi-colored velvet covering. They place a citron [*etrog*] or myrtle or a flower called *yona lapoov* on the chair. On the evening service of the day of the *milah,* they burn a lamp opposite the chair, and they . . . place a *Chumash* on the chair in honor of the *milah*."[113] Traditionally, Elijah is invited to every *brit milah,* and this ornate chair is reserved for him.

An intriguing tradition makes the women's sections of Kerala's synagogues distinctive. As one first enters the synagogue, a stairway leads to a covered ramp way to the women's section, locally known as *pennun-galude mâtom*. It is set back, rather than overlooking the downstairs area, as usual. A latticework ritual barrier (*mechitsah*) in front of the section separates the women from an almost unique Kerala innovation, a second bimah, just beyond the mechitsah and directly above the rear quarter of the male-occupied sanctuary. The only other place with a second bimah is the 1326 synagogue of Brussa, Anatolia, in the south of Turkey. Aaron Greenbaum, a South African rabbi who visited Cochin in 1966, speculated that the tradition of reading the Torah adjacent to the women's section may date from the Second Temple, when the public reading of the Torah at the conclusion of each Sabbatical year (*shmit-tah*) took place on a specially constructed bimah in the ezrat nashim.[114] The most important parts of the liturgy are conducted in such close proximity to the women's section to honor their high position within Cochin's Jewish community. The upstairs portion is supported by two pillars known as *yakhin* and *boaz*, "like the pillars that were in the Temple of Solomon." [115]

A small stairway in the northeast corner of the sanctuary reaches this upper pulpit, where the Torah is read on Shabbat and festivals. Sattu Koder writes that the most important prayer services of the year are conducted from this high bimah: morning services (*Shacharit*) on Shabbat and festivals and, on Yom Kippur, the evening (*Arvit*), morning, "Additional" (*Musaf*), afternoon (*Minchah*), and Ne'ilah (the penultimate Yom Kippur liturgy) services.[116]

The Cochin Synagogue's elegant clock tower was built by Yechezkel Rahabi II in 1761. The clock facing the synagogue is in Hebrew, the one facing Synagogue Lane is in western numerals, and the one facing the harbor is in Indian numerals. The clock has not worked within living memory.

Beyond the physical beauty of the synagogue is its spiritual beauty. Centuries of fervent prayers have left an echo of the spirit that remains palpable to this day. The Jew Town folks relate stories to convey their sense of the sacredness of their synagogue. Jacob Cohen tells of his grandfather, Yaakob Daniel Cohen, an émigré from Baghdad and a learned scribe and teacher during the last half of the nineteenth century. One day as Yaakob was alone in the synagogue, sitting in the anteroom writing some document or scroll, he heard the parochet in front of the Ark being pulled back, the door being opened, and the Sifrei Torah being removed. Yaakob was afraid to raise his eyes to the Ark, because he knew the noise was the angels conducting their prayers.[117]

Jews are not the only ones who appreciate the spiritual power of the synagogue: Muslims, Christians, and Hindus share a belief in its magical properties. The *shamash* of the synagogue, Jackie Cohen, told of two Hindu parents who visited the synagogue with their son, a young man in his twenties. They explained that the young man had just been offered a very desirable job in banking, but had become paralyzed on his right side and was unable to assume his duties at the bank. They asked if they might pray in the synagogue for his recovery, and upon receiving the sexton's permission, proceeded to prostrate themselves in a circle around the bimah. When they saw the ner tamid, they begged for a vial of its oil. They prostrated again and left, only to return the next day exclaiming, "This oil is a miraculous cure! Our son is starting to get some feeling back in his arm. Could we please have some more oil?" Jackie gave them more oil and replied, "You know, we don't believe in this sort of thing. Your kind of faith is very different from ours. But this is a house of prayer, and anyone can pray here. As long as you don't bring in any crosses, or anything like that, anyone can pray however they like." They returned a few days later, proclaiming their son's complete cure and begging for another vial of oil. Jackie thought this was getting to be a bit much, but gave them the oil anyway. Time passed, and Jackie received a letter from the family, again thanking him for the oil that cured their son's paralysis and allowed him to take up his position at the bank.[118]

Local people also ascribe curative properties to water from the synagogue's miqveh. Jackie Cohen's brother, Sassoon "Sunny" Cohen, tells of a Muslim woman who came to the synagogue one day, asking if she might take some water because a member of her family had become ill. According to Sassoon, such occurrences were not at all uncommon.[119] Generally in South India, the water at a shrine represents the beneficence of the deity associated with that shrine. The water's curative power is not restricted to adherents of any one religion. Just as water from the Cochin Synagogue miqveh is prized by everyone, so is the water from a fountain at the tomb (*dargah*) of a Muslim saint in Trichy, Tamil Nadu, valued equally by local Hindus and Muslims.[120]

THE *MUDALIARS*

The leaders of the Jewish community came to be known by the Tamil/Malayalam term *mudaliar,* meaning simply "headman." Sattu Koder conjectured that the title of mudaliar was conferred "in recognition of the privileges granted to Joseph Rabban in Cranganore."[121] First appointed by the maharajah of Cochin, the mudaliars had the authority "to enforce some punishments and to impose and remit fines, subject to the Raja's judgment . . . but capital cases were tried by the raja himself, and the [Dutch East India] Company had . . . some judicial power over them, too." [122] In short, both the foreign Dutch and the local Hindu rulers recognized them as heads of the Jewish community. The mudaliars also "became the rajas' close advisers, trusted counselors, and devoted agents." [123]

Nevertheless, the Jews and their patrons, the maharajahs, were never content under Portuguese rule, and having a common enemy further cemented their close bonds. Portuguese attitudes and policies were double-edged: in certain respects, the Jews in Cochin were allowed to prosper, as is evident from travelers' accounts of their town; however, in other senses, they were severely restricted. For example, in 1568, the king of Portugal proscribed Jews from making the sea voyage to India. Ominously, "captains were made responsible for ejecting them from their ships." [124]

Walter J. Fischel, the University of California at Berkeley historian who pioneered the study of Jews in India, summarized their condition under Portuguese rule. "All accounts agree that the Jews at the Malabar Coast were subject to contemptuous treatment and arbitrary taxes levied upon them by the Portuguese and that they were heavily restricted in their trade and oppressed by the Portuguese, though the raja of Cochin granted them, whenever possible, protection and special privileges." [125] Due to the oppression by the Portuguese, when the Dutch began to pursue their interests in Malabar they found the Jews to be ready, capable allies.

The Hindus and Muslims also opposed the Portuguese. One member of the Cochin royal family went so far as to invite the Dutch, arch rivals of the Portuguese, to help him by ousting the oppressors. In 1662, the Dutch, whose colonial interests were centered at Batavia, now in Indonesia, seized this opportunity to expand their influence and sent an expedition led by Commander Van Goens to Cochin. The Portuguese forces routed the Dutch, but the Jews, who had openly collaborated with the Dutch, suffered most from the loss. The enraged Portuguese vented their wrath in ferocious reprisals against the Jews. They burned the synagogue, including all of the Torah scrolls, holy books, and historical records—among them *Sefer Yashar,* the community's chronicle—and sacked Jew Town. The Jews fled to the hills, where they remained for the better part of a year until the Dutch finally defeated the Portuguese and established their rule in 1663.

Under the tolerant, commercially minded Dutch, the Jews' commerce and culture flowered to rival the glory days of Cranganore. "Under the Dutch," Fischel wrote, "Cochin became one of the most prosperous ports on the Malabar Coast, a place of great trade, a harbor filled with ships, streets crowded with merchants, and warehouses stored with goods from every part of Asia and Europe." [126]

As their economic fortunes rose sharply, Cochin's Jews were put into contact with Jews in Holland and throughout the Dutch empire, from Indonesia to New York. On November 21, 1686, they received a delegation from Amsterdam led by a refugee from Portugal, Moses Perreira de Paiva. "This impact of this delegation on the Cochin Jews," wrote Fischel, "was unprecedented and led to a close contact between the Jews of Amsterdam and Cochin which lasted all through the 125 years of Dutch rule over Malabar." [127]

The Cochin Jews wanted festival prayer books (*machazorim*) that reflected their own unique traditions. So they contracted the noted Amsterdam Jewish publisher Proops to produce the *Shingli Machazor*. A first edition was published in 1757 and a second, corrected edition, in 1769. Original editions are still used in the Paradesi Synagogue.

Upon his return to Amsterdam, de Paiva wrote *Notisias dos Judeos de Cochim,* an important source detailing the Jewish families and historical traditions of Cochin. His five days in Cochin were filled with receptions, prayers, music, and food. The Dutch delegation's welcome was so warm and enthusiastic, de Paiva wrote, "that if the King Messiah had come to them through the door, I do not know if they could have shown greater affection." [128] Then, as now, hospitality was a point of honor in Jew Town. De Paiva eloquently praised his hosts' cuisine: it was a "splendid lunch which David Raby gave us with such magnanimity that you, respected Sir, will have nothing to match its excellence, when God grants me the grace to return." [129] When the delegation traveled across the bay to visit the synagogues in Ernakulam, "In the middle of the river we met a boat which came to welcome us with . . . instrumental music and escorted us to the shore." [130] When de Paiva was leaving, "The *hahamim* [religious leaders], the leaders and also some persons from the other side [Ernakulam] brought with them choicest gifts and I did not know how to express my gratitude to them. I was very touched with the tears and sighs our imminent departure had caused. I was also affected by the love and kindness they bestowed on us and for their continuous receptions in gala dresses." [131]

The Jew Town folk told de Paiva their story: how they left Israel at the destruction of the Second Temple and went to Majorca, from where some seventy to eighty thousand of them went to India in 370 C.E. They showed him the copper plates and told him how the Jews were welcomed by Emperor Cheraman Perumal, who reigned "from Goa to Colombo," and how he made their leader, Joseph Rabban, the king of Cranganore. He learned that Jews from Majorca had brought "two trumpets with the Ineffable Name engraved on them from the Holy Temple" that were used "to announce the arrival of the Sabbath." In 499 C.E., they told de Paiva, another large group of Jews had arrived, but "they could not say from which part of the world they had come, as the knowledge they have is much confused because of the loss of the book named *Sepher Ayashar* . . . as a result of the plunder and destruction of the Synagogue and Jewish houses." De Paiva recounts their narratives: the quarrel between the Azar brothers, the struggles between the maharajah and the zamorin, and how they lost Cranganore and arrived in Cochin in 1512. [132]

In the seventeenth century, at the time de Paiva visited, the most famous family in Cochin was the Rahabis, variously known as Rabi, the anglicized Roby, and even Rabbi. Their fame was due, in part, to their prominence in trade and diplomacy. But it was also thanks to the many authors and scholars in the family—Yechezkel, David, and Naphtali in particular. The first patriarch of the House of Rahabi in Cochin was Yechezkel, who arrived from Haleb, Syria, in 1647, and gained his fortune as a merchant. His son, David, settled in Cochin in 1664. By the time of de Paiva's visit twenty-two years later, the Rahabi family was one of the most prominent in Jew Town.

When his father, David, died in 1726, Yechezkel II succeeded him as "Joods Koopman," the Jewish company man or chief agent of the Dutch East India Company. He embarked upon a remarkable career as leader of the Jews, advisor to the maharajah, and agent of the Dutch. He has been called "the Malabar's Kissinger," and he became "the towering and central Jewish figure in the economic life in Cochin during the eighteenth century, who served the governors and commanders of the Dutch East India Company for almost 50 years as merchant, diplomat and agent" [133] (see figure 7).

When the Dutch arrived in Malabar, they wanted "to secure for them-

Figure 7.   Yechezkel Rahabi (1694–1771), Jewish
merchant-prince of Cochin. (Courtesy of the late Sattu
S. Koder)

selves the maximum supply of pepper at the most favorable prices for
export to the European market," explained journalist T. V. Parasuram.

> The principal pepper-producing areas were, however, controlled at that
> time by four different kings, the King of Travancore, the Raja of Cochin,
> the Zamorin of Calicut and the King of Kolattiri or Calaesti . . . the Dutch
> had to conclude yearly commercial and peace treaties . . . with these local
> kings. . . . It was, therefore, considered necessary by the Dutch to combine
> force or threat with diplomacy. They had to choose a negotiator carefully.
> He must, of course, be loyal to the Dutch but loyalty was not enough. He
> must be patient and skilled in the art of negotiations, understand the psy-

chology of the kings and chieftains so that he could win their confidence, have the right contacts and be familiar with the local language, customs and manners of the region. The role was filled to perfection by Ezekiel [Yechezkel] Rahabi for almost half a century.[134]

Yechezkel II's home became "the meeting place of local rulers . . . from all over Malabar," as he was "one of the best-informed persons of his time. . . . He kept the Dutch Company representatives in Cochin informed about world affairs, military, political and economic changes, the movements of the ships of their rivals, the English and the French, troop movements of the formidable Zamorin of Calicut, the outbreak of wars among European nations, dynastic changes, the death of the King of Spain or Denmark, shipwrecks, confiscation by pirates, fluctuations of foreign exchange, market prices and other information of value."[135]

In addition to his career as a diplomat and community leader, "the great Ezechiel" pursued diverse business endeavors, including trade in pepper, cardamom, and cloth, as well as Chinese porcelain. He was a shipping magnate. His sloops bearing such names as Rachel, Daniel, Ashkalon, and Jerusalem, and emblazoned with the Star of David, plied the pirate-infested seas along the Indian coast, from Sumatra to Muscat, and from Colombo to Mocha.[136]

During this secure and prosperous era under Dutch rule, the "second golden age" of the Cochin Jews, literature and mysticism flourished along with commerce. Many lovely Hebrew songs and poems were composed in Jew Town. These Hebrew songs became part of the unique Cochini minhag and were anthologized in various liturgical books along with the songs of such Sephardi *hachamim* (religious leaders) as Yehuda Halevi, Moses ibn Ezra, Solomon ibn Gabirol, and Israel Najjara.[137]

Of Cochin's Jewish poets, Eliahu Adeni was the foremost, and of the mystics, Nehemiah Mota has had the greatest influence. Adeni, from Aden, Yemen, was the most prolific Cochin poet, but we know little about him beyond his poems and songs. The earliest known manuscript of the Cochin minhag was written during the seventeenth century. The *Seder Shirot Seder Bikashoth Seder Simchat Torah Milah V'Chupah*, which is believed to have been edited by mudaliar David Kastiel, contained 165 poems for Jewish holidays and rituals, many bearing Adeni's acrostic signature.[138] He was the only Cochinite to have an entire volume of his works published. According to his tombstone, he died in 1631.[139]

The influence of sixteenth- and seventeenth-century poet Nehemiah Mota remains tangible to this day. The Malabari Jews still honor his death anniversary on the first day of Chanukkah with a special banquet, followed by singing his Sephardic memorial prayer (*Hashkavah*).[140] His religious importance extends to the Paradesis as well. His tomb functions as the focal point of many vows, a spot for consolation in times of distress. More than that, Christians, Muslims, and Hindus make pilgrimage to his tomb. With the approval of the Jews, local Syrian Christians erected a lamp before the dargah.[141]

Who was this man who became patron saint of so many of Kerala's people? Unfortunately, Nehemiah Mota's cult never spawned the informative pilgrims' manuals, devotional songs, shrine histories, and hagiographies (*taskiras*) that provide fruitful material about Muslim Sufi saints, leaving us with only scattered references, vague memories, an inscription, and conjectures from which to reconstruct a portrait of South India's greatest Qabbalist. Yet Kerala's people refer to him still as "Naamia Muta," *muta* being a respectful term for "old man" in Malayalam.

The earliest scholarly reference—a vague and misleading one at that—to Nehemiah Mota is in the 1907 edition of the *Jewish Encyclopedia*, which states rather starkly, "In 1615 a false Messiah appeared among the Jews of Cochin." [142] During the rationalistic early twentieth century, almost every Jewish mystic was chided as a "false messiah."

We are not even sure where he was from or how he came to Cochin. Most authorities accept that Nehemiah Mota was from Yemen, although his sister, Saidi, who contributed so generously to the construction of the Paradesi Synagogue, was said to have been a native of Turkey.[143] Some Cochin Jews say he was an Italian Jew who came to Cochin via Yemen, while others claim he was Polish.[144] Even the public use of his songs varied mysteriously. The 1757 edition of the *Shingli Machazor* contained about twenty of Nehemiah's songs which, for unknown reasons, were deleted from the 1769 edition.

Many of the Jew Town folks talk about Nehemiah Mota only reluctantly. One friend of the community attributes their diffidence to the Jewish disdain for saint worship as bordering on idolatry, a conflict of sorts between folk traditions and Jewish beliefs still voiced by several men in the community.[145] To non-Jewish Indians, no conflict exists; perhaps that has helped sustain the more mystical aspects of Nehemiah Mota's influence, for in India communities often have *grama-devata* (village deities). For instance, early in this century, missionary Rev. Henry Whitehead observed these village deities' crucial role in alleviating childbirth anxieties. Typically, they began as people who—due to their supposed special powers or the eerie circumstances surrounding their deaths—are believed to continue to influence human affairs from beyond the grave, even to the extent that cults emerged to worship them.[146] The Naamia Muta of popular imagination resembles these village deities in several significant ways.

Typical of the cults of the village deities, the perceived after-death presence of Nehemiah inspired fear as well as blessings.[147] According to Gamliel Salem, fear is the reason local people maintain the tomb so well. In Jew Town folklore, if some piece of jewelry is missing from a household, the mistress of the house says within earshot of the suspected servant, "I'm going to Naamia Muta's tomb to get his help in returning my bracelet." If the servant had in fact pilfered the bracelet, he or she, fearing Nehemiah Mota's presence, immediately returns it.[148] There is a Hindu parallel to this practice. In one Tamil Nadu town, a village deity is especially known for her ability to adjudicate stolen property disputes. "This is certainly a simple method of doing justice . . . ," commented Whitehead, "and probably just as effective as the more elaborate and more expensive process of our courts of law. . . . To the practical British mind this seems the one really sensible ceremony connected with the worship of the village deities in South India." [149]

Mostly, it has been the women who make vows or light candles at Nehemiah's tomb. They often resort to such vows during a crisis—health, an employment opportunity, a long journey. It is not uncommon for a Cochinite to receive a letter from a relative in Israel, asking that candles be lit for some specified purpose.[150] At times, like her Gentile neighbors, a Jewish woman would vow to abstain from meat on a certain day each week if her husband recovered from an illness. One man in the community suffered several illnesses, and his wife had eventually limited her enjoyment of meat to the Sabbath.[151] These vows, especially when connected with Nehemiah Mota, resemble the general South Indian women's rites known as *nonpu*, "rituals of fasting, worship, praise and mythic reenactment that women perform without male involvement." Women are understood as "the source of a family's prosperity and continuity," and "a chaste wife . . . can save her husband from death. This she does by taking an oath . . . [which says that] if she is a [virtuous woman; an *ayshet chayil* in Hebrew, a *cumankali* in Tamil] . . . then the deity must make her husband recover; she puts herself on the line in no uncertain terms. [Believing that] only if she has been a devoted, chaste, and auspicious woman will the oath work." [152]

Nehemiah Mota's "adoption" by Hindus, Christians, and Muslims is not as unusual as it might appear. In India's popular imagination, the world is populated with spirits of astounding variety, even the occasional deified foreigner. "There are also cases of foreigners who enter this pantheon of deified human power figures," and often their tombs or graves "became known as a powerful holy place."[153] Through these popular, divinized figures, extrinsic religions such as Islam, Christianity, and Judaism became integrated into the "Hindu" culture of Kerala.[154]

MODERN TIMES

The first British ships visited Malabar in 1615, but it was not until 1797 that the English replaced the Dutch as overlords of Cochin. Cochin was never placed directly under the British Crown. Like Rajputana (now Rajasthan) and Kashmir, Cochin and Travancore remained autonomous princely states, nominally ruled by their maharajahs with the guidance of the British resident, or *dewan*. In Cochin, the British presence was confined to Fort Cochin and, later, to Willingdon Island, a naval base and customs facility the English built when dredging Cochin harbor.

The retention of Cochin's autonomy in the face of the economic, military, and political juggernaut of the British Empire, which consumed most of India, had good and bad effects on the Jews. On the positive side, they continued to receive the maharajah's protection and privileges, to which they had become accustomed. They were given a seat in the Cochin Legislative Assembly, and their youngsters were guaranteed admission to Madras University, the only university in South India at the time, or to medical colleges or other professional schools. The maharajah's government exempted the Jews from any duties, governmental or otherwise, on Shabbat and festivals (see figure 8). In general, the maharajah took his role as protector of the Jews seriously. Once he even overruled the British viceroy's decision to allow the Jewish cemetery in Ernakulam to be handed over to the municipal corporation for a development project, exclaiming, "I know that in every country in the world the Jews are persecuted, but none of this shall happen in my country!"[155]

On the negative side, however, the British neglected Cochin because they did not rule directly there, and this led to the deterioration of its economy. At first the British favored Calicut, within the boundary of British Malabar, as a trading center, and many mercantile activities moved northward. Eventually, Bombay emerged as the supreme west Indian port, superseding Cochin, Calicut, and Surat. Ironically, Bombay's development as western India's leading commercial and shipping center

Figure 8.   Jewish men of Cochin, early twentieth century. (From the catalogue
The Jews of India, p. 134, © The Israel Museum, Jerusalem; photograph courtesy of Tova Sofer and Reuven Sofer)

was due largely to Jewish émigrés from Baghdad, most notably the Sassoon family. But Bombay's development eroded the economic base of the
Cochin Jews.

MILESTONES AND *MINYANS*

Four unprecedented events marked the twentieth century in Jew Town.
The first was Indian Independence in 1947, enthusiastically welcomed
by the Jews. The second was the establishment of the State of Israel in
1948, cause of another joyous celebration in Jew Town. The third was
the gala celebration of the four hundredth anniversary of the Cochin
Synagogue in 1968. The fourth event seems less momentous, but it was
cataclysmic for the Jews of Cochin: one Shabbat during July 1987, for
the first time in its glorious history, there were no formal prayers in the
synagogue. The august Cochin Jewish community could not muster a
minyan, the minimum ten Jewish adult males halachically prescribed for
a prayer quorum. Indian independence, so welcomed by the Jews, had
paradoxically contributed to the demise of Indian Jewry. Although Jews

were loyal citizens who benefited from centuries of Hindu-Jewish amity, the political and economic realities of the mid-twentieth century weakened the community. In 1948 India's Jews rejoiced in Israeli independence, the fulfillment of the Zionist dream, but so many migrated to the new state that their home communities, small to begin with, were devastated irrevocably by the population loss.

The complex forces now leading inexorably to the extinction of Indian Jewry include economic and demographic pressures, the politics of competition among India's castes and ethnic groups, the profound impact of the Zionist vision upon religious Indian Jews, family and business disagreements, internal conflicts, and—some say—even a curse. In short, the demise of Indian Jewry has been attributed to everything *except* anti-Semitism.[156]

"Secularism in India does not mean animosity towards religion," said Prime Minister Indira Gandhi at the synagogue's quatercentenary celebrations on December 15, 1968. "It implies equal respect for all religions. . . . It is a matter of pride for us in India that all the great religions in the world are respected in our country. I offer my good wishes and say *'Mazal Tov'* (good luck) to all our Jewish citizens on the occasion of this quatercentenary celebration of the Cochin Synagogue"[157] (see figure 9).

On this singular day, the symbolisms of the Hindus and Jews perfectly coalesced. For the Cochin Jews, proximity to the highest levels of the host civilization had always been a source of pride and status. For centuries, close association with maharajahs was the key to their security and prosperity. Their history of such special relationships, based on mutual affection and respect, distinguished them from other Diaspora Jews, giving them a unique, coveted status among world Jewry. As Immanuel Jokobvitz, chief rabbi of the British Commonwealth, commented, "Through this outstanding event, your Congregation establishes a record unique in the annals of the Commonwealth and exceedingly rare in the history of our long-lived people. It is a ringing tribute to the perseverance and undaunted faith of our Jewish brethren in Kerala, no less than to the tolerance and friendliness of the Indian people who have never allowed their record to be besmirched by Jewish blood."[158]

For contemporary Hindus, tolerance is a matter of pride. Since most other major religions of the world do not value tolerance as highly, Hindus view it as one of their great contributions to civilization. Tolerance is also an important element in the political discourse of modern India as it struggles with tenacious ethnic, religious, communal, and linguistic conflicts. Thus, the presence of the prime minister of India at the syna-

Figure 9.   Indira Gandhi, the prime minister of India, is greeted in the Cochin Synagogue by (left to right) Sattu S. Koder, Elias Roby, Isaac Hallegua, and Samuel Koder. Gandhi's address was the highlight of the celebrations to mark the four hundredth anniversary of the synagogue in 1968. (Photograph courtesy of the late Sattu S. Koder)

gogue's four hundredth anniversary and the fact that the post office issued a commemorative postage stamp for the occasion meant status to both Hindus and Jews, albeit for thoroughly different reasons.[159]

The celebrations were as exotic as they were enthusiastic. Special archways bearing Hebrew and Malayalam greetings and blessings were constructed. Drummers beat traditional rhythms. A gold-caparisoned elephant, on loan from a neighboring Hindu temple, added the symbolism of royalty. All India Radio broadcast many of the speeches. An arts festival celebrated Keralan dance, drama, and music, while a symposium examined Jewish history and the role of minorities in India. Some ten thousand citizens of Cochin viewed an exhibition of Jewish antiquities and curiosities. Dignitaries, diplomats, scholars, religious leaders, and journalists attended from around the world. For one brief moment, all eyes were fixed upon Jew Town, and the Jews reveled in this celebration of their esteemed history. But the celebration heralded not continuation or new beginnings, but endings.

Other events of note were all closures, the end of ancient traditions, final ritual reenactments—the last wedding, the last brit milah, the last time the community baked matsah. The few elderly Jews who remain exude betrayal, abandonment, and desolation. Dust from commercial warehouses—once spacious Jewish homes—clogs the lungs, just as nostalgia for Little Jerusalem clouds the mind.

The saddest milestone came during July 1987. For several years it had often been difficult to gather ten men for Shabbat prayers. Lack of this quorum had caused the abandonment of the three traditional daily synagogue prayer services years earlier. Many other observances had disappeared, but Shabbat had always been different. "By the grace of God," commented Raymond Salem, "we have never missed Shabbat prayers—either Friday evening, Saturday morning, or Saturday afternoon. Whenever we're short of people, God sends us a foreigner so we can make *minyan.*" [160]

Four hundred and nineteen years of continuity were broken in July 1987, when the Shabbat minyan failed for lack of a tenth man. If the Cochin Jewish community's moment of death could be fixed, that was it.

JEWS AND THE CASTE SYSTEM

The story of the Cochin Jews interweaves legend with history, creating a charming narrative of honor and affection, of triumphs and a few defeats, of hospitality, of long-standing residence in Cranganore and ancient origin in Israel, a double-yichus—all of which served them well in creating a Jewish home in venerable India.

One aspect of their story, however, is less savory. The Cochin Jews evolved a pattern of social organization that reflected Indian caste values. Some Cochin Jews joined a liberal rabbi from Johannesburg in contemptuously describing this social system as "Jewish Apartheid," after the system of racial oppression in South Africa. The label is an exaggeration, to be sure, but in emulating the Indian caste system by developing subcastes, the Cochin Jews crossed the fine line of judicious accommodation with Indian society. Halachah was breached, as foreign Jews have admonished Cochin Jews ever since the issue was first raised in 1520.

India is a hierarchical society in which numerous castes "who may differ in their customs and habits, live side by side, agreed on the code which ranks them and separates them." [161] In Indian languages, a caste is called a *jati,* a "birth," indicating its hereditary character. The word *jati* is a cognate of the Latin *genus,* suggesting that in Indian thought, caste is a biological rather than sociological category.[162] Castes can be distinguished by three characteristics: "*separation* in matters of marriage and contact, whether direct or indirect (food); *division* of labour, each group having, in theory or by tradition, a profession from which its members can depart only within certain limits; and finally *hierarchy*, which ranks the groups as relatively superior or inferior to one another." [163]

The caste system is the basis for the well-known "Hindu tolerance." Hindus allowed foreign groups such as the Jews to flourish in India, following their own cultural and religious traditions, because they assume that different categories of beings would naturally have differing religious, behavioral, and moral codes.

For groups such as the Jews, one strategy for carving out an Indian identity was to become accepted as a caste in India. To do so, a group must interact with other castes according to the principle of hierarchy, remain separate as regards food and marriage, and display strict concerns about purity and pollution—the bedrocks of the caste system. This is precisely what the Cochin Jews did, especially through their unique observance of Passover. A group also achieves caste status by enacting appropriate symbols of status, as did the Cochin Jews with the display of royal symbolism in their distinctive Simchat Torah traditions. A group must narrate appropriate status-enhancing legends.

Of these four strategies for cultural adaptation to India's caste system, three—ritual enactments of purity, a show of royal status, and generation of an appropriate historical legend—posed no halachic difficulties for the Cochin Jews. Only with the fourth method, their proliferation into subcastes, did the Cochin Jews contravene Halachah and repeatedly defy rabbinic admonition and censure. These subcastes married only within their group, the practice of endogamy. And the "superior" group denied the "inferior" group a role in synagogue life. This internal division was purportedly based on one's descent from ancient Israel; however, some community members claim the distinction was based on skin color, the infamous white Jew/brown Jew/black Jew pattern of religious and social organization. Jews outside the white subcaste were denied religious equality in the Paradesi Synagogue and were not allowed to marry members of the white faction.

Jewish law states that a Jew is the child of a Jewish mother or someone who is converted to the faith according to Halachah. These definitions are halachic universals. As observant Jews, the Cochin Jews scrupulously followed these rules and regulations. However, they were also Indians. They created a resemblance to their fellow countrymen by adopting additional traits influenced by the Hindu caste system and applying them to their own religious and social conduct. Preservation of their identity depended on it, as did their coveted high-caste status in society at large. As a result, alien notions about a biological basis for Jewish caste identity were grafted onto halachic standards. Membership in a Jewish subcaste depended not only on a halachic conversion, but on perceived Jewish "substance" or "blood." The traditional Jewish identification of substance as blood underscores the role of the mother in conferring Jewish identity; yet the Cochin Jews' concern for the father's substance reflects the South Indian identification of substance with semen rather than blood.[164] Marriage and sexual relations were, therefore, of paramount concern, because if the Jewish blood of a couple was considered tainted, the Cochin community no longer recognized the offspring of that union as Jews.[165]

The first documented account of intra-Jewish strife in Cochin goes back to about 1520, when a letter of inquiry was sent from Cochin to the Sephardic world's preeminent *halachist*, Rabbi David ben Solomon ibn Zimra, in Cairo.[166]

The inquiry gave ibn Zimra ample background about the Cochin community. Of its nine hundred Jewish families, one hundred were meyuchasim, or "those with lineage, or yichus." Although they considered themselves the higher-status subcaste, apparently they were lower on the scale of wealth and influence. They refused to intermarry with their coreligionists—a "rich, devout and charitable group," close to the rulers of Cochin and dominant in the sea trade—whom they called "slaves," by which they meant descendants of manumitted slaves. The self-segregating group doing the name-calling was, by contrast, an impoverished minority that acted seemingly "out of jealousy and hatred." Their aloof, superior behavior, the anonymous petitioner noted, caused ongoing divisive arguments in the community.

After deliberating, the rabbi decided the two groups could marry, providing that the nonmeyuchasim first underwent symbolic conversion. *Tevilah,* ritual immersion before three witnesses which is ordinarily performed in the conversion process, was required to remove any stain of doubt regarding their previous manumissions and conversions. From that time forward, he declared, they were considered to be Jews. Those who persisted in calling them slaves were fundamentally wrong.

The rabbi's decision would seem to have taken care of the matter. It did not. The meyuchasim ignored his advice and wrote a similar letter a generation later, hoping this time for a ruling in their favor. Ironically, they appealed to ibn Zimra's student, Rabbi Jacob de Castro, in Alexandria. De Castro studied his teacher's arguments and reiterated that Jewish law permitted marriage between the two groups, the only prerequisite being tevilah for the larger faction. Again the meyuchasim disregarded this advice and segregated themselves. Their exclusionary behavior continued, despite rulings in 1882 and 1951 from rabbinical authorities who held to ibn Zimra's original decision, although to no avail.

Why did the nonmeyuchasim care whether or not the meyuchasim accepted them? Why would a large group that seemingly had everything clamor for acceptance by a tiny, self-segregating, impoverished faction? Obviously, the smaller group possessed something the larger group wanted: yichus, unquestioned Jewish status. Attested lineage ostensibly set the meyuchasim apart. Under the sway of Kerala's caste-based society, those claiming Jewish substance said they feared "pollution" and thus refused to mix with or marry those who could not prove the purity of their lineage. Their diffidence fit them neatly into the caste system. The meyuchasim never considered the nonmeyuchasim equals. While they recognized them as Jews, they apparently saw nothing else in common to warrant interaction.

Who were the meyuchasim, and why were they so intent on segregating themselves from their own people? When did divisions between these two factions become so pronounced? David Mandelbaum, one of the most astute scholars of Cochin Jewry, believed that the distinctions were introduced by Jewish immigrants from Europe and the Middle East.[167] Those described as meyuchasim in the early-sixteenth-century letter to ibn Zimra may have been mostly recent arrivals fleeing religious persecution in Spain and Portugal. Upon reaching Malabar, these foreign Jews were caught in a cultural dichotomy: they found a group of fellow Jews who were so utterly different—in language, dress, diet, and more—that they could not readily associate with them. Kerala's caste system, which they came to adopt, further exacerbated these social barriers. Wanting to carve a niche for themselves in their newly adopted society, they used whatever assets they had to their advantage. Aside from boasting about their Jewish lineage, the newcomers had greater Jewish knowledge than their Malabari counterparts, who had been somewhat cut off from the rest of the Jewish world. More important, the foreign Jews knew the languages and trade practices of the European merchants who came to South India. Because they could be useful to those in power, they eventually became powerful.

The meyuchasim were not alone in their exclusionary behavior. In-

deed, they mirrored Kerala's high-caste Christians and Muslims, who
shunned social or religious interaction with their own "lesser brethren"
to prove their purity and thus maintain their high status in the dominant
Hindu society.[168] During ancient and precolonial times, Kerala's Jewish
population was harmonious, though occasionally augmented by small
influxes of Jewish traders, a few of whom may have brought their families. Because there were so few foreign settlers, probably no formal social distinctions were drawn between them and local Malabar Jews.[169]
The mass migration of European Jews, entire families fleeing Spanish
and Portuguese persecution in the sixteenth century, abruptly changed
that dynamic. Ample documentation shows that these foreign Jews kept
to themselves, refused to mix with their coreligionists already settled in
Cochin, and ultimately drove a wedge between themselves and the others that only widened with time.

We can merely speculate why and when this polarity arose between
the local Malabar Jews and Paradesi, or "foreign," Jews, as they were
called. For centuries, foreign travelers' reports mentioned this segrega-
tionist behavior. Along with his other observations in 1686, Moses
Pereira de Paiva of Amsterdam noted that despite the two groups' com-
monalty of worship, cavernous fissures existed between them. The Paradesis kept their distance, religiously and socially, from the Malabar
Jews. They condemned intermarriage, refused to count a Malabar Jewish man as part of a minyan, and would not eat meat ritually slaughtered
by the other group. Why? According to de Paiva, "They allege as a reason they [the Malabari Jews] are slaves of slaves and they are mixed with
Canaanites, converts and Muslims."[170] Echoing the past, the Paradesis
denounced Malabaris as having tainted lineage, a belief they passed on
to foreign travelers, who usually heard only the Paradesis' side of the
story, since, after all, they were the ones who spoke European languages.

Understandably, the Malabari Jews grew angry with the Paradesis,
whom they accused of spreading slanderous lies about their origins. The
Malabari Jews countered that their lineage was actually more impressive
than the Paradesis'. Unlike these newcomers, they claimed, a number of
their Jewish ancestors had arrived in Kerala from ancient Israel more
than two thousand years ago. Traveler Rabbi David D'Beth Hillel was
"inclined to believe correct" the Malabaris' version of their history. In
1832, he recorded that they "believe themselves to be the descendants of
the Israelites of the first captivity who were brought to India and did not
return with the Israelites who built the Second Temple."[171] Moreover,
the story goes, those Israelites who remained in India were the first set-

tlers of Cranganore. Thus, they could claim not only ancient Jewish lineage but ancient Indian lineage, both highly respected in Kerala society.

The Paradesis vehemently refuted these claims and, over the course of time, developed their own origin story. They asserted that they were the only Jews descended from ancient Israel and, moreover, they were the true descendants of the original Cranganore settlers. Claiming Joseph Rabban as their own, the Paradesis repeatedly mentioned him in their letters and chronicles, sang his praises in their Hebrew and Malayalam folk songs, and symbolically likened a bridegroom to him in their wedding rituals. They embraced Joseph Rabban as an ancestral hero. Even today, some Paradesi Jews who trace their ancestry to Iraq or Spain, nonetheless speak proudly of their forefather, Joseph Rabban. The Paradesis also held the Hindu royal family in great esteem. They claim the royal family had protected them from the time of Sri Bhaskara Ravi Varma's rule in Cranganore through the reign of his descendant, the maharajah of Cochin.

Two distinctions were drawn within the Cochin community; while they often overlapped, they were not identical. The indigenous distinction drawn on halachic lines between meyuchasim, those with attested Jewish lineage, and nonmeyuchasim, those allegedly descended from slaves, is already clear.

The second distinction, established by European conquerors and immigrants, was no longer defined by one's ancestry but by the color of one's skin. The Paradesis and most European visitors and scholars perceived the "white" Jews as meyuchasim and the "nonwhite" or "black" Jews as meshuchrarim, descendants of slaves and converts. As mentioned, however, fair-skinned European converts were sometimes accepted as white Jews despite the obvious fact that they could not have Jewish lineage. Similarly, some dark-skinned Yemeni Jews who had proper lineage were considered blacks and were not accepted into the white synagogue. Our view of Cochin Jewish social stratification becomes confused when we conflate these two distinct systems of separation and prejudice. Keeping them separate gives us a clearer picture, even if Cochin Jews today often blend them.

This harks back to British India, a time of tremendous economic and social upheaval. Among the Cochin Jews, the worlds of the Paradesi whites and the Malabari blacks were turned topsy-turvy. The marked change in the two groups' relative economic fortunes no doubt was a sore point for the Paradesis, most of whom had dominated business as well as Indian Jewry's social and religious life since shortly after their arrival in Malabar. But by the mid-1800s, a number of Malabari families had become very wealthy from agriculture and domestic trade. Simultaneously, international trade, a field dominated by the Paradesis, moved north from Cochin to Bombay.[172] This trying period exacerbated the white Jews' already testy feelings for their nonwhite coreligionists. "This was a time of increasing hostility between Paradesis and Malabaris, and [brought] a serious split within the Paradesi congregation itself." [173]

During this time, many social issues came to a head in the Cochin community. The Paradesi whites, at a low ebb and perhaps eager to boost their bruised egos, wrote prolifically of their group's history. The narrative often reached grandiose proportions. As always, they portrayed their longtime rivals, the Malabaris, as the offspring of slaves and denied they had yichus from either ancient Israel or Cranganore. Not surprisingly, the Malabaris vehemently countered these charges, which they said were false, slanderous, and hurtful. Ironically, the situation resembled events between the two groups' ancestors three centuries earlier, when members of a large, prosperous faction tried to right what they considered a terrible wrong—being branded as slaves by a small, impoverished clique of foreign Jews. Appeals to eminent rabbis abroad had not resolved their unhappy situation centuries before. At this time of economic hardship for the Paradesis, nothing seemed to help, so they lashed out at the more prosperous Malabaris with poison pens. For their part, the Malabaris were determined to unshackle themselves from the hateful slave label.

But it was a faction within the Paradesis that seemed most determined to shake off its second-class status among Cochin Jewry. These were the so-called brown Jews, the meshuchrarim. Although *meshuchrarim* means "the manumitted ones," a reference to slaves freed by their Jewish masters and converted to Judaism, in fact the Hebrew word was used loosely by Paradesi whites to describe any fellow synagogue congregants whom they judged nonwhite. This subgroup did comprise manumitted slaves, but also the *yal'dei bayit* who were the offspring of white men and native women, often servants, as well as a number of darker-skinned Jews "of lineage" and converts. This derogatory—and for many factually inaccurate—label stuck, and the whites continued to use it long after the British abolished slavery in the mid-nineteenth century.

Unlike the Malabaris, who had seven synagogues to accommodate their people in Jew Town and neighboring towns and villages, the meshuchrarim did not have their own house of worship. Instead, they prayed at the Paradesi Synagogue, but not without difficulties. The Pa-

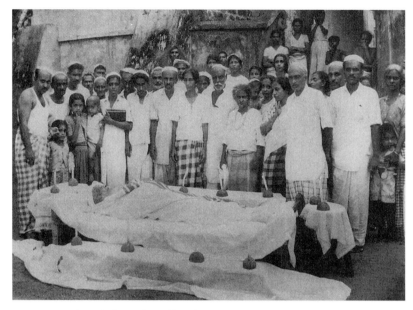

Figure 10.   Jewish funeral in Chendamangalam, circa 1940s. (Photograph
courtesy of P. T. Aron)

radesi meshuchrarim were not allowed to marry into the white faction
and were denied ritual equality. They could not chant certain liturgical
hymns, be called to the Torah to recite prayers or read from the Torah, or
bury their dead in coffins or, for that matter, in the Paradesi cemetery (see
figure 10). Every one of these prohibitions violated Jewish law. Moreover, meshuchrarim suffered the indignity of not being allowed to sit on
benches inside the synagogue; they were forced to stand or sit on the
floor of the synagogue anteroom, from where they could hear the religious services conducted by the whites.

   The meshuchrarim repeatedly tried to change discriminatory ritual
practices in the Paradesi Synagogue, but to no avail. By about 1840,
many meshuchrarim found their lowly status intolerable. Those who had
actively protested the religious inequalities were thrown out of the Paradesi Synagogue, whereupon they requested the maharajah's permission
to build a synagogue of their own in Jew Town. When permission was
denied in 1842, the meshuchrarim settled for conducting prayer services
in a Jew Town home. This, unfortunately, did not settle matters. After a
particularly ugly open quarrel between the white and brown factions on
Purim, the whites complained to the dewan, the British resident at Co-

chin, who directed a subordinate to ensure that no prayer services be conducted by the "group with impurity in the house appropriated for that purpose, and told [them] that they should walk submissively to the 'white' Jews." [174]

The next generation brought dramatic changes in the meshuchrarim's status. Most of these changes were embodied in one man, Abraham Barak Salem. Born into a poor family in 1882, Salem grew up to become the first university graduate among the meshuchrarim. He received his degree in law but seemed more interested in arguing cases for the masses on street corners than for one client at a time in a courtroom. Indeed, his public addresses on a hill in nearby Ernakulam were so frequent that the spot was dubbed Salem *Kunnu* (Salem Hill). He championed the underdog, striving to improve the lot of low-caste, low-paid workers such as boatmen and rickshaw drivers by actively working to organize labor unions. Outgoing and charismatic, Salem became involved in politics, cofounding and serving for many years on the Cochin Legislative Assembly. In 1929, as a delegate of the Native Princely States of Cochin and Travancore, he participated in the Congress Party's session in Lahore, where Mohandas K. Gandhi argued for Indian independence from the British.

Salem met many prominent Indian Congress leaders, but Gandhi made the biggest impression on him. At one time he called Moses and Aaron the "Gandhi and Nehru of ancient Egypt," describing both men as tireless "champions of the cause of the down-trodden." [175] Taken with the mahatma's teachings on nonviolent protest, Salem decided to use some of his mentor's tactics to further the cause of his own people within the Paradesi community.

In particular, he was impressed by the mahatma's campaign on behalf of the untouchables' right to use certain roads around the Hindu temple at Vykom, in neighboring Travancore State.[176] That campaign was inspired by Narayana Guru, a turn-of-the-century *Ezhava* (low-caste) activist who campaigned against brahmin orthodoxy and religious inequality in Kerala.[177] Emulating the mahatma, Salem staged various forms of *satyagraha* (civil disobedience) within the synagogue. Salem, like Gandhi, considered discrimination in the religious sphere the "most pernicious" of all imposed disabilities.[178] At one time he threatened a fast until death, although his most frequent protest was refusing to sit on the floor of the synagogue's anteroom. Instead, he stationed himself and his three sons on the steps leading upstairs to the bimah where the Torah was read, blocking the way of those called to recite blessings, who had to climb over them to reach the bimah.

Salem never gave up the fight. For decades, he continued to protest the white status quo, which still prohibited the meshuchrarim from burial in the Paradesi cemetery, sitting on synagogue benches, or being called to the Torah to recite blessings or read a portion of Scripture. (They were allowed to read publicly from the Torah only after the third *aliyah* blessing on Simchat Torah and could not be honored by being called by name.) Perhaps frustrated by the whites' unwillingness to change, Salem periodically held full prayer services at his home or attended them at the homes of other nonwhites, who also could not endure the humiliation in the synagogue. Salem's stamina—as well as his lawyer's oratory skills, used persistently to argue the group's case to any whites who would listen— finally paid off. A number of young Paradesi whites sided with him and protested their elders' actions. When the young men threatened to refuse to carry the heavy, metal-encased Torah scrolls for the Simchat Torah processions unless this unhappy situation were improved, at long last changes took place. Both sides accepted a compromise: two benches were set up at the back of the synagogue for the meshuchrarim. In addition, Mandelbaum reported during his visit to Cochin in 1937, "the *meshuhrarim* . . . may read from the Law on week days, though not on the Sabbath. These allowances still did not satisfy [A. B. Salem]." [179] In 1942, however, the rebel could record excitedly in his journal, "For the first time in the History of the Paradeshi Synagogue I got the chance, by stressing on the Law of the religious services regarding the reading of Torah, the privilege of reading the Maphtir of this Sabbath and Rosh Hodesh. May God be praised. . . . May the innovation become the order of the day!" [180] By the late 1940s, the meshuchrarim could bury their dead in the Paradesi cemetery, but in a separate section from the whites. In the synagogue, their men finally were allowed to read the Torah on the Sabbath as well as to recite blessings, although only the fifth of seven *aliyot*. These concessions were a significant start, although synagogue rituals remained far from equal—nonwhites still were barred from holding weddings or circumcisions, which they conducted instead in private homes.

Soon thereafter, migration to Israel weakened the community, and the remaining few, meyuchasim and meshuchrarim, white and brown, came to depend on one another more and more. Undermined by Salem's activism, along with modern education and values and the enervation of the depleted community, the subcaste structure of the community broke down. When a caste's position becomes weaker for political, social, economic, or demographic reasons, subcastes sometimes reaggregate into larger, more viable units.[181] The Cochin Jews are a model case. As A. B. Salem's son, Raymond, aptly put it, the whites finally acceded to the demands articulated by the oppressed meshuchrarim because "their wings have been cut." [182]

RITUALS OF POWER

In India, social identity involves social position, power, and place. Such social position is never simply a given but must be established ritually. The Cochin Jews used their observances, especially the so-called exotic aspects of their minhag, to position themselves within Kerala's complex caste system by ritually appropriating and enacting Indian symbols of power.

Among the most distinctive features of Indian civilization are two separate sources of power, social prestige, and position: the ascetic or the noble, the purely religious or the rich and politically powerful. In Kerala, the ascetics are the Nambudiri brahmin priests and the nobles are the Nayars. Both groups have maintained their stature on the basis of these two separate pillars since Manu's fourth-century codification of social law. The brahmins, who occupy one of the two apexes of the Indian hierarchy, are distinguished by symbols of purity: their pure food, their white clothes, their ascetic and scholarly lifestyle, and their self-distancing from sources of pollution (animal carcasses, meat, lowly born people, and agriculture). They maintain this distance through an intricate, hierarchical system of social interdependencies, customs, and taboos. Such purity is deemed an essential prerequisite to the efficacious reenactments of ancient rituals that constitute the brahmins' livelihood.

In Kerala, the ascetic lifestyle of the Nambudiri brahmins, the religious elite, are counterbalanced by the colorful, riotous deity processions of the Nayars, the dominant caste politically and economically. While the Nambudiris adore Brahman, an abstract metaphysical concept, the Nayars worship the life-embracing, erotic warrior-prince Lord Krishna, who embodies the kshatriya ideal. Their religion is neither intellectual (*jñani*) nor ritualistic (*karmi*), but emotional (*bhakti*). The Nayar nobility, residing at the second apex of the Indian hierarchy, traditionally employ the symbols of royalty, conquest, and wealth. Fine silks and jewels bedeck the kshatriyas and the maharajahs, in contrast to the pure, homespun white cotton of the brahmins.

In their minhagim, the Cochin Jews have foregrounded Judaism's inherent symbols of purity and nobility, but at the same time they have adapted some of Hinduism's priestly and royal symbols, creating one of the most intriguing systems of Jewish observance anywhere in the Diaspora. Embracing both of India's status-generating symbol complexes, they appropriated certain brahmanic symbols of purity in their unique Passover observances and adapted aspects of the Nayars' symbols of royalty and prosperity in their Simchat Torah observances and wedding customs. Moreover, they managed this syncretism judiciously, in keeping with the normal Judaic standards embodied in Halachah.

Judaism has ample indigenous resources that could easily be assimilated to reflect brahmanical priestly-ascetic symbols, including:

1. a hereditary priesthood of kohanim, paralleling the brahmins;
2. a fastidious system of laws of *kashrut,* or dietary regulations;
3. complex laws governing family purity (*taharat mishpacha*); and
4. ascetic tendencies in certain holidays, especially Passover and Yom Kippur.

Among Judaism's other resources comparable to the Nayars' noble-kingly symbols are the royalty symbolism (malchut) of the High Holy Days, the resemblances between the Torah processions (*haqafot* or *rodeamentos*) of Simchat Torah and Hinduism's deity processions, and the royalty symbolism traditionally ascribed to brides and bridegrooms. The minhagim of the Cochin Jews embody a creative synthesis that accentuates Jewish traditions connected with both the priestly and the royal sets of symbols, while at the same time incorporating comparable elements from Hindu traditions. These adaptive ritual observances serve as a means of periodically reaffirming the Cochin Jews' status in the Indian caste hierarchy, the *jati* system.

These three components of caste—separation (endogamy and food), division of labor (occupation), and hierarchy (status)—are all aspects of one overarching principle of purity and pollution.[183] The Cochin Jews obviously approximate caste behavior in their separation from other groups, which has been maintained through endogamy, and in their dietary restrictions. The Cochin Jews proliferated into four endogamous

subcastes: the Paradesi meyuchasim and the descendants of their manumitted slaves (the meshuchrarim) and the Malabari meyuchasim and the
descendants of their manumitted slaves (known as the *orumakars*). Their
observance of kashrut places them in a somewhat ambiguous situation.
On the one hand, in Indian eyes a strict and complex dietary code be-
stows high status. On the other hand, the meat in their diet resembles
low-caste practices. Cochin Jews, however, eat meat only at home, the
only place kosher meat is available. In public they frequent brahmin vege-
tarian restaurants, which meet requirements of kashrut while at the same
time reinforcing their high social position.

As for hereditary occupations, which are clear caste demarcations in
traditional Indian society, we simply do not have adequate evidence to
reach definitive conclusions. In modern times the Cochin Jews have been
professionals (attorneys, professors, engineers, teachers, physicians),
merchants large and small, and clerks. We have only meager evidence
about their life prior to their fleeing from Cranganore, where they were
primarily agriculturists and warriors. From the sixteenth century until
1957, when Kerala's communist government undertook vigorous land
redistribution, the community derived most of its income from coconut
estates owned by the synagogue and by leading Jewish families. In Hindu
tradition, landholding is the main criterion in determining if a caste is
dominant.[184] The Cochin Jews were also international spice merchants.
In general, however, occupation has not played a major role in the Cochin Jews' identity, at least as they have understood it. "Work, for many
of them . . . " wrote Mandelbaum, "was necessary and even meritorious
in its proper time and place, but was a practice that should not stand in
the way of ritual devotion or pleasure." [185]

Finally we come to the issue of hierarchy. How have other groups perceived the Cochin Jews within the dynamics of Kerala society? And how
has the Cochin Jews' concern about those perceptions altered their Judaism? For instance, their concern with purity at Passover is excessive
by the halachic standards, an excess best understood as a function of
their concern with maintaining their high status in the caste hierarchy.

Although the Cochin Jews have adopted many Hindu practices, they
have scrupulously ensured that their syncretic religious patterns do not
violate Jewish legal or ethical principles. In so doing, they have done
what Jews everywhere in the Diaspora have done, maintaining a distinct
identity while adapting creatively into their cultural milieu. This includes
their separation into subcastes, their removal of footwear in the syna-

gogue, their ritual use of Hebrew paralleling Hindu use of Sanskrit, and their observance of the dietary restrictions of kashrut. Some of their practices—endogamy, use of a sacred language, dietary codes, family purity—represent points where Jewish and Hindu values converge. Others—such as praying barefoot—point to more specific borrowings.

A number of the Cochin Jews' practices appear to have been borrowed from the highest Kerala brahmin caste, the Nambudiris. For example, the various Jew Towns in Kerala's cities were designed to be similar to the Brahmin Towns. Similarities in the economic organization of the communities may be more significant. In each case, individuals became dependent upon the synagogue or temple, which possessed vast estates. The Jews also resemble the Nambudiris in their emphasis upon yichus, seen in their focus on purity of descent and on their foreign origin; in their close association with the Cheraman Perumal emperors of Cranganore; in their relatively fair complexion; and in the use of a series of paintings in the synagogue or temple to narrate the community's "sacred history." [186]

The Cochin Jews have also had close links with the Nayars, the dominant caste politically and economically in Kerala. They established very cordial and fond relations with the Nayar maharajahs, including an intricate system of mutual dependence. The Jews enjoyed the maharajahs' hospitality and protection; for instance, the Cochin Synagogue was built beside the palace and royal temple by royal invitation. In return, they provided the maharajahs not only with their best soldiers but also with their liaisons with the world beyond Kerala's shores. Being part of an international people with commercial interests spanning the globe, the Jews used their expertise as traders, interpreters, and diplomats in the service of the maharajahs. Much of Cochin's legendary wealth was due to its relatively advanced position in such trade, a position managed for the most part by such Jewish leaders as the House of Rahabi.

Such proximity with a high caste tends to "rub off," and the Cochin Jews' behavior came to resemble many aspects of the Nayars'. For example, the social prestige and independence women enjoyed in Jew Town in part reflects the Jewish community's contact with the matrilineal Nayars. Once a "primary marriage" had been contracted with a Nambudiri man, Nayar women traditionally enjoyed autonomy in selecting partners. While Jewish women's sexuality is strictly governed, their autonomy is more generalized, as evidenced in their participation in religious education and, later, in professional achievement. In day-to-day interactions in Cochin, Jewish women and men are strikingly equal.

This equality cannot be attributed to modernization because it predates and in some respects exceeds it.

PASSOVER: AS PURE AS THE PRIESTS

The Cochin Jews secured a high place in the caste hierarchy by adopting aspects of the lifestyle and practices of Kerala's two highest castes. The complex dynamics of this process are clearly evident in the ritual observances associated with the festivals of Passover and Simchat Torah, which involve creative adaptation of the symbols of the Nambudiri brahmins and of the Nayars. Cochin Jews' Passover observances demonstrate another nuance of cross-cultural position building: how the ritualized exchange of food determines a group's relative status in the hierarchy.

In virtually every country where they have lived, Jews have adopted "additional observances" (*hiddur mitsvot*) on top of those required by Halachah, "which express the Jew's love of the *mitsvot* by embellishing them." [187] Passover preparations in Cochin are striking in this regard. In certain ways they are more fastidious than those found in other Jewish communities, even the very orthodox. Why do the Cochin Jews exaggerate their Passover observances? Why do they embellish them with additional stringencies?

The answer is complex, and it involves the value Hindu society attaches to purity and ascetic behavior. In emulation of the brahmin priests' concern with purity, these Jews foregrounded their own parallel traditions, and nowhere in Jewish tradition is purity more emphasized than in a disdain that borders on the obsessive for leavening (*chamets*) and anything touching leavening prior to and during the eight-day Passover festival. The Cochin Jews' fine balance between the worlds of Judaism and Hinduism is evident in their Passover observances, in which they have added to normative Jewish practice a form of asceticism that integrates them into Kerala's caste system. Cochin's Passover observances add another layer beyond its usual Jewish meanings—a celebration of the Exodus story, a commemoration of Temple sacrifices, and a springtime agricultural festival. This additional meaning is the reassertion of the group's high-caste status, actualized through exemplary group asceticism and a period of liminal separation from the non-Jewish world.

Asceticism is found in varying degrees in all of the world's religions, and its goals are said to be "absorption in the sacred" or "initiation or maintenance of contact with divinity, or some supernatural or transcendent being." [188] It usually takes five forms: "(1) fasting, (2) sexual continence, (3) poverty, under which may be included begging, (4) seclusion or isolation, and (5) self-inflicted pain, either physical . . . or mental." [189] Cochin Passover practices involve all but sexual continence, and stress fasting and isolation. The data from Cochin also suggest that status is as much an objective of asceticism as any "spiritual" goal.

Fasting generally involves either total abstention from all food or partial abstention from particular foods. [190] In Cochin, the Passover fast was partial. With respect to isolation, it is often an individual ascetic who is secluded, in accordance with the hermit ideal; however, a group may undergo a period of temporary liminal seclusion that often precedes rituals of status elevation. [191] In Cochin, where caste status is an integral component of Passover rituals, the community as a whole becomes isolated from its normal context prior to and during the festival. This isolation is a crucial component for the ritual establishment and celebration of Jews' status in the context of Hindu Kerala.

Passover practices throughout the Jewish world, of course, involve a modified fast in the form of abstaining from leaven and any foods or utensils that might have come into contact with leaven, or chamets— pronounced *hamas* in the sweet-sounding Hebrew of Cochin. Fasting is often connected with purity, purification, and removing pollution, as is the avoidance of chamets.

In Jewish homes worldwide, a month of work cleaning the home to eliminate chamets precedes Passover. This tradition is the origin of spring cleaning associated with Easter in Christian communities and simply with springtime among secularists. However, Cochin minhag— especially with regard to cleaning, separation, and purity—went markedly beyond standard halachic requirements and in uniquely Indian ways. This excess can be traced to the dynamic interplay of asceticism, diet, and caste in Kerala and to the Cochin Jews' periodic need—as "foreign" meat-eaters in a society that values vegetarianism—to reassert their high-caste status.

According to Halachah, preparations for Pesach, pronounced "Pesah" in Cochin, should begin thirty days before the festival, or just after Purim. [192] In Cochin, however, the Chanukkah candles had barely cooled before Pesach work, as it is called, began to warm up. First came the cleaning of the tea, chilies, tamarind, and spices to be set aside for Passover use. "Now the work for Pesach begins," Sarah Cohen said on January 15, when she bought a basket of tamarind for Passover cleaning. "Everything must start afresh for Pesach," she added, combining the motifs of special preparations and cleaning with the traditional understanding of Pesach as a "second new year," coming as it does during the first month of the Jewish lunar calendar.

Pesach work increasingly dominated life in Jew Town from the beginning of the month of Teveth until the middle of Nisan—about one hundred days. It became so important to the Cochin community that they believed if the women made even the slightest mistake in Passover preparations, the lives of their husbands and children would be endangered. "The legend is that they won't make it to the next Pesach. That's why women are more orthodox than men." [193]

The women scrubbed special rooms for storing Passover items and all utensils, pots, and crockery. Houses were painted or whitewashed soon after Purim. Not found elsewhere except among the Beta Yisrael Jews of Ethiopia and some Yemeni Jews, this minhag reflects the Hindu custom of whitewashing homes in preparation for the Holi festival. Yet whatever preparations were observed in 1987 pale in comparison with observance in days gone by. Sarah Cohen recollected, "The elders would scrape off all paint from the previous year, using coconut fiber, and then repaint everything. They say *hamas* would be there, too, so they would scrape it off." [194]

Wells were drained and scrubbed, lest they be polluted by a crumb of bread. [195] Each grain of rice for the festival was examined to ensure that it was free from defects or cracks into which polluting chamets might have found its way. After inspection, it was known as Pesach rice. Special Passover cushion covers and curtains replaced everyday ones. Wooden furniture was stripped and repolished. Barbara C. Johnson, an anthropologist at Ithaca College, documented many of these observances, and all of them evidence the traditional Jewish concern for avoiding any contact with chamets, carried to a remarkable degree of fastidiousness. [196]

Making wine—either fermented *yayin* or fresh *mai*—was a major undertaking in Jew Town and represents an instance in which halachic and Hindu concerns for purity perfectly overlapped. Judaism's abhorrence of idolatry manifests itself in severe restrictions about wine. Since wine was used to consecrate pagan idols, any wine that might be so used is forbidden to Jews; therefore, only wine made by Jews is considered kosher. These wine restrictions come to resemble Hindu taboos about food preparation because they go further and hold that if Jewish-made wine were even *touched* by a Gentile, it would become forbidden because, as Halachah assumes the Gentile to be religious, he or she would likely dedicate some of the wine to the gods. [197] The Cochin Jews take one more step that reflects Hindu practice regarding food purity: if even the shelf or table upon which the wine sits is touched by a Gentile, the wine becomes taboo.

Similar scrupulous restrictions governed matsah. After grains of wheat were obtained, many hours were spent inspecting each for cracks or breaks that might indicate leavening due to contact with water. This inspection was performed three times: first by non-Jewish servants, then twice by Jewish women (or, rarely, a Jewish man). After the third inspection and the removal of all broken grains, non-Jews could touch neither the wheat nor its containers nor the shelf on which it rested. As with the wine preparations, Cochin observance exceeds halachic norms and reflects Hindu practice with these extra prohibitions.

The Jews of Cochin traditionally ground the wheat at home, but in recent times their diminished numbers have led to some modifications. In 1987, Passover wheat was ground in the nearby, Hindu-owned Kanchana Flour Mill, which had been specially cleaned the previous evening by the compliant proprietor. Jewish women brought the wheat early the next morning and cleaned the milling machinery a second time themselves. To prevent any contact between the wheat and non-Jews, the miller touched only the machinery. The women poured in the wheat kernels and collected the flour, which was then returned to Jew Town for sifting.

The climax of Pesach work was *massa* day. Early that day the women and young people gathered in the courtyard of Queenie Hallegua's vast home. The Gentile servants could perform only two jobs: tending the coconut husk fire (charcoal was mixed with the husks as an innovation in 1987), which heated flat iron griddles, and scouring the special mixing bowls, called *legen,* with "a bit of clean new coconut fiber and the soapy substance from a small green soapnut fruit, which the Jews use only for Passover washing, because it is thought to be particularly pure." [198]

Water that had been drawn from a purified well and cooled by standing overnight in special earthenware jugs kept solely for this purpose was used to knead the flour.[199] This had to be done quickly, for the water could be in contact with the flour only eighteen minutes before baking, or the flour was considered leaven. The massa was then rolled out using *kozhali,* hollow brass cylinders filled with metal beads, which were used only for this purpose and which produced a sweet, bell-like sound. Blessings were said over each household's batch of flour, usually around two kilograms, and the obligatory *challah* (the portion of the dough that during Temple days was set aside for the kohanim) was thrown into the fire. The matsah was baked on the hot griddles. The whole process used to be accompanied by the sounding of the shofar and the chanting of Passover songs and sections from the *Haggadah*.

The purity associated with the kohanim in the Temple was later transferred to all of Israel as "a nation of priests," especially but not exclusively regarding the kashrut system of food purity. The table (*shulchan*) in every home replaced the altar (*shulchan*) in the Temple. Jewish restrictions about food are in many ways analogous to the brahmin's restrictions concerning food purity, and such restrictions are identity markers for both groups. The methods of preparing "emblematic" foods in Cochin during the partial fast of Passover—massa in particular, but wine and other consumables as well—exceed halachic norms at crucial points, many of which resemble high-caste Hindu taboos about possible pollution by contact with *kaccha* (cooked) food. As Yosef Hallegua put it, "Pesach is the *cleanest* holiday."

The Passover jokes and complaints we heard tended to reinforce the ascetic quality of Passover preparations and observances in Cochin. Since the ascetic's self-infliction of pain may be psychological as well as physical, such banter is significant. Despite dinner tables laden with steaming buriyanis and curries, our 1987 hosts said the meals were too meager to sustain life—"the fasting feast" theme. "Bread fills up the holes in a diet," complained Jacob Cohen. Gamliel Salem, the community's most unabashed skeptic, joked, "Just because Moses did these things so long ago, we all have to suffer now. What rotten nonsense!" Community members recalled non-Pesach meals at the brahmin-run Krishna Cafe with an exaggerated fondness. This particular form of banter, comparing brahmin (or Jain) food with Jewish food during Passover, closely connected them to the status associated with food exchange in India.

Seclusion and isolation are common ascetic practices, but an intriguing variant was practiced among the Cochin Jews. Usually very gregarious, they became increasingly isolated from their non-Jewish friends during the month or two prior to Passover, culminating in almost total isolation during the eight days of the festival itself. However, they missed their usual connectedness with their Hindu neighbors. In 1987, Passover coincided with the local Hindu festival Vishu. Sarah Cohen complained, with a real feeling of loss, "It's too bad that Vishu falls during our Pesach this year. Otherwise we would all go to the [Hindu] temple [for Vishu] and mix with our Hindu friends and take our lunch with them."

The Jews' gradually increasing isolation became apparent by the festival of Purim. A month before Passover, Pesach work so dominated and consumed the Jews that they had little time for interactions outside of the community. Cochin Jews generally enjoy sharing food and conversation with their Hindu, Christian, Jain, Muslim, and Parsi friends on any occasion. In fact, they particularly enjoy intercommunal exchange of special foods—such as cakes for the Jewish new year, Rosh Hashanah—but not during Passover.

The Cochin Jews believed that the only way to avoid chamets completely was to avoid their non-Jewish friends. "For eight days I cut off everything. If I see my friends," Isaac Ashkenazi said, "they may offer me a cup of tea or some food. Actually, Pesach is a very hard time for us." Sarah Cohen warned, "Don't go outside [of Jew Town]. You might make a mistake and eat or drink something you can't have." While they would have enjoyed meeting friends or going to the local brahmin restaurant, the Krishna Cafe, the Jews scrupulously avoided both. "The main thing," according to Reema Salem, "is that we take nothing from outside." During the Passover festival, the Cochin Jews' universe did not extend beyond Synagogue Lane.

Avoidance of chamets thus translated into the temporary avoidance of non-Jews. Only one family regularly invited outsiders to their Seder: Sattu and Gladys Koder, the leaders of the community, who have traditionally borne the responsibility for the group's external relations. Some believe that the presence of a non-Jew at the Seder table "pollutes" the ritual.[200] This exclusion, however, was so contrary to the Cochin Jews' usual gregarious instincts that, on occasion, they compromised by aligning two dining tables under one table cloth, maintaining the ritual separation of tables, quite literally, under cover so as not to offend their gentile guests.[201]

But the Cochin Jews' Passover isolation from their neighbors was temporary and ended with a celebratory reaggregation into Kerala society, a charming "hamas party" hosted by neighbor D. B. Khona, an influential businessman and lay leader of the local Jain temple.[202] The temporary suspension of hierarchical societal interactions led to a reaffirmation of that hierarchy in a ritualized reaggregation, enabled by the host community's leadership. Thus the Cochin Jews' separation and isolation, ritually bounded by Pesach work and the hamas party, were both temporary and communal.[203] This isolation is part of the ascetic, self-inflicted pain of Passover, although the pain was more psychological than physical—at least for the men. Cochin men anticipated Passover with dread and bemoaned it as "the fasting feast" and "a nuisance festival" when there was "*nothing* to eat." Interestingly, leaven became overvalued prior to and during Passover. Men repeatedly protested that they needed "a cold beer"—something only rarely drunk in this community. Discussions of desired but forbidden foods increased as Passover drew nearer, often accompanied by vigorous protests. These complaints were made in half jest, but that does not diminish their psychological effect.

The women's suffering was more physical. They had to prepare their large homes for the festival, a pain exacerbated by the terribly hot weather of the premonsoon months. The temperature on massa day 1987 was 102° and the humidity was high; in the baking area, the temperature must have surpassed 120°. Perspiration quite literally boiled off, causing painful skin burns. The very real pain associated with Pesach work was verbally reinforced. "Cleaning the wheat, a backbreaking job," said Sarah Cohen. Summing up, she added, "During Pesach you die from the work, and then there is no food to eat!"

While poverty as such is not a virtue in Judaism, the Cochin Jews went to great expense in the annual repainting or whitewashing of their large homes, in hiring workers to drain and scrub their wells and water tanks, and in stripping and repolishing their furniture. Painting a large house cost between 6,000 and 7,000 rupees (in 1987, more than U.S. $500, a sum greater than India's per capita GDP), while employing casual workers to clean their wells cost at least 60 rupees ($5). To fulfill Passover traditions, many families willingly incurred expenses they could not afford.

As noted, Cochin's Passover embodies four of the five general forms of asceticism: fasting, in the modified form of avoidance of leaven, which went beyond the requirements of normative Judaism; a temporary isolation of the community from non-Jewish Cochin; self-inflicted psychological and perhaps even physical pain; and a degree of expense that posed real financial difficulties, this approximating the theoretical concern with poverty. The only missing ascetic criterion is sexual continence.

Despite the ascetic character of Cochin's Passover observances, the festival has its humor in offhanded comments that reflected very serious issues, such as the community's place in the larger society of Cochin. One example of the serious implications of Passover humor is the Cochin Jews' exaggerated longing for a snack at the Krishna Cafe. In India, and the south in particular, every town has brahmin-run restaurants. The Hindu dietary rule of thumb is that "the cook must be as pure as the eater," so one implicitly acknowledges another's equal or greater purity by the simple act of taking food. Brahmins have the strictest dietary regulations of any caste in India, except for the Jains. That everyone is willing to eat food cooked by a brahmin is evidence of the caste's high status.[204]

To joke about missing a Krishna Cafe meal is to point out that, for the duration of Passover at least, even pure brahmin food is not pure enough. The special requirements for avoiding chamets during Passover added a layer of food taboos that ipso facto carry high status. As the French anthropologist Louis Dumont succinctly put it, "superiority and superior purity are identical."[205] This drama of purity and status, played out nightly in Jew Town, is another indication of the Jews' high-caste status.[206]

On a typical week night in Jew Town, a car pulled up to Elias Koder's house at 7:30 P.M. sharp, as it had done nightly for more than fifteen years. The car belonged to D. B. Khona, whom everyone called Bapu-sait, and who carried his usual array of stainless steel tiffin carriers filled with snacks into Elias's house. A few minutes later Koder's Jewish neighbors, Jacob Cohen and I. C. Hallegua, strolled inside. Dr. Panikar, a Hindu surgeon, was usually last, coming directly from a nearby hospital. Occasionally V. K. Hamza, a Muslim lawyer, also dropped in, as did P. M. Jussay, a Syrian Christian newspaper editor. With all "members" taking their places around a huge table, the drinking club came to order.

A teetotaler himself, Koder nonetheless made sure there was plenty of rum, whiskey, and mixers to go around. And go around they did, literally, on a lazy Susan that seemed to be in perpetual motion as the men reached for refreshments. As the drinks continued to flow, so did the conversation. It included business, politics, risqué jokes, gossip, and quite often, religious matters.

Bapusait played the role of provider for the group because as a Jain he was subject to the most stringent dietary regulations of anyone, beyond even the brahmins. Anything from his kitchen would be pure enough for anyone; however, more than such reasoned practicality was at stake in the issue of who provided the food.

Given the Jews' isolation from the non-Jewish world during Passover, one might have expected the drinking club to be suspended during the festival. It was not, however, so maintaining the club's meeting assumed great symbolic importance. As Passover drew closer, more and more conversation turned to the festival's dietary requirements. Whiskey and beer could not be taken, of course. Brandy was acceptable because it was made from grapes rather than a suspicious grain. Discussion ensued. Indian brandy was, in fact, a grain product, flavored to resemble its European model, and technically should be avoided. Samuel Hallegua suggested that they drink only French cognac during Passover, an idea that was lauded until someone mentioned the exorbitant price that a bottle of imported brandy fetched on the Ernakulam black market (more than U.S. $50). Despite religious scruples, they decided to make do with Indian brandy.

As the discussion turned from drinks to snacks, Bapusait became especially curious. "Could you eat parched corn? How about flat rice pancakes?" When he learned that flat rice pancakes would be acceptable, he quickly offered to bring them. "No, because we don't know what else is in your kitchen, what has been cooked in your pots, where hamas [chamets] could be found," Jacob Cohen replied.

Bapusait was undaunted. "I will buy new pots to cook your pancakes and will only carry them on new plates. Could you eat them then?" At this point the conversation broke down into laughter. "We just can't take anything from outside," the Jews said, and Bapusait was crestfallen. Eventually he satisfied himself with bringing delicious mangoes (Passover falls during mango season in Kerala), as fresh fruit is *kosher le-Pesach* (kosher for Passover). That everyone enjoyed the discussion did not diminish its significance; by "out-brahmining the brahmin," the Jews established their status during this period of liminality. Even the purest Jain food was not pure enough, temporarily.

The celebration of Passover's conclusion culminated at Elias's house in a hamas party hosted by Bapusait. He brought *iddli*s (steamed rice flour), *puri*s (puffy fried flat bread), sweetmeats, and other treats that had been temporarily forbidden. The Jews relished the chamets—Gamliel Salem had been yearning "to eat hamas like hell" for days—thereby ending their liminal period of abstinence from certain foods and from contact with their non-Jewish friends. At the same time Bapusait resumed his role as provider, ritually reintegrating the Jews into the larger Kerala society and hierarchy. The Jews' high status thus ritually reestablished, they returned to and reaffirmed the society in which they had lived so happily for so long.

SIMCHAT TORAH AND SYMBOLS OF ROYALTY

Every spring in the ritual observances of the Passover festival, the Cochin Jews reassert their high place in the caste hierarchy by demonstrating their purity in accordance with the brahmanical-ascetic apex of power. Every autumn, on the other hand, in the ritual enactments of the High Holy Days and Simchat Torah, they give precedence to a different set of symbols, symbols of royalty and wealth, in accordance with the kshatriya-noble apex of power represented in Kerala by the Nayars. This emphasis on symbols of royalty represents a natural extension of the liturgical theme of the autumn High Holy Days, which celebrates God's kingship, *malchut* in Hebrew. *Avinu Malkenu,* "Our Father, Our King," one of the most popular prayers, is unique to the season. Beginning with the morning service on Rosh Hashanah and continuing through Yom Kippur, prayers focus on God's attribute of royalty or nobility (see figure 11). In Cochin, indigenous songs enhance this symbolism, as do the unique manner of displaying Torah scrolls and the joyous afternoon processionals on Simchat Torah. Through these festivals, royalty becomes the leitmotif of the autumn holy days.

The two-day festival known in Cochin as Shmini concludes the fall cycle of holy days. Most synagogues in the Diaspora observe two separate festivals, Shmini Chag Atseret and Simchat Torah, but in Israel, the two are celebrated together in one day. Shmini Chag Atseret commemorates the additional sacrifices offered at the Temple after Sukkot, and Simchat Torah is a nonbiblical celebration of the conclusion of the yearly cycle of Torah reading and the beginning of the new cycle.[207] In Cochin, Shmini is of enormous significance, arguably the community's most distinctive autumn observance. The synagogue, brilliant and colorful at any time, is utterly dazzling on Shmini. The whitewashed walls and dark wooden benches are covered with golden satin. The shimmering walls reflect the blazing oil lamps encircling the pulpit (*tevah*), suffusing the dainty prayer hall with a light that borders upon the supernal. All around the upper half of the walls hang parochets, "curtains" made of deceased Cochini women's festive sarongs, in green, gold, blue, red, and white embroidered silks. The impact is enhanced by the aroma of string upon string of freshly plucked jasmine flowers hanging among the many chandeliers and oil lamps.

The most striking decorations transform the *Aron Hakodesh* (Holy Ark). A special temporary ark called a *kule* is constructed between two tall silver pillars. The platform is covered with gold-embroidered, red Benarsi silk. All seven Torah scrolls are on display, replete with gold, jewel-encrusted crowns, and silver finials (*rimomim*). The effect is completed by a canopy of red and gold silks, topped with the lid of the synagogue's famous solid-gold kiddush cup, the one used to break the Yom Kippur fast a fortnight before and to sanctify every bride and bridegroom in Cochin for centuries.

The synagogue becomes a vision of eternity.

Figure 11.   Yosef Hallegua sounds the shofar for Rosh Hashanah in the
Cochin Synagogue, 1986. (Photograph by Ellen S. Goldberg)

In 1986, the Simchat Torah prayers increased in intensity through each
of the festival's three services, those on the first evening being the most
subdued. The synagogue was crowded for Arvit (evening) services. Indian Jews from as far away as Bombay, Trivandrum, and Madras, not to
mention Ernakulam and Alwaye, were present, as well as Jewish travelers from Switzerland, South Africa, England, Israel, and the United States.
As the seven *haqafot* (processions) commenced, men and women produced songbooks and filled the synagogue with haunting Shingly tunes,
melodies composed centuries earlier in Cranganore, ancestral home of
the Cochin Jews. Bottles of rum, brandy, and whiskey began to appear
in the corners and recesses of the building—as well as in the women's
section—as dancing, jumping, and clapping accompanied the singing.

By Shacharit prayers the next morning, the mood had become all the
more festive. The high spirits were enhanced by the "petrol" drunk to
enliven the steps of the younger men, who carried the Torah scrolls, as
well as the chants of the older men and the women. As the men caught
their breath after each circumambulation of the tevah with the heavy,
metal-encased scrolls elaborately bedecked with crowns and rimomim,
a fellow celebrant would invariably tap one of the men's shoulders, a
naughty grin on his lips, and invite him to share "Petrol! Petrol!" The
scroll would be passed to other eager arms, and the two would abscond
to the crowded apartment of the shamash, the caretaker, adjacent to the
synagogue. Bottle after bottle of liquor filled his dining table, as well as
boiled potatoes and eggs to ease the absorption of the spirits. Half a po-
tato and a healthy shot of brandy later, the reveler would be back in the
procession, singing *shirot* (songs) more loudly than ever and, quite literally, jumping with delight.

The *Haftarah* (prophetic reading) for Simchat Torah was sung in
Shingly cantillation and pronunciation, as were its blessings—an especially beautiful chant. Shingly or Cranganore, of course, was the site of
Indian Jewish sovereignty, so the use of Shingly cantillation and pronunciation linked the festival with Jewish nobility.

The three afternoon haqafot in the courtyard outside of the synagogue building are unique among Jews throughout the world.[208] A red
coir mat was laid around the synagogue. The younger and stronger men
carried the scrolls while older men sprinkled rose water on the celebrants. In recent years, as the congregation dwindled, people worried if
there would be enough young, able bodies to complete the seven circumambulations with the heavy scrolls, while in the past, they worried,

instead, if there would be enough rounds to give everyone a chance to carry the beloved scrolls. Mandelbaum observed the children's eager participation in 1937. "The younger men try hard to have the honor of carrying them. There are two small scrolls which are carried by boys. I noticed one little fellow tearfully pleading with his father that he might have the privilege of bearing the *sefer*. The privilege must be purchased, and when the father finally nodded his assent, the boy went bounding off in an about face of emotion, to tell his friends of his luck." [209]

All—men, women, children—lustily chanted unique Cochini Hebrew songs proclaiming their love of Torah. According to local tradition, the entire liturgy for the afternoon haqafot was composed in Cranganore. The older men led the processions carrying handwritten songbooks, walking backwards as they sang, facing the scrolls as one would a monarch. The women, dressed in brilliant saris and kerchiefs, sang no less enthusiastically. This festival was the only time women freely entered the main hall of the synagogue.

After the haqafot, the synagogue emptied as everyone headed home for a rest. Almost everyone. During the 1930s Cecil Koder introduced yet another festivity to Simchat Torah observances: water fights. Reminiscent of streets during the riotous Hindu festival, Holi, Synagogue Lane on Simchat Torah afternoon became a jocular battleground. Celebrants poured pails of water over any and every unsuspecting head, followed by a recent addition, rotten eggs that had been hidden away and painted with Hebrew festive greetings. Some elders scurried to bar their doors, but most accepted a rotten egg and pail of water as their due. In any event, they had time for a shower before Minchah prayers. Mandelbaum aptly commented upon the seemingly chaotic merriment:

> On this day the tears in the social fabric are mended. All quarrels are supposed to be patched up on *Simchat Torah,* and many dissentions really are smoothed over in the general merry-making. The least of the congregation enjoys the honor of reading the blessings before the Law together with the most distinguished. Women are allowed to come into the synagogue hall to kiss the sacred books. At noon the young people dine in houses other than their own. Wine and arrack flow copiously and some men become gloriously tight. Like drunken men the world over, they crack muddled jokes and bawl out catchy tunes. But in Cochin the tunes that they sing in their groggy animation are synagogue melodies, hymns and paeans to the Lord of Israel. [210]

After taking a rest, the Jews returned to their synagogue for Minchah prayers at 6:30 P.M. The Cochin Simchat Torah Minchah is a unique,

highly significant service, with origins in Shingly. A 1503 letter by Moshe
ben Abba Mori of Shingly reads, "And we have a custom, and the second holy day of *Shemini Atzeret,* after praying the additional service
(*Musaf*), they bring eight Torah scrolls, in precious drapes and chains
and golden pomegranates, outside the synagogue, and utter song and
praise and thanks in a loud voice and circle three times and pray *Mincha* (the afternoon prayer)."[211] The special afternoon service's importance in the community is clear. When Yaakob Daniel Cohen established
a Hebrew-Malayalam printing press in Jew Town in 1877, his first publication was the liturgy for this occasion (*Seder Minchah Simchat Torah,*
published in 5637/1877). The service includes the liturgy for the three
haqafot as well as the longest *Kaddish* in the world.[212]

Arvit prayers followed the Minchah. Then came another unique, intriguing Cochin observance. The Torah scrolls were placed on chairs
and benches, and as everyone—men, women, and children—sang shirot in the synagogue hall, the congregation dismantled the temporary
ark. Ritually and methodically, they carefully removed the Benarsi silks
and then the silver pillars. Finally, they disassembled the wooden planks.
Throughout, they sang shirot. At the conclusion, the young people
started singing and dancing an Israeli folk dance, the *hora,* and when
they were completely finished with dismantling the ark, they sang the Israeli national anthem, *"Hatikvah"* ("The Hope").

Once again the Jew Town folks walked from their synagogue to the
tiny street. Sattu Koder's measured steps and restrained demeanor set
the pace. They walked past the "tree of light," a huge candelabra with
seventy-two lights ablaze. The entire community escorted the eldest
member to the door of his house, sneaking longing glances back to the
metal-and-fire tree. The restraint of this final ritual act of the fall cycle
was a striking counterpoint to the animated ark dismantling and hora
dancing. Everyone sang the Indian national anthem, a counterbalance
to "Hatikvah." Just before entering the doorway, Sattu proclaimed with
a wave, "God bless everyone," and everyone replied in one voice,
"L'shanah haba b'Yerushalayim" ("Next year in Jerusalem!"). Someone
thought to adapt the Hebrew adage to better fit their circumstances and
shouted out, *"L'shanah haba b'Cochin"* ("Next year in Cochin!"), a ral-
lying cry that echoed along Synagogue Lane until everyone had retired
into their homes, exhausted from a full month of festivals.

Three aspects of the Cochin minhag for Simchat Torah are creative
responses to their Hindu environment in Kerala, borrowing and adapting Hindu symbols of royalty and nobility: displaying their Torah scrolls

on a temporary ark(kule), adding afternoon haqafot outside of the synagogue building, and ritually dismantling the kule. Hindu practice is defined by each particular community of Hindus, determined by caste and
geography, as well as other factors. There is no one normative version
of Hinduism, but rather a dazzling array of local traditions. The symbols
of royalty and nobility are generally promoted by the dominant caste of
the region, which in Kerala is the Nayar caste and, in Cochin, the Pe-
rumpaddapu family in particular.

Like most royal families, the Peramppadapus are devotees of Lord
Krishna, the erotic warrior-prince god of the Vaishnava pantheon. The
maharajah's temple, which abuts the Cochin Synagogue, is known as the
Pazhayannur Shri Krishna Temple, and it is not surprising that the Indian nobility opted to worship a god who sprang from their own community of rulers and warriors. The Jews could adapt the symbols of a
royal Hindu god because of their own metaphors of God's kingship
(malchut), the dominant liturgical theme for the High Holy Days. This
required only an exaggeration of ritual themes already inherent in Judaism, not the adoption of alien symbols.

Every Hindu temple has its own deity and an annual festival for that
deity. During the festival, the deity image is generally displayed on a
wooden cart (ratha, or chariot). Often these chariots are enormous, such
as the one in the famous cart festival at the Shri Jaganath Temple in Puri,
Orissa. More than a million Hindus participate in Shri Jaganath's festival, pulling the three-hundred-foot cart down Puri's main road. At the
conclusion of such temple festivals, the deity's image is ceremoniously
disposed of, often by tossing it into a river or ocean.

The three elements characteristic of Hindu temple festivals—display,
procession, and disposal—are also characteristic of Simchat Torah in
Cochin. Like a Hindu deity, the Torah scrolls are removed from their
usual holy abode, the Jewish Aron Hakodesh, paralleling the Hindu
sanctum sanctorum, and displayed on a temporary structure, the Jewish
kule, paralleling the Hindu ratha. Like the deity, they are carried through
a public area, in this case the synagogue courtyard. As the deity's image
is disposed of at the end of the festival, so the temporary ark—not, of
course, the Torah scrolls—is ritually demolished. These three unique aspects of the Cochin minhag serve as the means by which Hindu royal
symbols and rituals are adapted and Judaized.

The ingenuity of these adaptations is an instance of Jewish adaptive
cultural genius. Finding ways to participate in the Gentile world while
maintaining fidelity to Jewish observance has been the challenge to Jews

in all four corners of the Diaspora. In India, a culture not merely tolerant of religious diversity but affectionately supportive of it, Jews have
adapted to Hinduism while adhering to normative Judaism's standards.
They created a well-balanced, ritually established identity. They judiciously merged traditional Jewish metaphors and symbols of nobility
with borrowings from Hindu practice in order to connect their community with one of India's axes of power. By appropriating both the ascetic and the royal symbols of power, Cochin Jews integrated themselves
into Kerala's predominantly Hindu social order.

LEAVING COCHIN

The Cochin Jews provide a particularly fine example of how a small religio-ethnic community can locate itself within a larger society. First,
they fashioned a bipolar story that linked Jerusalem and Cranganore,
Cheraman Perumal with Joseph Rabban, indeed, Judaic and Indic civilizations. Their story reverberates well in both worlds, so much so that
the two worlds became fused in one identity. Second, they reflected
Hindu social values by emulating its caste system, even to the point of
violating Judaic halachic principles. In so doing, however, what they lost
in terms of approval from a distant Jewish world, they gained from their
more immediate Indian neighbors. Third, by periodic ritual enactments
of the symbols of the two axes of power in the caste hierarchy of Kerala,
they achieved a secure place in that hierarchy. In some instances, they
foregrounded strands from within the Jewish (guest) community's traditions congruent with the symbols of the Hindu (host) culture, while in
other cases they borrowed Hindu symbols directly. By so doing, this
guest community retained its unique identity at the same time that it located itself within the larger host society.

Having acculturated into Kerala, Cochin's Jews were able to live fully
Jewish lives. Never experiencing discrimination, they were learned, pious, prosperous, and secure. They contributed to Judaic and Indic civilizations, and when conditions allowed, they fulfilled themselves by making mass aliyah to Israel. The Cochin Jews achieved continuity through
their own learning and creative adaptability, as well as through the tolerant embrace of their neighbors.

About eight hundred miles to the north, around Bombay, an entirely
different story of Jewish continuity occurred. The Bene Israel, too, lived
in India for centuries, leading pious lives and maintaining a distinct

identity. But there the similarity ends. Truly, the case of the Bene Israel suggests that a simple reliance upon God can be as effective in maintaining identity as were the erudition and judicious acculturation of the Jews of Cochin. While we may marvel at the Cochin Jews' resourcefulness, in the case of the Bene Israel we may witness "the finger of God," *etsbah Elohim.*

TWO

An Identity Transformed

The Bene Israel

A gala celebration is under way at Bombay's Maghen Hassidim Synagogue. Hundreds gather in the synagogue's courtyard, enjoying the pleasant evening air and munching *samosas* and *bhel-puri.* As at so many Indian communal gatherings, Bombay's Jews are enjoying a talent show. A group of teenagers in brightly colored satin costumes perform Punjabi folk dances, and the emcee tells the audience that the troupe will soon participate in a dance celebration in Israel for which they are raising funds.

An elderly, wiry gentleman starts a conversation with me. He is a retired corporal, having served first in the British and then in the Indian army. Proud of the Bene Israel's military heritage, he regales me with story after story of his exploits maintaining order after partition in 1947 and about his battlefield experiences in Kashmir. Finally, he directs the conversation to where he wanted it to go all along: metaphysics. Mixing references from the Hebrew Bible with some from the *Upanishads,* he describes a mystical experience that he felt had transformed his life. "I have seen *olam haba* [the world to come]," he says with an extravagant gesture. "I have seen olam haba, and this world is *nothing*." He clicks his tongue for emphasis. "Nothing. Compared with olam haba, this world is nothing."

It was an impressive testimony and a revealing one. This gentleman conveyed a quintessential Hindu idea in a Jewish vocabulary. According to the Advaita nondualist school of Hindu thought, the empirical world is known as *maya,* "magic." Maya is likened to a snake, which at twilight is erroneously perceived in place of a rope lying coiled at the foot of a tree. Just as the experience of the snake is *subrated* by the subsequent experience of the rope, so this world is subrated by the mystical experience of Brahman. The Hindu cognoscenti subrate the magical illusion with the Real, or "this world" with olam haba in my friend's story.

In Cochin, Sarah Cohen's description of the side-by-side harmony between Hinduism and Judaism provided a metaphor for the *acculturation* of the Cochin Jews. She envisioned Judaism and Hinduism as equals, the one not reducible to the other, but both interacting harmoniously. In a very similar way, this old soldier's mystical comments expressing Judaism through Hindu concepts gave me a metaphor for the Bene Israel's *assimilation.*

In other ways as well, the Bene Israel Jews of Bombay and the nearby Konkan coast are a perfect counterpoint to the Cochin Jews. The Cochin Jews established and maintained their identity through the construction of an origin legend that reflected both Indian and Jewish status, through the skillful adaptation of Hindu symbolic and ritual elements within the framework of Judaic law, and through the emulation of Indian social structure. They were actors in the finely balanced drama of Indian Jewish identity.

The Bene Israel, on the other hand, were more reactors—albeit creative ones—than actors. They clung to highly attenuated, vestigial Judaic observances and, through a series of serendipitous encounters with other Jews, Christian missionaries, British colonialists, and Indian nationalists, were transformed from an anonymous, oil-pressing caste of the Konkan coast into modern, urbane Jews. Their transformation is so unlikely that one is tempted to see therein divine, rather than human, agency.

IDENTITY AND REFERENCE GROUPS

The world outside of India first heard of the Bene Israel in a 1768 letter from Yechezkel Rahabi of Cochin to his Dutch business partner, Tobias Boas. Rahabi wrote, "Jews known as Bene Israel are distributed all over Maharatta province [today's Maharashtra state], living under the Moguls. They live in tents, they own oil presses, some of them are soldiers, they know nothing as regards their faith except to recite the Shema and rest on the Sabbath."[1]

Rahabi's letter is the first unambiguous reference to the Bene Israel,

Figure 12.   Different styles of dress worn by the male members of a Bene
Israel family, Bombay, early twentieth century. (From the catalogue *The Jews of
India*, p. 126, © The Israel Museum, Jerusalem; courtesy of the Ethnography
Department archive, The Israel Museum, Jerusalem)

even though Bene Israel historians claim that earlier documents refer to
their community. The most renowned of these documents is a letter of
1199–1200 by Maimonides (Moshe ben Maimon, better known as the
Rambam), in which he commented that "the *Mishne Torah* [the Rambam's encyclopedic Torah commentary] . . . has enlightened Jews as far
as India. They have nothing of religion except that they rest on Sabbath
and perform circumcision on the eighth day." [2] More than five centuries later, the situation seemed static, according to a 1738 letter by the
Rev. J. A. Sartorius, a Danish missionary in Madras, who reported rumors about the existence of such a group of Jews in western India: "They
have not the books of the Old Testament nor do they understand Hebrew but Hindustani . . . , the language of the country where they reside.
What they know of religion is not yet ascertained except that they make
use of the word 'Shema' as a formula of prayer of doctrine. . . . They practice circumcision as a part of their religion. They wear turbans and a long
dress reaching to their feet, and long trousers, just as the Mohammedans
do [see figure 12]. They do not intermarry with other Indians, but keep
to their own people." [3]

Since the time of Sartorius's letter—if indeed it refers to the Bene Israel and not, as is more likely, Jews of Arabic origin who were known to have settled in Surat by the mid-eighteenth century—these isolated, low-caste oil pressers of the Konkan coast have evolved into the fifty-thousand-strong Jewish community known as the Bene Israel, 90 percent of whom now live in Israel.[4] Having distinguished themselves in India in civil and military service, academics and the arts, environmentalism and business, the Bene Israel today look back over the last two centuries and see cultural and religious change so profound that it transformed their very sense of identity.

ORIGIN LEGEND

The time of the Bene Israel's arrival in India cannot be ascertained, but when Christian missionaries came to the Konkan in the early nineteenth century, that is precisely what they wanted to know. Missionary Rev. J. Henry Lord was one of the first to record the Bene Israel's origin legend, which he called "sensational and romantic."

> Some sixteen or eighteen hundred years ago, they say, their ancestors were wrecked on Indian shores. . . . They came as refugees from persecution and political overthrow, but speedily found themselves again involved in disaster ere they reached the shores on which they had intended to establish their new home. Only fourteen of their number—seven men and seven women—survived the shipwreck, and these were cast ashore at a village called Nawgaon, in the close proximity of Alibag, the present chief town of the Kolaba Collectorate, and situated about twenty miles south of Bombay. Here they buried the bodies of their comrades, as many as were washed ashore. Near a burying ground containing some five hundred other graves of members of their community, the Bene-Israel of to-day show two mounds said to contain the remains of their shipwrecked ancestors, males buried in the tumulus to the north, and the females in the one to the south.[5]

Over the years, this legend has been transformed into pseudohistory.[6] The Bene Israel's arrival has been grafted onto the legend of the ten lost tribes, and their origin has been pinpointed to the northern kingdom of Israel. Each Bene Israel historian tried to refine what had gone before, even pointing out the similarity between their own origin legend and that of the local brahmin caste. The Chitpavans also claim an extrinsic origin, arrival by shipwreck, and a common ancestry from seven surviving couples.[7] From Navgaon, the Bene Israel spread throughout the villages of the Konkan coast, where they became oil pressers (*teli*) (see

Figure 13.   Bene Israel family pressing oil in Revdanda, 1992. (Photograph by Joan Roth, from the catalogue *The Jews of India,* p. 109, © The Israel Museum, Jerusalem; courtesy of the Ethnography Department archive, The Israel Museum, Jerusalem)

figure 13). They maintained, or seemed to maintain, some attenuated Judaic observances.

Just as the Bene Israel's identity went through profound changes after the mid-eighteenth century, so did their observance of Judaic holy days, laws, and customs.[8] Their "religious evolution," as Bene Israel author Benjamin J. Israel aptly called it, was shaped by their encounters with "reference groups," higher-status communities who provided them with templates for their evolving identity.[9] According to Bene Israel tradition, their evolution began during the twelfth century with a mysterious figure named David Rahabi.

Moving from legend to ascertainable history, a series of significant encounters propelled the Bene Israel's transformations of identity. Lower-status religious or ethnic communities, especially immigrant groups, often emulate a higher-status group's customs, mores, and folkways. Like other groups that climb a social hierarchy, the Bene Israel interacted with several significant reference groups.

The first such encounter, which the Bene Israel consider their "first awakening," was with Jews from Cochin, beginning with David Yechez-kel Rahabi (1721–1791), the son of the author of the 1768 letter.[10] Many Bene Israel project this fateful meeting backward in time to the twelfth century, when they were discovered by the legendary David Rahabi, "David the Egyptian." Some believe this David to be Maimonides's sea-faring merchant brother, who, in fact, died in a shipwreck en route to India in 1176.[11]

Paradoxically, the "second awakening" of the Bene Israel was sparked by contact with Christian missionaries.[12] In 1813 the British government lifted its ban on missionary activities. Soon thereafter, American, Scottish, and English missionaries established mission schools for Jews in the Konkan.[13] Expecting easy work in converting such uneducated Jews, the missionaries began by translating the so-called Old Testament into Marathi. Instead of converting them, access to the Bible confirmed the Bene Israel's identity as Jews. The missionaries also taught them Hebrew and English. As soon as the Bene Israel knew enough of the holy tongue, they translated Hebrew prayers into Marathi and composed Indian-style devotional songs known as *kirtans*. The Bene Israel studied English avidly, and it became their passport to Bombay, to the modern world, and to Jews elsewhere.

In Bombay, the Bene Israel encountered their third and fourth significant reference groups: the British and the "Baghdadi" Jews—actually Arabic- and occasionally Persian-speaking Jews who had recently migrated to the empire's newest frontier town to seek their fortunes. Bene Israel became clerks and soldiers for the British Raj, entered the middle class, and became modern. But their relationship with the Baghdadis was more complex and difficult. The Baghdadis, in an effort to be seen by the British as European, came to hold themselves aloof from the Bene Israel and all things Indian. This painful chapter in Bene Israel history is the focus of an excellent book by Pace University historian Joan G. Roland.[14]

Apropos of twentieth-century nationalism, two powerful nationalistic movements spawned the next reference groups to have a major impact on Bene Israel identity (as they did on the Cochin Jews): the Indian independence (*Swaraj*) movement and Zionism. Finally, as they migrated and adapted to Israeli society, the Bene Israel's identity was again transformed. In modern India, they were seen as Jews and understood themselves as Jews. But in Israel, they are seen as Indians, just one more ethnic group (*edah*) among all the others.

Each of these six reference group encounters had a deep impact on the

Bene Israel's understanding of who they are, on their social organization, on their professional life, and on how they lived their religion and culture.

Turn-of-the-century writer Ahad Ha'am coined an oft-quoted phrase about the centrality of Shabbat to Judaism: "It is not so much that the Jews kept [preserved, guarded] Shabbat, but Shabbat preserved the Jews." [15] His words are nowhere more applicable than to the Bene Israel. Observance of Shabbat, and little else, distinguished the Bene Israel from other groups in premodern Konkan society. Before they established contact with Jews elsewhere, the Bene Israel were known as *Shanwar Telis,* (Saturday Oil Pressers), because they abstained from work on Saturdays. This quirk attracted the curiosity of Jews from Cochin, and contact with them eventually resulted in the Shanwar Telis' reclaiming their Jewish identity. Perhaps without their tenacious hold on a vestigial Shabbat observance, the Saturday Oil Pressers never would have become Bene Israel.

Nothing is known about the Shanwar Telis' style of observing Shabbat beyond abjuring work and resting their animals, but one folk story emphasizes the importance they placed on Shabbat:

> There was a family of Talker residing in Sarsuli, a village near Tale Khar where also there was a Bene-Israel congregation. His name was Abraham alias Bandu Shet Talker. He had a big family consisting of sons and daughters. One Saturday afternoon, two Hindu neighbours came to Bandu Shet and asked for the loan of his cart. Bandu Shet replied that it was his Shabbath [*sic*] and as such everyone, even his cattle, was resting and nobody was supposed to work. The Hindu neighbour again said that he was asking for the cart and not for his bullocks. To which Bandu Shet replied that he did understand the position, but as such a thing had never occurred in the past, even putting his cart on its wheels, he could not take the risk of doing it and thus contravene the age-old customs of his forefathers. No one in the family knew Hebrew or had any Hebrew education. What was significantly noticed was the unshakable belief in the traditional practices of our forefathers.[16]

As a result of their tutelage under Cochin Jews during the eighteenth century, the Bene Israel became more cognizant of normative (which is to say, halachic-rabbinic) Judaism's rules for Shabbat observance. David Yechezkel Rahabi brought three young men from leading families back with him to Cochin, where he trained them in the rudiments of Judaism. He gave them the title of *kaji,* and when they returned to the Konkan, they assumed religious and communal leadership. As they became more prosperous, the Bene Israel hired Cochini cantors (*chazzanim*), who taught the community.

As Bene Israel migrated to Bombay, entered the civil service, and assumed lower-middle-class professions, however, their Shabbat observances became attenuated. Saturday is a working day in India, and Bene Israel felt they had no choice but to adapt Shabbat to the needs of their new workplace. Thus, Friday night rather than Saturday morning became the focus of Shabbat—much as has happened among many western Jews, especially in the Reform movement. Saturday morning services at one of Bombay's leading synagogues, Tifereth Israel, began at 7:00 A.M. and concluded by 9:00 A.M. to allow for a full day's work after prayers. To facilitate such an early conclusion, much of the Musaf ("Additional") service was deleted.[17]

If Shabbat is the primary Judaic observance, the Shema prayer is the primary creed, or affirmation of faith. Reciting the Shema ("Hear, O Israel, the Lord is Our God, the Lord is One!") at crucial moments—the moment of death, especially, but also at moments of danger—is regarded as a sign of piety. Although they had forgotten the Hebrew language, prayers, and most Judaic observances, Bene Israel somehow preserved the Shema and extended its range of usages, as mentioned by Rahabi and Sartorius. Since they did not know any other prayers, the Shema became their all-occasion expression of religious sentiment and affirmation of identity. Whenever prayer seemed appropriate, they intoned the Shema.

Bene Israel often illustrate the centrality of the Shema with stories of its miraculous, protective powers:

> During the days when Siddi Nawab of Janjira was ruling over Tala, and Peshwa, the Viceroy of the Maratha King, over the neighbouring parts, there lived one Shelomo Abraham Talker who was a rich oil-presser and who owned many agricultural lands and cattle in the Tala Village. Being a man of importance and of God-fearing nature, he was respected not only by his community and villagers, but even by the Muslim and Hindu rulers. The courtiers of both the rulers used to come to his residence and enjoy his hospitality. But as the relations between the two rulers became strained, it was reported to the Court of the Peshwa that Shelomo was conspiring with the help of the Siddi ruler to overthrow the Hindu rule. Accordingly, Shelomo was called to the Court of the Peshwa, and when he reached there

with four of his associates of whom Shimon was one, Shelomo noticed that he was not given his usual place of honour. Shimon suspected foul play and warned Shelomo to be on his guard. When the charge against Shelomo was read out, he flatly denied it and declared openly that God of Israel would protect him. According to the custom of those days Shelomo was ordered to be thrown at the feet of a mad elephant, but Shelomo was not afraid. He kept on repeating the Shema Israel, the only refuge, solace, prayer and weapon of the Bene-Israel of the ancient days. When he was thrown before the elephant, there happened a miracle and God of Bene-Israel rushed to the rescue of Shelomo. It is said, the mad elephant, no sooner saw Shelomo, at once became quiet and picked him up by its trunk and instead of dashing him to the ground placed him on his back royally and majestically. There was a commotion in the audience, the Peshwa repented, the innocence of Shelomo was proved and he was immediately given a special seat of honour in the Court. Not only that, to compensate him for the loss of prestige, he was given a Jagir of the village of Gangli in the Mangao Taluka.[18]

In telling this tale, Bene Israel establish a link with the biblical story of Daniel, who survived a lion's den through the type of faith exhibited by Shelomo Talker. In their ongoing construction of a Jewish identity, the Bene Israel employed the strategy of grafting their experience in India onto Bible stories. At the same time, they affirmed the Shema's centrality.

Especially in India, as demonstrated in Cochin, food taboos distinguish one group from another. In this regard, Indian and Jewish values overlap. Just as a caste's interactions with other castes are limited by caste-specific dietary codes, so has the Jewish observance of kashrut enforced social distance from the gentile world. According to Bene Israel tradition, kashrut was another vestigial Judaic observance by which the Shanwar Telis were recognized as "lost" Jews. Once David Yechezkel Rahabi became nearly sure that the Shanwar Telis might really be Jews, he devised one last test to ascertain their identity. Haeem Samuel Kehimkar recounts the incident: "Although David Rahabi was convinced that the Bene-Israel were the real descendants of the Hebrews, he still wanted to test them further. He therefore, it is said, gave their women clean and unclean fish to be cooked together; but they promptly singled out the clean fish from the unclean ones, saying that they never used fish that had neither fins nor scales. Being thus satisfied, he began to teach them systematically the tenets of the Hebrew religion."[19] The four defining characteristics of a caste include prohibitions against dining with other castes, enforced by dietary codes. Kashrut served this purpose. The other three major caste markers are taboos against intermarriage known as endogamy, hereditary occupations, and ranking within a social hierarchy.[20] Clearly, traditional Bene Israel exhibited all four characteristics, and most modern scholars view them as a caste.[21] Yet, for a variety of reasons, several Jewish scholars are reticent to do so.[22] They argue, in essence, that caste is limited to a specifically Hindu sacred canopy of social stratification, viewed as "a mystically sanctioned, pre-ordained [system of] inter-dependence."[23]

Sociologist Hugh Tinker summarizes this controversy: "There might be two basic definitions of the Bene Israel: one, describing them as Jews who live in India, and the second as Indians whose religion has, under influences exerted during the last two centuries, become increasingly identified with Judaism."[24] Those who adhere to the former implicit definition downplay the perspective of caste, which after all is very Indian and not very Judaic. Most Bene Israel, whose Jewishness has been challenged both by the Baghdadis in Bombay and by the rabbinate in Israel, tend to take the former, "Judaicist" stance, probably motivated, in part, by a desire to demonstrate their Jewishness. Yet, as Tinker observes, "The Bene Israel possess an alternative personality, a discarded identity, which still affects their life in Bombay city today," and "They might have remained an obscure Hindu caste with a vague folk-memory of foreign origin (like so many other castes and clans in India) had it not been for the intrusion of the west."[25]

The Konkan groups known as Teli (oil pressers), which included the Shanwar Teli subgroup, were ranked rather low in the caste hierarchy. Indeed, even after the Bene Israel migrated to Bombay and succeeded in various professions, the hurtful epithet of Teli was occasionally hurled against their schoolchildren.[26]

Like many other castes, the Bene Israel divided themselves into subcastes: Gora, or White, and Kala, or Black.[27] This division had nothing to do with skin pigmentation. The Goras were believed to be descendants of the seven original shipwrecked couples, while the Kalas were stigmatized as descendants of concubinage between a Gora Bene Israel and a gentile woman, usually low caste.[28] As is so often the case in India, the two subcastes abstained from both intermarriage and interdining, and one subcaste was considered "purer." Goras thought Kalas were polluting, especially in regard to food, as one informant reported. "My mother used to get furious when Kala came near her cooking utensils, and would push them away. She would not allow Kala to touch any utensils which she used for food."[29]

Although Gora and Kala Bene Israel attended the same synagogues (unlike the white and black Jews of Cochin, who maintained separate houses of worship), Kala were not permitted the same honors as Gora. For instance, Kala could not be offered wine for kiddush until all Gora had drunk theirs.[30]

While hierarchy is an essential component of the caste system, this hierarchy is not always as rigid as it looks. In his influential work *Religion and Society among the Coorgs*, sociologist M. N. Srinivas described the process by which a lower caste takes on certain higher-caste, especially brahmin, attributes. He calls this process "Sanskritization," reflecting the determining role of the Hindu sacred language in the brahmins' status. By Sanskritization, Srinivas demonstrates, castes may rise in the hierarchical framework of Hindu society.[31]

As long as the Bene Israel used Hindu castes as their reference groups, Sanskritization abounded. For example, the Bene Israel abjured eating beef, and until fairly recently considered it nonkosher. They also shunned widow remarriage and propitiated certain Hindu deities, especially Sitali, the "Cool One," the goddess said to inflict smallpox upon those who displease her.

As the Bene Israel came into contact with the Cochin Jews, then the Baghdadis, then the Zionist movement, and finally Israeli society, their points of reference changed. The role that higher caste Hindus once played came to be filled by various Jewish groups. As the Bene Israel became acculturated to Jewish norms, they modified their self-understanding and their sense of place within India. Rather than emulate high-caste Hindu behaviors—Sanskritization—they emulated more knowledgeable Jews, in a process of "Hebrewization." This resulted in an elevation of status in the eyes of both Hindus and Jews, according to informant Yakobeth Warulkar of Pen.[32]

Part of Hebrewization involved shedding their Indian-defined caste identity and substituting one acceptable to the Jewish world.[33] This attitude was reinforced by the Baghdadis in Bombay, who had made the British their primary reference group. As the British adopted condescending attitudes toward India and things Indian, the Baghdadis did the same—including looking down upon their coreligionist Bene Israel. The more-Indianized Bene Israel then found themselves in an intractable dilemma. The group who had become their status reference now sneered at them.[34] This painful rejection was repeated when they began aliyah to Israel, only to find their Jewishness questioned by a chief rabbi who came from Baghdad.

After most Bene Israel moved to Bombay, they found themselves in a new world—modernized, westernized, and Hebrewized. This was the beginning of the end of their Indian identity. "From approximately 1750 until 1940, the Bene Israel were involved in a process of multiplex adaptation. The first strand, an all-India rather than a specifically Bene Israel phenomenon, was the modernizing, westernizing ethos introduced by the British. This process was more crucial to the Bene Israel than to most other Indians because it signified the end for them as an Indian 'sub-caste.'"[35]

Although only twenty miles away, Bombay was eons apart from rural Konkan. The Bene Israel left behind their comfortable niche in caste-bound Konkan, together with their bullock-powered oil presses.

RITUALS AND OBSERVANCES: ELIAHU HANABI AND THE *MALIDA* RITE

Eliahu Hanabi ("Elijah the Prophet") is the Bene Israel's biblical touchstone, a template of identity whose importance to them has increased in modern Israel. The folk tales and notions about Eliahu Hanabi and his propitiation in the *Malida* rite are unique to the Bene Israel. This unique complex is central to their religion and emblematic of their identity. As Shalva Weil notes, "Although many other aspects of Bene Israel religious life differentiate them from their co-religionists, no single item plays such a central role in defining their exclusiveness. . . . [Eliahu Hanabi] has become one of the core symbols of Bene Israel identity. . . . It has become synonymous with defining one's 'Bene Israelness,' and is believed in by even the most indifferent."[36]

The Eliahu Hanabi/ Malida complex is an outstanding example of how great religious cultures interact in the performance of rituals. Bene Israel beliefs about Eliahu Hanabi are similar to others in the Jewish world, but in their religious life the prophet "stands exalted almost to the status of a patron saint of Bene-Israels and the deep veneration for him is unflinching and unwavering."[37] The Bene Israel relocated Eliahu Hanabi's mission to India, where it is a perfect cultural fit. The veneration of a leading religious personality is often found within extrinsic (non-Indian) religions in India, most commonly in the cults of Muslim Sufi leaders.[38] Finally, the Malida form of worship derives directly from Konkani Islam and Hinduism. The Eliahu Hanabi/ Malida rite complex directly reflects the interactions among Judaism, Islam, and Hinduism in Konkani culture.

> [Eliahu] . . . is the most popular personality in Hebrew history, the patron saint of Jewish life. . . . [He is] the gentle comforter, the solicitous friend,

the chivalrous companion of the weak and the oppressed. . . . [It is he] who opens secret doors through which the martyred escape, who provides dowries for the unfortunate daughters of the poor, who saves the defenceless victims of powerful swindlers. There is a chair for him at every circumcision, and a cup of wine on every Passover table. He is stationed at the crossroads of paradise to welcome every worthy person. He weaves garlands for God from the prayers of the truly pious. He will be the precursor of the Messiah, ushering in the new world in which the sufferings of Israel and all peoples will be no more.[39]

Eliahu Hanabi is said to have appeared among the Bene Israel in ancient times at the Konkan village of Khandala and to have promised them redemption in the future.[40] The Bene Israel connect this key event with the biblical story of Eliahu's ascension to heaven in a chariot of fire (II Kings 2:1–11). Perhaps the appeal of this theme was enhanced by the Bene Israel's proximity to Muslim culture, with its emphasis upon the legend of the Prophet Muhammad's ascension to heaven from Jerusalem. The Bene Israel relocate Eliahu's ascension to Khandala, site of several massive rocks. One boulder is emblazoned with white scars they say are marks left by the wheels of Eliahu's chariot and by the hoofs of his horses. Khandala remains the favored site for the veneration of Eliahu. According to Bene Israel traditions,

> It is said that on this eve [15th of Shevat], Elijah the Prophet visited the people of Khandala, a village about three miles from Alibaug, and about eighty miles from Bombay. There was a loud thunder and lightning that night, and the people of the village came out to see what had happened. What they saw was a vision of a white bearded holy figure mounted on a white horse ascending to heaven. Immediately the Bene-Israels of the village (Khandalkars) recognised that the . . . figure was no other than Prophet Elijah. The next morning the people again visited the place and saw to their amazement a long stripe of mark of a horse's hoof on the rock. The people were convinced of the vision they had seen and of the identity of the Prophet Elijah.[41]

Eliahu is propitiated in the Malida rite, which clearly derives from local Muslim and Hindu customs. For this reason, and because no pre-Rahabi account cites the Malida, Bene Israel author Rebecca Reuben suggests "when David Rahabi revived Judaism among the Bene Israel he deliberately substituted the Prophet Elijah for the numerous local Indian saints invoked for help against the evils of life."[42] Weil describes the rite:

> [T]he women prepare five different kinds of fruits, usually a coconut, a date, almonds, apples or an orange and another seasonal fruit such as a

banana, which they place in a dish on top of *melida,* a composition of rice
flour and sugar. The mixture is piled up and covered by the fruit and a
rose or myrtle leaf is placed in the centre. Frankincense is burned by the
side. Five pieces of liver are placed by the side of the dish. . . . A respected
male is selected to lead the chant over the offering and the participants re-
peat the *Shema,* and the words "Eliahu Hannavi" about a dozen times.
They recite *Veyitenlekha,* the blessing normally said after the *Havdala,* the
prayer recited at the termination of the Sabbath, when Elijah is believed
to appear in Bene Israel homes. After the officiating reader has made a
blessing over a cup of wine, he then picks up each fruit in a set order and
recites the appropriate blessing over each. . . . Each fruit is distributed in
turn, first to the person on whose account the ritual is performed, and then
to the other participants. After the fruits have been consumed, the *melida*
mixture is blessed and distributed in similar fashion. No food is left over.
The flower or the myrtle which adorned the *melida* is also blessed, and
petals or sprigs are distributed. The company then partakes of festive meal
consisting of *chapatis, papud* (unleavened wafers fried in oil), *gharries*
(wheat flour or rice flour cakes), livers or gizzards of chickens, and rice.[43]

The dish was once called *khundache nave tabak,* a "dish offered in the
name of God." Malida is the Muslim and Hindu term for the rice flour
mixture, but history does not reveal when this rite became known by
that name.[44]

The Malida rite is performed on three types of occasions: "cyclical
rites associated with the calendar [such as holy days]; *rites de passages*
which demonstrate the linear progression of the individual through birth
to death [such as *brit milah*s or weddings]; and non-repetitive individual rites [such as thanksgiving for a boon, or in fulfillment of a vow]."[45]
These three types of occasions order Bene Israel life in many ways, but
the Malida is their most distinctive adaptation of local custom. It is
most commonly performed in association with vows. In India generally,
vows are personal, intense, religious behaviors. Typically undertaken by
women, vows form a bargain between the petitioner and the deity or
saint, especially in the face of a health or employment crisis, or a long
journey, or to obtain a boon such as university admission, a lucrative
position or contract, or high marks on an examination. Like their counterparts in Cochin, sometimes a Bene Israel woman will promise to abstain from meat on certain days of the week or to undergo some other
such austerity in exchange for a specific outcome such as a family member's recovery from illness. These vows, described as "rituals of fasting,
worship, praise and mythic re-enactment that women perform without male involvement," reflect Indian conceptions of a woman's *shakti*

Figure 14.   Malida ceremony at Khandala in 1987. (Photograph by Ellen S.
Goldberg)

(power).[46] Very often, the fulfillment of a vow involves some ritual display of the petitioner's devotion to the deity or saint; for the Bene Israel
this means sponsoring a Malida rite.[47] If the vow is particularly crucial,
the rite may be coupled with pilgrimage to Khandala (see figure 14).
Bene Israel believe that a native of Khandala must redeem her vow
there.[48] In Israel, they substitute a cave near Haifa that is associated with
Eliahu Hanabi.

In India, the Eliahu Hanabi/Malida complex is a Judaic identity
marker. Since "It contains a variety of types of religious expression—
ritual, pilgrimage, folktale and song—but it requires no specialist knowledge either to participate or to officiate," this complex was ideally suited
to the Bene Israel.[49] They may have derived the Malida rite from Hindu
food exchanges between a worshiper and a deity. In Hindu worship, food
is offered to the deity. After the deity consumes the "essence" of the food,
devotees receive the remains, which are called *prasadam* (grace). Since it
is seen as a gift from the deity, the food itself is considered holy. The
alternative source is the Muslim analog known as *slametan*, feasts at
the *dargah* (tomb-shrines) of Muslim saints that employ the parched rice
Malida mixture.[50] Nevertheless, the Malida ritual's Judaic referent (Eliahu Hanabi) and purported biblical origins made it central to Bene Israel identity in India. Even in Israel today, they still love Eliahu Hanabi

and perform the Malida rite for him. While the Haifa cave has replaced Khandala as the pilgrimage site, this set of beliefs remains both "a statement of personal belief and an important identity-marker." [51] In Israel, instead of establishing Bene Israel as Jews vis-à-vis Hindus and Muslims, it distinguishes them from the myriad *edot* (ethnic groups) in contemporary society. Eliahu stayed with the Jews during the full circle of their transformation in identity, from Shanwar Teli to Bene Israel; from Jew in India to Indian in Israel.

CALENDRIC RITUALS

Two calendric occasions necessitate the Malida. [52] Since Eliahu Hanabi is associated with *Habdalah,* the rite marking the conclusion of the weekly Shabbat, Bene Israel Jews recite prayers to him then, either in the synagogue or at home, in an abbreviated Malida. When Habdalah is associated with the fulfillment of a vow, the full Malida rite is performed. Bene Israel also celebrate *Tu B'Shevat,* the early springtime new year for trees, with a unique, extensive Malida rite.

With the significant exception of the Eliahu Hanabi/Malida rite complex, the religious life of Bene Israel closely resembles that of other eastern Sephardic communities. As with many such communities (North Africa, the Balkans, and among the Malabaris), the Sephardic rite was superimposed on older Judaic customs. The Bene Israel were influenced by their Cochini teachers, whose *nusach* (liturgical melodies) they still follow, by their Baghdadi neighbors, and more recently, by Israeli culture. These influences are most strongly felt in their calendric observances. As with Jewish communities everywhere, there was more room for local creativity in life-cycle rituals. When Bene Israel practices conform to eastern Sephardic norms, there is no need to describe their observance; however, the Bene Israel religious culture is unique in many ways.

All Sephardic Jews begin the liturgical year with forty days of penitential prayers known as *S'lichot,* held before dawn each morning beginning thirty days before the New Year itself, Rosh Hashanah. But the Bene Israel refer to this period as Ramazan, the Persian name for the Arabic month of Ramadan. Many pious Bene Israel men and women copied the Muslim practice of fasting from sunrise to sunset each day, except on Shabbat. [53]

While Bene Israel observance of Rosh Hashanah, called *Naviacha san* (new year holiday), does not differ significantly from other communities, the importance they attach to the *Tashlich* ceremony is distinctively

Bene Israel. Tashlich is the symbolic casting away of sins, wherein peni-
tents toss bits of bread into a river or ocean while reciting verses from
the prophet Micah. It may be performed at any time between Rosh
Hashanah and Yom Kippur, and modern observance is limited, except
among the Orthodox. But in Bombay, more than 60 percent of the Bene
Israel participate in Tashlich at one of three sites. During the late 1960s,
1,500 to 2,000 Bene Israel gathered between morning and evening
prayers at New Ferry Wharf in Bombay for Tashlich.[54] Tashlich's popu-
larity among the Bene Israel may be attributed to its similarities with
Hindu water purification rites: "This, then, might be an example of acculturation of an otherwise unimportant ritual becoming significant because of its acceptability in the particular Indian context where water
purification is highly honored."[55]

Bene Israel called the fourth day of the new year *Khiricha san* (the
holiday of *khir,* a pudding made with coconut milk, sweets, and nuts).
This Bene Israel harvest festival was the analog to Sukkot, some two
weeks later. Bene Israel would burn frankincense, recite the Shema, and
enjoy khir.[56] Now Bene Israel celebrate Sukkot and have all but forgotten Khiricha san.

Traditionally, the Bene Israel called Yom Kippur *Darfalnicha san* (the
festival of closing the doors). The day before, they observed the ritual of
Malma, bathing in hot and cold water. On Yom Kippur itself, Bene Israel would dress in white, remove their footwear, lock their doors, avoid
all contact with Gentiles, and remain in their houses from five o'clock
one evening till seven o'clock the next, during which time they would
fast and pray.[57] Aware of the Bene Israel custom, their Hindu neighbors would tend their cattle for them on this solemn day. After the fast,
"The elders received the homage of the young persons who fell at their
feet. Even wives fell at the feet of their husbands, and this glorious and
soul stirring custom is rigidly observed in villages even to this day. In
cities like Bombay, the custom is gradually disappearing, due to western
influence."[58]

The Bene Israel observed the day after Yom Kippur as *Shila san* (the
stale holiday), likely so called because no fresh food had been prepared
the previous day. Under the influence of their Cochini teachers, the Bene
Israel transformed the stale holiday into Simchat Cohen, "the rejoicing
of the priests," a unique Indian Jewish festival commemorating the hereditary priests' day of rejoicing after the arduous temple sacrifices the
day before.[59]

In a uniquely Bene Israel twist, Yom Kippur and Simchat Cohen observances actively intertwined their beliefs about the dead. These festivals "may be connected with the Bene Israel belief that the souls of the dead visit their relatives on the day before Yom Kippur and remain until the night of *Shila San,* during which time one invokes intercession by the dead for the granting of a good new year. Just as on the afternoon before Yom Kippur they had held a Hashkaba (memorial prayer) and Malida service calling on three generations of ancestors to come and be with them for Yom Kippur so, on the morning of *Shila San,* after Hashkaba, the ancestors were requested to go away." [60]

Bene Israel had forgotten Sukkot. Instead, they celebrated the Khiricha san festival two weeks earlier. After instruction from David Yechezkel Rahabi, however, they reinvigorated their observance of Sukkot, which became an important festival. Annually during the mid-nineteenth century, they erected palm-thatched *sukkot* (booths) and celebrated for nine days. By the time fifty years had passed, the Bene Israel had come to eat all their meals for eight days in the *sukkah.* They carried the *lulav* (a bundle of a palm frond and myrtle and willow branches) and *etrog* to their synagogues and concluded the holiday with a joyous Simchat Torah.[61]

The Bene Israel also turned a minor holiday, Tu B'Shevat, also known as *Rosh Hashanah Leilanoth* (the new year for trees), into a major festival. Fixing it as the date of Eliahu Hanabi's mythic visit to Khandala, they called it *Elijah Hanabicha Oorus* (the fair of Eliahu Hanabi). According to Bene Israel tradition, "sound philosophy" connects Eliahu Hanabi and Tu B'Shevat. Bene Israel historian E. M. Jacob Gadkar says, "Spring time is symbolic of Elijah the Prophet who will at his coming, transform all waste and barren lands into fruitful landscapes, and, just as the naked trees and the bare earth once again clothe themselves with blossoms and fruits so will the dead once again awake when He, the Messiah shall appear." [62] On Elijah Hanabicha Oorus, Bene Israel make pilgrimage to Khandala, recite prayers of thanksgiving for the earth's bounty, and perform Malida, using "a twig of subja and a censer filled with frank-incense burning therein." [63]

Kehimkar suggests that David Rahabi introduced Tu B'Shevat to the Bene Israel but that they later transformed its observance into an *oorus,* a religious fair in the style of the Muslims.[64] Note the use of *oorus,* the Muslim term for a religious fair honoring a Sufi saint, instead of the parallel Hindu term, *mela.* After most Bene Israel migrated from the Konkan to Bombay, the site of the oorus shifted from Khandala to Bombay's first synagogue, Sha'ar Harahamim. Eventually, the synagogue's Cochini chazzan objected to the oorus; he held that "though Elijah the Prophet might have appeared to them as they believed, yet to celebrate the day in the manner in which they did, with such an exaggerated degree of festivities, was almost the same as worshipping him, an act which is opposed to the very spirit of their faith." [65] Most Bene Israel continue to observe Tu B'Shevat by performing the Malida rite at home. In Israel, many make pilgrimage that day to the Eliahu cave near Haifa. [66]

Once Purim was introduced to the Bene Israel, they observed it like Jews everywhere. They changed only the name by which the Feast of Esther was known, calling it *Holicha san*, but this was an intrinsically Indian modification. Holi is a Hindu festival, celebrating both the goddess Holika and the god Krishna. Holi and Purim are similar: both festivals fall at the same time of year, and both include masquerades, inebriation, gift exchanges, and raucous merrymaking.

In contrast, the Bene Israel preserved Passover even during their long isolation from the rest of world Jewry. For eight days, Bene Israel celebrated the holiday they called *Anasi Dhakacha san* (the festival of closing the jar). Kehimkar describes their observance: "They abstained from using the sour liquid [used in food preparations], as well as any leaven, during the period of the feast . . . [although t]hey had forgotten the object of this holiday as observed in memory of the deliverance of their ancestors from Egyptian bondage." [67] During Passover, most Bene Israel also abstained from tea, sugar, jaggery (coarse brown sugar made from palm sap), and ghee (clarified butter), and many would whitewash their homes in addition to scouring their utensils and pots. [68]

The publication of a bilingual Hebrew-Marathi Haggadah (Passover text) in 1846 was a major event in the Bene Israel's history, "a milestone in the process of linking the 'Bene-Israel' with their Jewish heritage." [69] For the first time, they could read a Judaic liturgical text; and it became so popular that it was republished again and again. The Haggadah's bountiful illustrations instruct the reader about preparations for and performance of the Seder. Its content is similar to the haggadot of the Jews of Cochin, Yemen, Baghdad, and Livorno, with one exception: it outlines four occasions for washing the hands. In addition to the three usual hand-washings at the beginning of the ritual, before the meal, and prior to reciting the grace after meals, it calls for a unique hand-washing after the recitation of the ten plagues.

When the fast of Tisha B'Av was introduced to the Bene Israel, they called it *Birdiacha roja* (fast day of the bidda), after the *bidda* (bean) curry eaten with rice at breakfast. At this meal, "A large dish is filled

with a little cooked rice, a few chappaties, cooked *bidda,* liver of a fowl
or goat, dates and banana, some sweet-smelling leaves or twigs, and a
small glass of brandy. All present stand around the dish and recite *Hashkavah* for the departed. The eldest member of the family pours out a little
brandy as libation and blesses each item and tastes it." [70] Otherwise,
Bene Israel observe Tisha B'Av like Jews elsewhere, and like other Jews,
they observe the period from the seventeenth of Tammuz (the fast day
commemorating the breaching of the walls of Jerusalem) until the ninth
of Av (the fast day marking the destruction of both the First and Second
Temples, the expulsion from Spain, and other calamities) as a period of
semimourning, abstaining from meat and new clothing from the first to
the ninth days of Av.

LIFE-CYCLE RITUALS

Eliahu Hanabi and the Malida rite are also significant components of
auspicious life-cycle events. As outlined in the life-cycle section, Malida
is performed for a brit milah, or the reenactment of the covenant by circumcision, and for the parallel rite for naming a baby girl. Malida is also
performed at engagements and weddings. [71]

Some religious rituals follow the calendar, celebrating the rhythms of
nature. Other calendric rituals commemorate historical events, such as
the exodus on Pesach or the destruction of the Temples on Tisha B'Av.
Mystical themes, such as the creation of the world, structure Rosh Hashanah and Shabbat. Specific rituals also arise at times of crisis, which
in India often involve protection, pilgrimage, and vows.

Rituals following the rhythms of an individual's life mark the stages
of pregnancy, the birth and naming of a child, education, marriage, and
death. In Bene Israel culture, the most distinctive of these life-cycle rites
were associated with marriage, pregnancy, and birth. In a detailed and
exhaustive chapter on Bene Israel life-cycle rituals, Israeli scholar Shirley
Berry Isenberg notes that Bene Israel "[r]ites of passage typically involve
both religion and folkways." [72] This is true for Jews everywhere, as seen
in life-cycle rituals. The mechanisms of Judaism's acculturation to its
host cultures are seen most readily in these life-cycle rituals. Yet Bene
Israel wanted to be acceptable to other Jews, so as they learned standard
Judaic practices, they let many of these borrowings from local Hindu
and Muslim culture fall by the wayside. [73]

For many years, however, local culture shaped Bene Israel customs.
Author Haeem Kehimkar described many of their distinctive practices

in *The History of the Bene Israel in India,* written in 1897 but not published until 1937. Kehimkar evokes their life in the late 1800s in portraits of customs and rituals dealing with pregnancy, circumcision, and marriage. He describes unique practices surrounding pregnancy in which a pregnant woman was "fed daintily with sweet things, her hair is very beautifully dressed and decorated with garlands of flowers, and she is dressed in rich clothes." [74] Conversely, she was denied all these fineries for four or five months after delivery.

A woman's first pregnancy was marked by a special ceremony, held during the middle of her seventh month:

> At home, the pregnant woman was presented with five fresh fruits which were placed in her lap. Then she, her husband, and a few others together had to cross a body of water in a boat. For Bombay and surroundings, the Mahim creek, in north Bombay, was the popular place for the boat ride of the ceremony. From the boat, the pregnant woman dropped a coconut into the water. Upon returning home, she donned a new sari and new green glass bangles, and participated in a *Malida* ceremony during which Elijah the Prophet was invoked and asked to grant the woman a safe childbirth. Then a small dinner party was held. [75]

This demonstrates the borrowing of local folkways. Offering a coconut to the sea is common among local Hindus, and pregnant women in northern India often wear green glass bangles. As coastal people, Bene Israel regarded this ceremony as a way to protect the child from the dangers of the sea. [76]

For her first birth, a woman retired to her parents' home; she bore her succeeding children in her marital home. A midwife, who was paid between one-half and five rupees plus a pound of rice and one coconut, supervised the birth in an unventilated room. "As soon as labour pains began, the mother-to-be was fed gruel with a certain leaf (*lepidum sativum*) added to it, and, if in labour too long, she was given hot milk with pepper to drink. Immediately following the delivery, she ate a few pieces of nutmeg, 'for warmth.' A brass or copper plate was beaten to announce the birth to others in the house." [77]

And as for the newborn:

> Drops of cold water are then sprinkled on the body of the babe to encourage it to respire, and at the same time to ascertain that it is alive. The child is then laid in a winnowing fan and has its navel cord cut. It is also made to lick castor oil and honey. Its body is rubbed with the white of an egg that it may have no eruptions on the skin. It is then bathed in lukewarm water. ... True it is that some foolish and superstitious families do bore the nostril of the first child born alive (the right nostril if a male and the left one if

a female) if the mother has been unfortunate enough to lose the first four
or five of her children. This custom has probably been borrowed from the
Hindus.

No sooner is the child bathed, wrapped in swaddling cloth and laid on
a cot than the mother bathes and lies down by the left side of her babe. The
knife with which the navel-cord has been cut off is kept under a pillow that
is placed at the side or the head of the child. The reason for this practice
is that the child may not be afraid of anything. As soon as the babe wakes
after a short sleep, it is taken in the arms and made to lick the juice of a
piece of perched aloe mixed with honey. A few drops of the milk of a cow
or a she-goat are put into its mouth, at intervals, with a piece of cotton or
cloth clout. A dim lamp is purposely kept burning in the room in order
that the child may not acquire a squint, or any other defect in sight.[78]

The new mother did not leave the delivery room for a week. For the first
three days, she ate only dry coconut, dates, chicken soup, spices mixed
with jaggery, and ghee, as well as a mixture of dill seed, jaggery, and coconut milk to ensure lactation. The mother kept her head, ears, and body
wrapped and wore sandals, and she and the baby bathed twice a day for
twelve days, and once daily thereafter. The baby's body was rubbed with
turmeric and egg whites after each bath.[79] Like Jews in many cultures,
Bene Israel feared the evil eye (*ayin ha-ra*) and malevolent spirits during
the crucial first week of life. They employed a *janta*, or exorcist, who provided amulets and lockets for protection.[80]

Visitors—female relatives only—were received on the third day, ex-
changing gifts of cloves and nutmeg for sweet pan (arecanut and sugar
rolled in a betel leaf). On the fourth day, the mother was allowed weak
tea; on the fifth day, a party was held for female friends and relatives;
and on the sixth, a party was given for the males.

The women's party was known as *Panchvi* or fifth:

The invited guests gather between seven and eight in the evening, each provided with a coconut which is a symbol of fruitfulness. A low wooden stool
is placed in the middle of the room in which the confinement actually took
place: a white handkerchief is spread over it and a copy of the Scriptures
is now-a-days placed on it; but formerly only a lamp with five lighted wicks
was suspended from the roof in the centre of the room. Sitting at some distance both from the stool and the lamp, the woman who has been lately
confined stretches forth her hand in the direction of the copy of the Scriptures and the lamp and kisses it in a token of gratitude to the Almighty for
having removed the cloud of darkness which had overhung her and for
having shown her the light of a lamp again. Her lap is then filled with five
dry dates as a symbol of fruitfulness. Presents are given to the child by its
relatives in the shape of a silk frock and jari cap, and of gold or silver
bangles. The guests partake of a feast provided by the child's father.[81]

The mother left the room only on the seventh day, holding the baby and crossing the room's threshold several times as she was sprinkled with water mixed with turmeric. The baby was placed on a clean, white bed, and boiled gram (chick peas or other pulses) and coconut pieces were laid around the child. Local children "who had been invited to the party went in turn near the child, and said 'Come away, child! let us go to play and eat a dish of rice cakes on the sixth day.' When the boy or girl had taken some of the boiled gram from beside the child, he or she ran away, and while doing so, was struck with a twisted handkerchief by one of the other boys or girls." [82]

Bene Israel held the naming of a female child on the sixth, twelfth, thirtieth, or even eightieth day after birth, either at home or in the synagogue. A cup of milk and honey was placed on a stool covered with a white towel in the middle of the room, and the chazzan or kaji chanted verses from the *Song of Songs*. Visitors recited blessings and sang Marathi and Hebrew Jewish songs.

Flora Samuel, a Bene Israel writer and community leader, described a Bene Israel naming ceremony for infant girls, called a *barsa,* held on a baby's twelfth day. The child was simultaneously introduced to her gaily decorated cradle and to her name by her aunt. The barsa was directly borrowed from local Hindu culture, down to the detail that children had to appear to "steal" the sweets prepared for them, in emulation of legends, song, and dances associated with young Krishna, who would steal butter and sugar from his mother's larder. This rite was also performed for boys, but it did not include naming. Boys were named in the synagogue at the brit milah on the eighth day. Samuel conjectured that the barsa's purpose was to introduce the baby specifically to Gentile neighbors, since Jews would have attended the brit milah in the synagogue, from which Gentiles were excluded. [83]

Circumcision rites were more complex. On the evening before the circumcision, celebrants placed a chair on the western side of the room where the ritual was to take place. They used a silk curtain to cover the chair, which was reserved for Eliahu Hanabi, patron of all brit milah ceremonies, and placed a Chumash upon it. They put a citron and either *subja* twigs or myrtle on a white-covered table opposite Eliahu Hanabi's chair. Between the chair and the table, two more chairs faced each other: one for the *mohel* (circumciser) and one for the *sandek* (godfather). The Bene Israel's brit milah mirrored the practice of Jews everywhere, but their festivities were unique:

On the morning of the circumcision the child is taken in a palanquin or in a carriage to the Synagogue accompanied by friends and relatives. The mother remains at home, as she may not enter the synagogue before the purification which takes place on the fortieth day. If the circumcision is delayed owing to the child's illness, she takes her child to the synagogue on the fiftieth day after the birth. On the entrance of the party into the compound of the Synagogue, juice of dry grapes or raisins and a plate containing a cup of oil, and a piece of lint of some cotton are taken inside and placed on the table where two candles are lit. The child is generally carried from or to the palanquin or the carriage into or from the synagogue by the maternal-uncle. Presents are given to the child by its relatives after the circumcision is over. They are in cash, or consist of ornaments of gold or silver. Batasas (sugar cakes) are then distributed, and the party breaks up. Some of the relatives accompany the child home, where they cut the citron, break a coconut or two and invoke Elijah the Prophet. . . . A cock is killed on this occasion, cooked and given to the circumciser and members of the family; but the parents of the circumcised child do not partake of it.[84]

On the twelfth day after birth, parents bathed the child and placed it for the first time in a cradle to the repetition of *B'Shem Adonai* (In the Name of God).[85] The family broke coconuts, sprinkled water on the baby, and sang a unique Bene Israel song:

Jo jo, my child,
My seed or pearl,
Keep your eyes
From crying, my treasure, jo jo.

I waved your cradle
of sea-weed, my child;
Lie quietly,
Sleep, my sweet, jo jo.

I'll lay you in it,
You'll sleep pleasantly;
I'll pray to the Above,
The Lord of the world, jo jo.

My milk has quieted you,
Has sweetened your lips,
And within the hand of God
I shall deliver your soul, jo jo.

I washed your flesh,
I pitied you dear;
In the Name of the Lord
I put you to sleep, jo jo.

Your shirt is green,
Your matlet is silk;
The Pipalpan is yellow
And pure are the pearls, jo jo.

Your cradle is of Sandalwood,
Your cushion of silk;
Grandmother will come
And will sing you to sleep, jo jo.

I'll thread pearls for you
To decorate your neck;
Your mother will dress
Her head with flowers.[86]

In Judaic tradition, a woman is ritually impure for forty days after the birth of a male and for eighty days after the birth of a female (Lev. 12:1–5). Bene Israel followed complex purification rites. First, the mother shaved the baby's head because Indians, in general, and Bene Israel, in particular, regard it as improper to allow the hair, which the child had while in the womb, to grow on after its birth. The mother then returned to her confinement room and bathed with cold water. Attendants had stirred the water with subja twigs while reciting biblical verses (I. Chron. 29:11–13 and Nehem. 4:5), adding more verses for a female child. Then, the mother bathed her child with warm water and purified herself by washing with warm, and then cold, water.

Celebrants then held a plate of ten or twenty balls of boiled rice flour over the child's head. As the balls rolled off the plate, the gathered children caught them and gobbled them up gleefully. That evening members of the immediate family held a Malida ceremony. If the mother were confined at her parent's house, her husband would send a message inviting her to come back home after her purification. The mother's parents bought her new clothes and bedecked the baby with bracelets or bangles, and, for girls, pierced the baby's ears and provided earrings. When the mother and child reached home, guests waved a small quantity of cooked rice called *ambat bhat* over their heads and then threw it away, as a protection against malevolent spirits.[87]

The Bene Israel performed a number of minor rites at various stages of a child's development. Since they had no kohanim, they did not know about the rite of *Pidyon Haben* (redemption of the firstborn) until their Cochini teachers introduced it. Bene Israel never universally practiced Pidyon Haben, unless a Cochini, Baghdadi, or foreign kohen happened to be in the locale.

Sometime between age one and two, a girl's ears were pierced in four places for four kinds of pendants and her nose was pierced for a nose-ring.[88] Since smallpox was a constant fear in the area, many Bene Israel used to propitiate Sitali Devi, the smallpox goddess, to ask protection for their children. One modern Bene Israel reported:

> The only Hindu custom that my mother followed, and which I remember, is the worship of Mata ["The Mother," an appellation of Sitali Devi] on the occasion of bathing a child who had suffered an attack of smallpox, or chicken pox, or even of measles. This was done at the time of announcing the end of the segregation of the family due to illness. There was great fear of smallpox as a fatal disease. The difference between the Hindu worship of Mata and that of the Bene Israel being that the Hindus visit the goddess' temple on this occasion, while the Bene Israel honor the child who has recovered from the disease. On this occasion some foods are distributed to other children as well.[89]

When a child took her or his first steps, "The mother takes a coconut, breaks it in front of the child's feet, and divides the kernel and dates or sugar among the children."[90]

Long ago, Bene Israel adopted the Hindu practice of child marriage. When a married girl reached her twelfth birthday, her family held a "skirt-ceremony" to mark her puberty:

> On this day, the relatives came in at about eight or ten in the morning, when the girl and her husband were bathed. The boy then put on fine clothes, the hair of the girl was combed and decked with flowers. As soon as this was over, five married women went to her and made the skirt of her saree pass over her head from the right to the left. The boy and the girl were made to sit on low wooden stools side by side. Sugar was then put into their mouths, and the girl's lap was filled with almonds, dry dates, betel-nuts etc., and grains of rice were thrown over her body as a symbol of fruitfulness.

Of all rituals, life-cycle rituals tend to be the most embellished by local cultures, especially marriage customs. This is true for the Bene Israel as it is for Jews around the world. Kehimkar, who is quite aware of this process, introduces his discussion of Bene Israel marriage customs by enumerating their reliance on local practices:

> Before we begin to treat of marriage we shall enumerate some of the customs introduced amongst our people in imitation of local usages. Fixing an auspicious day for marriage; calling out five unwidowed or unmarried women, as is done on every auspicious occasion; putting on bangles on the wrist of the bride a day previous to her marriage; waving copper or sil-

ver coin round the bride and bride-groom (not to avert evil, like the Hindus, for the latter throw the same afterwards to people of the lower castes in order that evil may be averted from the pair and be transferred to these low people, whilst among the Bene-Israel, the pieces are presented to the very sisters of the bride and bride-groom); throwing rice on their bodies as a sign of fertility; rubbing their hands and feet with Mendi (Henna); fastening together the hems of their handkerchiefs as a symbol of union; the tying of a necklace (Laccha) of glass and golden beads round the neck of the bride at the conclusion of the marriage ceremony; making the newly married pair tear out rolls of leaves, held between the teeth, from the mouths of each other; making them play the games of odd and even; the bridegroom's going away from the bride in pretended ill-humour; the hiding by the bride-groom of a betelnut or some ornament which is to be searched for and found by the bride; the breaking of the bangles and of the Laccha (wedding pendant), worn by a woman, after the death of her husband; and the discontinuing of the use of the nose ring by a widow.

For Kehimkar, writing at the close of the nineteenth century, it was a matter of pride that "most of the local customs have gradually been given up by our people during the last fifty or sixty years," especially child marriages.[91]

As Bene Israel transformed themselves from Shanwar Telis into modern Jews, Kehimkar describes precisely what happened. Although many Bene Israel marriage customs were borrowed from Hindu culture, their practices—even before their Jewish revival—differed from local practice. The Bene Israel bride wore a green sari for her henna ceremony, whereas Hindu brides wore red. Bene Israel brides wore a different number of bangles than their Hindu counterparts, and the Bene Israel held a unique wedding pendant ceremony.[92]

In both traditional Jewish and Hindu cultures, parents arranged the marriages. Even today, parents play a large role in selecting their children's mates, although the youngsters' wishes are not disregarded. In the mid-1800s, the boy's family would send two matchmakers to the girl's family: a male to speak with the prospective bride's father, and a woman to speak with her mother. If the match were approved, negotiations ensued about the presents the boy's family would give the bride and the household items, clothing, and jewelry the girl's family would provide. As an engagement unfolded, sugar took on a major symbolic role. The boy's family brought sugar to the girl's to symbolize their engagement agreement. A few days later, the girl's family would hold an espousal party at their home for relatives from both sides. Five women fed sugar to the girl and her mother, who sat on stools, reciting *B'Shem Adonai*

Figure 15. Bene Israel couple, Karachi, 1902. (Photograph courtesy of Eva Digorkar, Dimona, Israel; reproduced with permission of The Israel Museum, Jerusalem)

(In the Name of God). Guests ate sweet rice and pan. In the evening, community elders and the boy's father returned to the girl's house, and the chazzan or kaji fed sugar to the girl and both fathers, all seated on stools. Then the matchmaker announced the betrothal as snacks and pan were served.[93]

In the Indian style, a few weeks later the groom would ride a horse or be carried in a palanquin in a procession to the girl's house. A chazzan singing Maimonides's Thirteen Principles of Faith, *"Yigdal Elohim Hai,"* led the way, as torch bearers and musicians accompanied the groom (see figure 15).

When they arrived, the groom would sit opposite the bride and her mother, both on stools covered in white. A ring and a plate of sugar were placed between the couple. The chazzan or kaji gave the ring to the groom, who placed it on the bride's left forefinger, reciting three times, "Behold, thou art betrothed unto me by this ring according to the law of Moses and of Israel." The couple and both fathers were given sugar again, and the bride's father gave a ring to the groom, completing the betrothal.[94]

In most Jewish communities, including in Cochin, the betrothal (the *erusin* [the "acquiring" of a wife], also known as the *kiddushin* [consecration]) and the wedding itself (the *nissuin* [elevation] of the couple) were performed one right after the other, so seamlessly that most Jews were unaware that they were two distinct rites.[95] But the Bene Israel held their weddings some time after the betrothal.

Before the wedding, the congregation held a Hashkavah to invite ancestors to the event. The service was called the Wedding *Ud*, for the fragrant tree resin burned at the rite, creating a distinctive aroma the Bene Israel associated with memorial services.[96]

Wedding preparations took weeks. A colorful tent was erected for the ceremony. Five women prepared the feast. Like their Hindu neighbors, the women applied turmeric and attached mango leaves to the handle of the bride's new rice mill. But unlike their neighbors, Bene Israel gave no credence to astrology in planning their weddings, in determining neither the suitability of the match nor the auspicious time for the ceremony.[97]

The day before the wedding, both bride and groom took purification baths. Then, a female bangle-seller came to the bride's house to place five green glass bangles on her right wrist and four on her left. Attendants applied turmeric (*haldi*) to the bride and groom's heads and forearms. After eating rice pudding, the bride and groom sat on a white cot. The bride wore a green sari, bedecked with flowers. Then, attendants applied henna to their hands and feet.[98]

At noon on the wedding day, guests enjoyed a festive meal, featuring a Malida plate in the center of the table. In days gone by, the groom's head would be shaved and he would take more ritual baths. The groom and his male guests sat in the wedding tent, while women guests gathered in the homes of the bride and groom. As music played in the tent, the groom's parents gave symbolic gifts of auspicious foods (rice, wheat, unrefined sugar), saris, cloths, and gold and silver ornaments. Then the bride and her father entered and sat on stools between the men's and women's sections of the tent. They examined the gifts and the bride donned the jewelry.[99]

Sometimes, the groom, bedecked in a highly decorated turban, dagger, and tinsel-covered coconut as a symbol of fertility, would ride a caparisoned horse to the girl's house, but these Muslim- and Hindu-inspired customs had been discarded by the early 1900s.[100] Today, the synagogue has replaced the tent as the wedding venue.

In a unique Bene Israel tribute, the groom, standing under the tent's canopy, welcomed the bride to the wedding with a song by Israel ben Moses Najara (1555–1625), "Yonathi Ziv":

> My dove, the splendour of your beauty is like Orion and Pleiades,
> And for your love, I shall sing a song in three verses:
> Oh most lovely of all maidens, sleep has fled from my eyelids because of my desire (for thee).
> Thy lips are like lilies giving forth fragrance, like lovely myrtle,
> Thine eyes are like those of a dove, burning like a flame of fire,
> Thy speech is more pleasant to me than the song of singers and musicians cooing with might and strength.
> Rejoice, for I shall soon [re]build the city most defiled on earth,
> And the children of Syria and Seir shall I break like the breaking of a bottle.
> I shall deliver thy foot from fetters,
> I shall be angry with thy enemy, with a rage like that of a warrior.
> Let not thine hands slacken any more, gazelle.
> Do not fear, I shall visit the remnant of thy flock, my chosen Israel.
> I shall feed them on every mountain and island.
> I shall bring them back from the land of wandering and I shall rehabilitate wasted cities.[101]

Under the *chuppah* (wedding canopy), the couple watched with both fathers as a special elongated ring called *akda* or *akkara* was put into a goblet of wine or grape juice.[102] After blessings, the groom drank half the cup, then the chazzan chanted the wedding contract (*ketubah* in Hebrew, called *akhtama* by Bene Israel). The groom handed the ketubah to the bride, who passed it on to her father for safekeeping. After wedding songs, the refilled cup was blessed and shared by bride and groom. Like their Cochini coreligionists, the Bene Israel did not break a glass under the groom's foot.[103]

Next, the bride's father tied a *laccha* around her neck. The laccha is the Hindu equivalent of a wedding ring in that it is never removed and is an emblem of a woman's married status.[104] This gold pendant, worn suspended around a woman's neck on a string of black glass beads, often identifies her caste. In northern India, it is called a *mangal-sutra* (blessing-thread) and in the south, it is a *tali.* Today, Bene Israel women wear a laccha in the shape of a *Maghen David* (Star of David) within a circle.[105]

The couple sat side by side, their fathers behind them, as someone tied together the hems of both pairs' clothes or their handkerchiefs, symbolizing the union of the couple and the families. The couple then kissed the Torah scrolls in the Ark and left the synagogue. The bride rode in a palanquin, the groom on horseback, accompanied by music and fireworks, to the bride's home, where a feast was held.[106]

SYNAGOGUE LIFE

The establishment of the first Bene Israel synagogue in Bombay in 1796 once again transformed the community's religious life. Before that, the Bene Israel's Judaism was "centered on home ritual." [107] Because their traditional occupation of oil pressing meant that only a few families could earn a livelihood in any one village, synagogues were not feasible, given such a widely scattered Jewish population among the Konkan's villages. As Israel elaborates,

> Congregational worship was usually arranged at the house of the most prominent family, temporary booths being built for marriages. Burials were made in Muslim cemeteries at places where Bene Israel cemeteries did not exist. Every male was taught the technique of ritual slaughter (this continued to be done by Bene Israel living outside the large centres of Jewish concentration until fairly recent times); almost every male could conduct the services; and after the visit of David Ezekiel Rahabi, hazans were employed. The kajis probably toured whenever required to settle disputes and attend important ceremonies like circumcisions and marriages.[108]

By the time their first house of worship was built in Bombay in 1796, a number of Bene Israel had migrated to the new, developing British metropolis in search of a comfortable, middle-class life. In Bombay, for the first time Bene Israel lived in a concentration of sufficient magnitude to use and maintain a synagogue. Samuel Ezekiel Divekar, also known as Samaji Hassaji, a British army officer, built the synagogue, apparently in fulfillment of a vow made when Sultan Haidar Ali of Mysore released him from captivity during one of the three Anglo-Mysore Wars of the eighteenth century.[109] The synagogue, at 254 Samuel Street (named for its builder) in Bombay's Israel Mohalla section, was first called Masjid

Bene Israel, according to Rabbi David D'Beth Hillel, an emissary from Israel who visited Bombay during the late 1820s.[110] By the time Kehimkar wrote about it at the end of the nineteenth century, the synagogue had become known by its present name, Sha'ar Harahamin (Gates of Mercy).[111] Today, Bene Israel informally call it the Samaji Hassaji Synagogue.

More synagogues followed as Bene Israel communities of sufficient size evolved and accrued adequate wealth. Bombay's second synagogue, Sha'ar Ratzon, was built in 1840, followed in rapid succession by synagogues around Konkan and in districts of Bombay: Beth El in Revdanda in 1842; Maghen Aboth in Alibag in 1848; Talekar Synagogue in Talla in 1849; Kenesseth Israel in Mangaon in 1849; Beth El in Panvel in 1849; the Bene Israel Synagogue in Worli, Bombay, in 1852; Beth Ha-Elohim in Pen in 1863; Hesed-El in Poynad in 1866; Sha'ar Shalom in Janjira in 1869; Kenesseth Bene Israel in Bombay in 1872; Ambedpur Synagogue in Alibag in 1874; and Sha'ar HaShamaim in Thane in 1879. Tifereth Israel, the largest and arguably most active Bene Israel synagogue, was built in Bombay in 1886, the same year Sha'ar Tephilla was built in Mhalsa, followed by Etz Hayim in Bombay in 1881, Beth El in Ashtami in 1892, Orle Israel in 1896, Maghen Hassidim in Bombay in 1931, the Bandra Bene Israel Prayer Hall in Bombay in 1930, and the Kurla Bene Israel Prayer Hall in Bombay in 1946. Rodeph Shalom, India's only Reform (or Liberal) synagogue, built in 1925, was inadvertently damaged during the Muslim-Hindu disturbances in January 1993. In other cities, Magen Shalom was built in Karachi in 1893, Succath Shelomo in Pune in 1921, Maghen Abraham in Ahmedabad in 1933, and Judah Hyam Prayer Hall in New Delhi in 1956.[112]

As synagogues became the focal points of Bene Israel communities, their Judaism became increasingly similar to mainstream Judaism elsewhere: Hebrewization. For example, the position of the kajis, their unique religious leaders, was replaced by congregational leaders known as mukkadam, a Muslim term. They included the elders, known by the Marathi term *aschogla,* as well as a treasurer, cantor, circumciser, scribe/teacher, and sexton.[113]

The Bene Israel learned mainstream Judaism from Cochinis—the chazzanim they employed as well as the teachers who inspired them. During the mid-nineteenth century, "in matters of ritual, the Bene Israel were almost wholly in the hands of teachers from Cochin."[114] The Cochini nusach is still followed in Bene Israel synagogues today, although a smattering of Ashkenazic tunes has been added. In years to come, three other groups—the Baghdadi Jews of Bombay, the Christian missionaries who came to evangelize the Bene Israel but paradoxically ended up confirming their Jewish identity, and western Jews associated with Zionism and the Jewish Agency—deepened this Hebrewization process, but the Cochinis were the reference group for the Bene Israel's synagogue life and liturgy.[115]

Like most religious institutions in India, synagogues owned significant tracts of land. In rural areas, sharecroppers rented synagogue-owned farmland, and in cities, merchants leased synagogue-owned shops. Revenues accrued to the synagogue treasury, to pay salaries for the chazzan, sopher, or shamash, and to fund maintenance and charity.[116]

Bene Israel synagogues range from modest to elaborate. Throughout their history, they have resembled Sephardic synagogues elsewhere, with a *tevah* (*bimah* or altar) at the center and a women's section upstairs. An elaborately carved, wooden *heichal* (cabinet) on the eastern wall holds metal- or wood-encased Torah scrolls. Special *parochets* (curtains) veil the heichal. An ornate wooden chair for Eliahu Hanabi sits to one side of the heichal. Men sit on chairs or on the benches that line three of the synagogue's walls. Decorations include distinctive Bene Israel brass *chanukiyot* (Chanukkah lamps), *mezzuzot* (biblical verses on parchment kept in a decorative case affixed to door posts), a *ner tamid* (eternal light), and chandeliers. Many Bene Israel synagogues have large courtyards where nonreligious public gatherings can be held. Typically, the synagogue maintains a *miqveh* (ritual bath) in an outbuilding in the courtyard.

For the most part, Bene Israel synagogue rituals follow Cochin traditions, but some of their synagogue customs are unique. For example, when Bene Israel leave their synagogues after prayers, they practice an elegant custom known as *hath boshi* (hand-kissing). Lord was the first to describe it:

> Emanating from the chief minister . . . it passes throughout the congregation . . . from . . . senior [to junior]. Extending the arms with the hands flattened out, and in the position of the thumbs being uppermost, the person approached takes the hand between both of his own, similarly held, and the junior then probably places his remaining hand on the outside of one of those of the person already holding his other hand. The hands of each are then simultaneously released and each one immediately passes the tips [of his fingers] to his mouth, and kisses them. He then passes on to receive the same from, or to bestow the same on, another; and so on, till all in the Synagogue have saluted one another.[117]

Lord interpreted this custom as analogous to "the kiss of peace known amongst the early Christians," but a Parsi (Indian Zoroastrian) observer argued that instead it derived from the Zoroastrian practice known as *hamazor,* passing along blessings at the conclusion of Parsi rituals.[118]

As in any Jewish community, Bene Israel congregants have their share of debates about ritual propriety and halachic standards. As well as being a pioneering historian, Kehimkar was a reformer of religious observance. He worked to establish the Israelite School, to enable Etz Haim Prayer Hall members to pray in Hebrew, to appreciate sermons, and to publish religious books. He labored to enhance the community's general Judaic life.

> Some of Kehimkar's other proposed synagogue reforms were: recitation of prayers by the congregation in unison; shortened services, in order to enable worshippers to attend office on Sabbath; no more celebrations with dancing and eating to be allowed to take place within the synagogue; and no more bidding for the privilege of being called up to the *bimah* for blessing or reading from the Torah.[119]

IN ISRAEL

During the first half of the twentieth century, the Bene Israel were caught between two strong nationalistic movements: the Swaraj movement for Indian independence from Great Britain, and Zionism, the movement that led to the establishment of the State of Israel. All three of the Bene Israel's reference groups—the Indians, the British, and other Jews—were involved in conflicts. The Bene Israel loved and admired both their Indian neighbors and their British patrons, yet by this time their transformation into Jews was irrevocable, despite harsh treatment from the Baghdadis.

The marginal position of the Bene Israel, indeed of all Indian Jewry, became clear in 1938, when a Jewish delegation met with Mohandas K. Gandhi. When they asked the mahatma what their role should be in the Indian-British struggle, he replied, "Although I would welcome your help in our freedom struggle, I would advise you not to take part as a community since you are so small you would be crushed by three mighty conflicting forces of British imperialism, Congress nationalism and Muslim separatism." [120]

Yet the Bene Israel initially were ambivalent about Zionism. They mistrusted "foreign" Jews because of their unhappy experiences with the Baghdadis. Many adopted the prevailing Indian view of Zionism as a British incursion into Arab territory; however, the fact that fringe elements in the Swaraj movement embraced Hitler's cause helped propel the Bene Israel toward the British and Zionism.[121] Ultimately, the vast majority of Bene Israel opted for life in Israel; therefore, modern Israeli society became the last in the historic chain of reference points marking the transformation of their identity.

When the Bene Israel arrived in Israel, one of their worst fears was realized. The chief Sephardic rabbi, Itzhak Nissim, himself from Baghdad, was all too aware of the Baghdadis' doubts about the Bene Israel's Jewishness, and he was inclined to believe the *lashon hara* (malicious gossip) emanating from Bombay and Baghdad. The controversy involved the two related but distinct questions of origin and lineage. The origin of the Bene Israel is simply beyond the historian's ken, given our current state of knowledge. The second is knottier because Judaic law (Halachah) governs marriage and divorce. When a marriage is not ended according to Judaic law but the woman remarries anyway, the offspring of the second marriage are tainted with *mamzerut* (bastard status), since she is technically still married to her first partner. Jewish communities that are beyond the reach of the rabbinate (such as the antirabbinic Karaites, and possibly the Beta Yisrael of Ethiopia and the Bene Israel) run the risk of rampant *mamzerut,* a taint (*pagam*) that disqualifies them and their offspring from marriage with other Jews. This issue caused the greatest halachic difficulty.

The controversy spread beyond rabbinic circles to the political realm. At one point, to protest being labeled bastards, Bene Israel, who are called *Hodi'im* (Indians) in Israel, conducted a *satyagraha* (civil disobedience à la Gandhi) on the steps of the Kenesset (Israeli parliament). Despite his predilections and much to his credit, Rabbi Nissim conducted a thorough inquiry. He consulted previous rabbinic writings and interviewed Bene Israel elders.[122] As a result, he published a halachic ruling including all relevant rabbinic documents, travelers' accounts, and scholarly writings. The report concluded, in essence, "that (1) the Bene Israel were Jews, and (2) that there was no evidence that could cast doubts on their family status and divorce procedures."[123] Curiously, it was the Bene Israels' fidelity to a Hindu custom that had kept them within the strictures of Judaic law. Divorce and remarriage are prohibited in Hinduism. Due to the process of Sanskritization, the Bene Israel emulated their Hindu neighbors in abjuring both, so the problem of irregular divorce and remarriage had not arisen in their case. This coincidence relieved them of the burden of presumptive mamzerut.[124]

The matter was thus settled, or so it seemed. But, as recently as 1997,

an Ashkenazic rabbi in Petah Tiqveh refused to register a marriage between a Bene Israel *sabra* (native Israeli) and her Ashkenazic groom. The
matter caused a brief controversy, but world rabbinic opinion was virtually universal in support of the young woman. The hard-line rabbi was
suitably castigated and the marriage was celebrated.[125]

Despite such occasional encounters with ignorance or bigotry, Bene
Israel have flourished in their new/old home. Today, their population
in Israel is ten times as great as in India, 50,000 or more compared
with 5,000. Despite their growth in numbers, however, Bene Israel still
struggle with an outsider status. For generations, the Bene Israel were
Jews in India. Now they are Indians in Israel.

THREE

An Identity Aloof

Baghdadi Jews of the Raj

The *Lal Dewal* (Red Temple) is Pune's most famous landmark (see figure 16). Its steeple dominates much of the old British cantonment. Ar-
chitecturally, the imposing red brick structure would be more at home
in England than in India, but Pune was born of a British aesthetic. Once
a hill station for Bombay's elite, known for its salubrious climate, Pune
has become a metropolis in its own right, better known today as the locale for Rajneesh's mega-ashram.

Every taxi driver knows Lal Dewal, but few know that it is the Ohel
David Synagogue. Sir David Sassoon built it in 1867 to serve Bombayites during their summer residence. A small Jewish colony of merchants
who catered to the vacationers were year-round members. These days
only a few Baghdadis pray there, shopkeepers mainly, who prefer Ohel
David's stately solitude to the bustling activity at the nearby Bene Israel
synagogue, Succath Shelomo. In fact, even a Shabbat *minyan* (prayer
quorum) is rare at Ohel David, so I was delighted to find I was the tenth
man one Shabbat when I visited. This number, precisely ten, posed the
halachic conundrum that serves as my metaphor for the adaptive skills of
the minuscule communities of pioneering Baghdadi Jews that once dot-
ted India. During the nineteenth century, Jews from Darjeeling to Lucknow, Varanasi to Hyderabad, managed to live Jewish lives, virtually in-
visible among so many Hindus and Muslims.

Since the community is Sephardic, Ohel David's kohanim performed

Figure 16. *Lal Dewal* (Red Temple)—Ohel David Synagogue, Pune, 1987. (Photograph by Ellen S. Goldberg)

the *duchan* rite of the priestly blessing almost every Saturday. (Ashkenazic Jews outside of Israel reserve this rite for holy days and festivals.) According to local custom, Pune's Baghdadis forbid a kohen to perform the duchan rite with bare arms. I was unaware of this nuance. For the better part of a year I had duchaned bare-armed in the Cochin Synagogue, but my short sleeves posed a problem for Pune's Baghdadis.

Ten men were present, so we could recite the priestly benediction. But since my arms were uncovered, I could not duchan. As a kohen, however, I also could not remain in the room without participating while others duchaned because that would be tantamount to casting doubts upon my *kehunah* (priesthood), which no kohen is permitted to demean. However—and here is the catch—if I stepped out of the room, the prayer service would lose its mandatory quorum. Under Jewish law, no man may leave a prayer service when he is the necessary tenth. I could not leave because I was the tenth, and I could not stay, because I am a kohen.

The Baghdadis created a compromise. They reasoned that if I stood in the synagogue doorway, I would simultaneously be sufficiently present for the minyan and sufficiently absent to avoid insulting the kohen heritage. To me, this exacting halachic compromise symbolized the adaptability at the core of the Baghdadi identity. The compromise was ersatz-Halachah, to be sure. Yet it typified the cultural creativity that characterized Baghdadi life in India. Having little choice in the matter, the Pune Baghdadis were willing to reason their way through a halachically complex situation. Having no rabbi to consult, no time to send a question to an authority in Jerusalem or London, they managed. Their grandparents in Monghyr or Dhaka, and their great-grandparents in Calcutta or Bombay, must have managed the same way when those were Jewish frontier towns 150 years ago. They managed by adapting, yet by adapting they became increasingly aloof from Jews and normative Judaic practice elsewhere.

By the middle of the eighteenth century, a few Arabic- and Persian-speaking Jews had established a community in Surat, a port city 165 miles north of Bombay.[1] Slowly at first, then ever more rapidly, these *Mizrachi* (Eastern) Jews filled a commercial-entrepreneurial vacuum in the emerging British port cities of Calcutta, Bombay (now Mumbai), and Rangoon (now Yangon in Myanmar, formerly Burma). By the early nineteenth century in Calcutta, by the mid-nineteenth century in Bombay, and by the late nineteenth century in Rangoon, Jewish communities were not only established but had already begun their meteoric rise in wealth, status, and creativity. These towns became cosmopolitan centers with Jewish schools, kosher markets, and ritual baths. The Jews there became known in India as Baghdadi Jews, a name that masks their diverse roots in Baghdad, Aleppo, Damascus, Basra, Yemen, Persia, Afghanistan, Kurdistan, Bokhara, Tunisia, Cochin, and elsewhere.

Like the Bene Israel, the Mizrachi Jews acquired their Baghdadi identity via a series of encounters with other groups, both Gentile and Jewish. The composition of these reference groups varied, though Jews in both Calcutta and Bombay emulated the British. In Bombay, the other reference groups were the Bene Israel Jews, who had already established two synagogues before the Baghdadis arrived, and fellow commercially minded Middle Eastern minorities, most notably the Parsis. In comparison, trading caste Hindus (such as the Marwaris) and fellow minority groups (notably Armenians and Anglo-Indians) became reference groups for Calcutta's Jews.

A FOUR-STEP JOURNEY OF JEWISH IDENTITY

History transformed Baghdadi identity in four stages: early history, the 1857 Mutiny period, post–World War I, and post–Indian and Israeli independence. During the early period, their Judaeo-Arabic identity subtly shifted, and they became "Arabian Jews of India and the Far East," reflecting their interactions with the cultures they encountered in Calcutta. After the Mutiny of 1857, they began to distance themselves from things Indian and to identify with the British instead. Following World War I, they wanted to be identified as "European." Thereafter, they were torn by the powerful forces of competing nationalisms: the Indian independence movement and Zionism. During the 1930s, the Baghdadis received thousands of Ashkenazim who were seeking refuge from Nazism. This rescue effort strengthened their ties to Zionism and to Britain. After Britain was compelled to grant independence to India in 1947 and to Israel in 1948, most Baghdadis left India. Highly Anglicized Jews went to London; those more influenced by Zionism went to Israel. Paradoxically, those who remained in India developed an Indian-Jewish identity, something that had not been done before. But by then the community was inexorably heading toward extinction. Today, whether they live in Israel, London, Singapore, Bombay, the United States, or Canada, the Baghdadis maintain a cosmopolitan "Diasporized Baghdadi" identity.

THE EARLY PERIOD: TO 1857

During the early period of India's Baghdadi communities, the pioneers established themselves commercially. They began with the culture and religious life they brought from home. For Calcutta's first Jewish settlers, Aleppo was home, but they were soon outnumbered and overwhelmed by Iraqi Jews from Basra and Baghdad. In Calcutta, a Baghdadi identity was superimposed upon a substratum of Aleppan identity. The Baghdadi image was in turn modified by the impact of significant numbers of Yemeni, Persian, Cochini, and Bene Israel Jews. In Calcutta especially, close trading and family links to satellite communities to the east—Rangoon, Penang, Singapore, and Shanghai, satellites useful in the burgeoning opium trade—helped to create this new sense of self. Occasional visits to Penang or Rangoon for bar mitsvah celebrations or weddings enhanced the Calcutta Jews' sense of being part of a diasporized community, a process described as "transculturation."[2] The Calcutta Baghdadis' identity was also shaped by local reference groups, Armenians mostly, but also Marwaris, British, Portuguese, Greeks, Anglo-Indians, and Chinese.

For the first Jews in Bombay, home was unequivocally Iraq, and the community coalesced by following in the traditions established by its towering Iraqi leader, Shaikh David Sassoon. The Bombay community was Baghdadi from the start, with flavorings from Cochin, Yemen, Persia, and Afghanistan, and a tortured relationship with the numerically superior Bene Israel. For societal orientation, the Bombay Jews turned to the Parsis and the British as reference groups.

In both cities, the Jews' Baghdadi identity soon became transformed subtly into "the Baghdadi diaspora of India and the Far East." This reshaping of identity occurred, in part, because of the cosmopolitan character of these diaspora communities. Up until the Mutiny of 1857, the Baghdadis occupied a "greytown" social position between the elite British and other Europeans, and the "native" Indian population. The trauma of the Mutiny, however, led to another shift in identity, from the greytown of Asiatic Jewry to increasing identification with the British.

THE EARLY PERIOD IN CALCUTTA

Shalom Obadiah Hakohen established the first Baghdadi community in India in Calcutta in 1798. As he was lured by the commercial promise of the British capital, his success there attracted a Jewish community in his wake.[3]

Born in 1762 in Aleppo, a provincial city of the Ottoman Empire, now in Syria, Hakohen left home at the age of twenty-six and meandered first to Baghdad and then to Basra before sailing to Surat via Bombay in 1790. Though only in his early thirties, Hakohen became the leader of the Surat's Jewish community, home to sixty-five Arabic-speaking Jewish merchants, a synagogue, and a cemetery.[4] He traded briskly with his partners in Basra, dealing in ivory, indigo, coffee, Arabian horses, rose water, coral, textiles, and Venetian glass. Hakohen and his partners gradually expanded the scope of their trade to Cochin on the Malabar Coast, to Calcutta on the Bay of Bengal, and eventually east to Siam and China and west to Arabia and Zanzibar.[5]

Although Hakohen left his diary for 1789 to 1834, virtually from his arrival in India until his death, we cannot ascertain why he moved from Surat to Calcutta in 1798. Perhaps, ever perspicacious, he sensed the decline of Surat and the emergence of Calcutta on the east and Bombay on the west as British India's leading coastal trading centers. Perhaps, since he was also ever contentious, disputes forced him to leave. Whatever propelled him, his journey included visits to new and old Jewish communities in Bombay and Cochin.

When he arrived in Calcutta, several British-Jewish trading houses were already active, most notably Lyon Prager "who carried on a prolific diamond trade between Bengal and London."[6] Significantly, Hakohen either chose not to settle near his British coreligionists or was not allowed to. Instead, he rented and later purchased houses from Armenians, with whom Calcutta's Baghdadis maintained a close relationship for centuries. Until the Baghdadi elite moved to southern Calcutta between 1900 and 1950, they shared the city's greytown with Armenians, Anglo-Indians, Greeks, Portuguese, and others not pale enough for the European "whitetown" quarter, yet not at home in the Indian "blacktown."[7] Like the Jews, the Armenians were relatively affluent, Middle Eastern, and commercial. What is more, the Armenians arrived in Bengal first. They settled there in 1655 and had maintained a community in Calcutta since 1690.[8] The Armenians became the Baghdadis' trading partners as well as their neighbors and generally helped them settle into their new environment.

Hakohen set about developing his trade in silks, fine textiles, diamonds, and indigo. He was also a skilled jeweler, so accomplished that he was appointed court jeweler in Benares, Lucknow, and the Punjab. Although his jewelry business required extended residence at various courts, he continued to develop and maintain trading contacts. He traded with Surat, Madras, Dhaka, Murshidabad, Benares, and Bombay, where he became enmeshed in a nasty dispute with Jacob Semah, leader of the local Baghdadi community. Quite soon it became obvious that his businesses required help, so he employed Jews from Aleppo and Cochin, thus giving birth to a Jewish community in Calcutta. Tiny satellite communities sprang up along the River Ganges, and Hakohen hired agents to purchase silks and agricultural commodities.

The Jews traded many agricultural products, including opium. Grown all along the Gangetic Plain during the nineteenth century, opium was the source of many Jewish fortunes. Jewish life in these early-nineteenth-century Ganges market towns is difficult to imagine today, but somehow these outpost traders observed kashrut and kept Passover, raised families and buried their dead in places like Bhagalpur, Ghazipur, and Dinapur. They returned to Calcutta only very briefly, perhaps to find a bride for a son. Otherwise, the items they required were sent to them: matsah for Passover, a *ketubah* (marriage contract) or a *get* (divorce decree), a new prayer book, and a packet of Judaeo-Arabic newspapers.[9] To keep an eye on opium production, they lived in these Jewishly remote towns, shipping the prized black tar down the Ganges to Calcutta. There, Jewish merchants bought chests of opium at government auction and shipped them to members of their extended families in Penang, Singapore, Hong Kong, or Shanghai. They traded the opium to Chinese merchants in exchange for tea, which they sold for gold in England.

This opium trade was so lucrative for all concerned—for the Jews and the Marwaris, their only competitors, as well as for the British—that England went to war with China twice, in 1839–42 and in 1857, when Beijing tried to halt the import of the vitality-sapping narcotic. By the time China succeeded in banning opium trafficking in the early twentieth century, the Sassoons of Bombay had switched to textiles. Calcutta's Jewish elite—the Ezras, Gubbays, and other families—had moved on to real estate and manufacturing.[10]

By then, the economic base had long been established. In 1806, Hakohen assured his own succession by sending to Aleppo for Moses Dwek, who came to Calcutta to marry Hakohen's daughter. Then, in 1811, as the Calcutta community grew, Hakohen established a prayer hall near the Armenian Church. Dwek led the prayers and attended to the family's business ventures in Dhaka and its trade with Muscat. A diarist like his father-in-law, Dwek became a leading figure in the community after Hakohen died in 1836.

Gradually, Jews in Arabia, Persia, and Yemen learned of the good fortunes of the fledgling Calcutta community. The trickle expanded. By 1825, the community had more than one hundred members, but immigrants from Iraq outnumbered the original Aleppan settlers. The community became known as Baghdadis because of this newer group.[11]

As the community grew, Hakohen's small prayer hall became inadequate, and a large house was converted into Calcutta's first synagogue, Neveh Shalom, in 1826. The prosperous community accelerated payment of the mortgage and settled it in just five years. Growth continued so quickly that when a new building was erected in 1856, the community had already outgrown it. Rather than serving the entire congregation as planned, the newer structure became a second synagogue, Beth-El (see figure 17). It served the community along with Neveh Shalom until late in the century when a third synagogue, Maghen David, opened.[12]

In this synagogue and others added later, the Baghdadis expressed an identity that clearly was not Indian but was not exactly Baghdadi, either. While numerically supreme, they were relative newcomers to Calcutta, and the community was decidedly multicultural from the start, encompassing Jews who were Iraqi, Aleppan, Yemeni, Persian, Cochini, Bene Israel, Tunisian, and even Italian, from Livorno. Still, Hakohen's economic supremacy and Dwek's religious leadership assured that Syrian traditions, especially their unique Torah cantillation, would become permanent in Calcutta's minhag. The continuing community preference for *tallitot* (prayer shawls) from Aleppo also reflects Syrian tradition.[13]

The community also coalesced as it grew. The loosely knit groups formed a common clan. They were no longer simply Baghdadis, but *Baghdadis*. Calcuttans Flower Elias and Judith Elias Cooper defined members of the local Jewish community as "Jews of Arabian origin who went to India and the Far East," or perhaps they were best called simply "the Jews of the Raj," as another community member, Mavis Hyman, suggested.[14] Perhaps this latter nomenclature is most apt, as their sojourn in India roughly paralleled that of the British. These Jewish immigrants were attracted to India largely because of the opportunities the British presence afforded, and they left India soon after the British did. The Baghdadis were never intrinsically Indian as the Bene Israel or Cochinim were.

Through their synagogue life, they maintained connections with home. Except for Torah reading, Calcutta's synagogues followed the

Figure 17.　Beth-El Synagogue, Calcutta, 1987. (Photograph by Ellen S. Goldberg)

Baghdadi rite, one of the oldest in world Jewry.[15] They also maintained their religious connections through letters posing Judaic legal questions to *chachamim* (rabbis), mostly in Baghdad, but also in Persia, Yemen, and Israel.[16]

Baghdadis gave *Sifrei Torah* (Torah scrolls) additional prominence in their synagogues. Typically, a family would hire a scribe in Iraq to write a scroll to honor a departed relative. They would commission a case to be carved in China, a task overseen by Baghdadis in Shanghai or Hong Kong. Families stored their memorial scrolls in the *heichal* (storeroom for Sifrei Torah) of their synagogue, to be read on the anniversary of the honoree's death or on other dates significant for the family.[17] Synagogues in Bombay, Calcutta, or Rangoon might have one hundred or more scrolls in their heichals. Baghdadis also beautified their synagogues with velvet, cashmere, or silk *parochets* (curtains placed before the heichal), embroidered with gold and silver thread, magnificent hangings that were also used to cover caskets at funerals.[18]

Baghdadis reflected Iraqi custom in their use of *Sefer Haftarah*, scrolls of the Hebrew Bible's prophetic writings. Apparently this custom is unique to Baghdad and those who follow its traditions, as Moses Dwek commented when he saw a Sefer Haftarah in Calcutta for the first time.[19]

Calcutta's Jews generously supported shrines in the Holy Land and in Iraq, where the tomb of Ezra Hasopher (the Scribe) at El-Ozeir is the most important Jewish shrine.[20] Indeed, Ezra is considered the patron of all Baghdadi Jews, assuming a role similar to that of Elijah among the Bene Israel and of Nehemia Mota among the Cochin Jews. Ezra is associated with the festival of Shavu'oth, as Elijah is associated with Lag B'Omer and Nehemia Mota with the first day of Chanukkah. Iraqi Jews routinely invoke Ezra when embarking on a journey or any dangerous undertaking; Iraqi women transact their vows with him, a popular custom among India's Baghdadis.[21]

Even today, Baghdadi synagogues display *tsedaqah* (charity) boxes to benefit foreign shrines, usually in Iraq, but in Israel as well. The labels on scores of silver boxes announce their purpose: supporting the tomb of Ezra or a Sephardic Yeshiva in Jerusalem or the shrine of Kabbalist Shimon bar Yochai near Tsfat. Also popular, especially among Baghdadi businessmen, were the shrine of Rabbi Meir (the great teacher in the *Mishna*, also known as *ba'al haness,* the master of miracles) near Tiberias, and the burial site of the patriarchs and matriarchs, the Cave of Machpela in Hebron. By supporting such shrines and institutions Baghdadis ritually connected and reconnected themselves both to their mother country, Iraq, and to the Holy Land. Their identity was created and re-created as they made such connections between Calcutta, Iraq, Israel, and elsewhere.

Charity, however, was not entirely routine. Emissaries (*shlichim*, sing. *shaliach*) from Iraq and elsewhere began visiting Calcutta and Bombay during the nineteenth century, soliciting contributions to support shrines, destitute communities, or *yeshivot* (rabbinical seminaries).[22]

Chachamim also routinely made the journey east in search of donations. Apparently these visitors became tiresome, given a comment by a writer in Calcutta's Judaeo-Arabic newspaper, *Paerah:* "They should be called . . . Hakhamim Abu Amama, Hakhams by virtue of their turbans, which were larger than usual. These . . . did not put on even a 'Fez' . . . in their native cities. When they reached Suez on their way to India, they used a small cloth covering for their heads. At Aden, further East, they tied a scarf; the closer they got to India the larger the turban, till at the place of destination it became quite unwieldy!"[23]

The Calcutta Jews maintained their Baghdadi identity in their homes as well as in their synagogues (see figure 18). By speaking and writing in Arabic, by wearing Arabic clothing, by living in the greytown neighborhoods favored by Middle Eastern people, by following the close familial traditions of the Middle East, and by enjoying essentially Middle Eastern food (albeit a bit spicier than in West Asia), the Baghdadis not only expressed their roots, but transmitted their evolving culture to subsequent generations born in India. The so-called Mutiny of 1857 closed off this early period of identity building. This traumatic event propelled India's Baghdadis to abandon their familiar Middle Eastern cultural roots and to seek European status and identity. Part of that process was to emulate the British by rejecting all things Indian.

THE EARLY PERIOD IN BOMBAY

In Bombay, this process of identification with the British was more painful than in Calcutta, because the Bombay Baghdadi community was more or less superimposed onto the older Bene Israel community. Relations between the two Jewish groups had always been harmonious, until Bombay's Baghdadis began to identify with the British against the Indians. Then, the Bene Israel—who were proud to be Indian—bore the brunt of the Baghdadis' emulation of British snobbery.

The Bombay Baghdadi community dates to the 1790s when Jacob Se-

Figure 18.   Moses Elias in his home in Calcutta, 1986. (Courtesy of the photographer, Frederic Brenner)

mah arrived there from Surat. The community's growth was fueled and enriched by turmoil in West Asia. From 1817 to 1823, Jews sought asylum from persecution by the governor of Baghdad, Daoud Pasha. Others came from Meshed, in eastern Iran, to escape forced conversion. Ottoman and Persian Jews already had come to view the British in nearly messianic terms, so when their homes became unsafe, they made their way to Bombay, the boomtown being developed as Britain's premier port in western India.[24]

Figure 19.   Shaikh David Sassoon (1792–1864).
(From the catalogue *The Jews of India*, p. 141; © The
Israel Museum, Jerusalem; courtesy of the Ethnography
Department archive, The Israel Museum, Jerusalem)

Actually, Bombay had a Jewish history before the Bene Israel arrived in the eighteenth century. The islands that came to make up the city had once been the private botanical preserve of Garcia de Orta, a Portuguese Jewish botanist and physician.[25] The Bene Israel preceded the Baghdadis there and had erected their first synagogue by 1796.[26] But the Baghdadis soon became so prosperous that they utterly dominated the city's older Jewish population. This domination began in 1828 with the arrival of Shaikh David Sassoon (1792–1864) (see figure 19). Sassoon was a native of Baghdad, where his father, Sassoon B. Salah (1750–1830), was *nasi* (Jewish community leader) of Baghdad and chief treasurer of the local Ottoman rulers, the *pashas*. David Sassoon inherited his father's position, but had to flee to Basra to escape Daoud Pasha's plunder. From there he made his way to Bombay, where he carved a niche for himself among the Parsis and British, who dominated the city's import-export trade. Beginning with opium and expanding into real estate and textiles, Sassoon became patriarch of one of the wealthiest and most expansive Jewish families in the world, "the Rothschilds of the East."

Sassoon's family dominated Bombay as no one family ever did in Calcutta, even the Hakohen-Dwek dynasty. His businesses were so successful that it became known throughout Jewish Asia that any Jew in need of employment could find it in Sassoon's mills. Sassoon's eight sons spread out around the world and eventually established the Sassoon empire not only in Bombay and Calcutta but also in Singapore, Hong Kong, Shanghai, Kobe, Molucca, Baghdad, Amsterdam, London, and New York. Sassoon's philanthropy was as grand as his business. He built Bombay's first Baghdadi synagogue, Maghen David, in Byculla in 1861. He also built the Ohel David Synagogue in 1863 in Pune, a hill station retreat from the heat, popular among Bombay's elite. His grandson, Sir Jacob Elias David Sassoon, built Bombay's other Baghdadi synagogue, Kenesseth Eliyahoo, in 1884 (see figure 20). The grounds of Maghen David included a hostel for Jewish travelers, a *miqveh* (ritual bath), and a *Talmud Torah* (religious school). The Sassoon family also constructed hospitals in Bombay and Pune, a medical research institute, orphanages, museums, docks, schools, libraries, and other charitable institutions.[27]

The Baghdadis' philanthropic largesse resembled that of another commercially minded Middle Eastern minority in Bombay, the Parsis. These descendants of Zoroastrians came to western India in the eighth century, fleeing the Arab conquest of their native Iran. The Parsis were the Baghdadis' most significant reference group in Bombay, much as the

Figure 20.   Kenesseth Eliyahoo Synagogue, Bombay, 1987. (Photograph by Ellen S. Goldberg)

Armenians were in Calcutta. Zoroastrians and Jews go back a long way together, to the seventh century B.C.E., when King Cyrus of Persia defeated Babylonia and allowed captive Jews to return to Israel. Cyrus even helped to finance construction of the Second Temple. Settled primarily in Bombay, the Parsis—India's most educated and wealthiest minority— provided a role model for the Baghdadis. Like Jewish charity, which began close to home and spread outward, Parsi philanthropy began within its own community, but it did not stop there. They built schools, art institutes, research centers, and libraries.[28] Even today, every Parsi in India is promised a university education, even abroad, at community expense. In a striking example of intercommunal philanthropy, the leading Parsi industrialist, Sir Jamsetji Jijibhoy, and Shaikh David Sassoon built the Gateway to India, Bombay's most famous landmark, an arch through which virtually all pre-aviation-era travelers entered India. Parsi-Jewish amity continues to this day, symbolized by Maestro Zubin Mehta's leadership of the Israel Philharmonic Orchestra.

David Sassoon's son Abdullah, also known as Albert (1818–1896), reinvested his father's opium earnings in huge textile mills. The Sassoons and industrialists such as the Tatas effected the industrialization that dominated nineteenth-century Bombay. Abdullah built the city's shipping docks and a high school, erected statues, and became a leading advisor to the government. His brother Elias David Sassoon (1820–1880) established the family's interests in Shanghai in 1845.[29] Another brother, Solomon Sassoon (1841–1894), a noted Hebraist and Talmudist, ran the family's commercial enterprises, expanding them to encircle the globe. But Solomon's wife, Flora (1859–1936), was perhaps the most eminent Sassoon luminary, a dominant figure in turn-of-the-century Bombay. She truly internationalized the family businesses as she continued its philanthropic endeavors. A pious Jew, she was said to always include a *shochet* (ritual slaughterer) and at least ten men in her retinue when she traveled, so she would never lack kosher meat or a prayer quorum. Bombayites remember her today, thanks to the dominant Flora Fountain near Victoria Station and Bombay University, a popular landmark meeting spot. Flora also led the family's gradual relocation to London, where she moved soon after the turn of the century.[30]

The Baghdadis were also significantly affected by the Bene Israel. When the Baghdadis first arrived in Bombay, they were only too happy to pray in Bene Israel synagogues, bury their dead in Bene Israel cemeteries, and eat meat the Bene Israel had ritually slaughtered. In a sense, the Baghdadis' arrival in a city with a preexisting Jewish community mirrored what happened elsewhere, in the United States, for example, when newly arrived Jewish immigrants encountered an established community. In America's northern cities, German Jews tended to look down on their coreligionists from Poland and the Ukraine, whom they considered backward, superstitious, and generally undesirable. At best, they would deign to help the "greenhorns" become more Americanized, like themselves, discarding sidelocks and black coats for proper Yankee garb. In the process, they offered charity or a job. In Bombay, however, the situation was reversed. The newly arrived Baghdadis were more cosmopolitan than the established Bene Israel. Since political and economic power in Bombay rested with the British, to be "native" was to be dispossessed, and most Bene Israel were thoroughly Indianized when the Baghdadis arrived during the early nineteenth century. While becoming Americanized might help the Polish Jews to advance in America, becoming Indianized like the Bene Israel would have disenfranchised the Baghdadis. Rather, by the middle of the century, after a brief period when the Baghdadis benefited from and relied upon Bene Israel institutions, they had superseded their reference group to become instead the Bene Israel's patrons, offering them employment and charity and schooling them about the ways of powerful foreigners.[31] This relationship was to be radically altered after the Mutiny of 1857.

BETWEEN THE MUTINY AND THE GREAT WAR (1857–1917): IDENTIFICATION WITH THE BRITISH

Only British understatement could dismiss the tempestuous events of 1857 as a mutiny. Indian historians call this bloody military revolt by the Bengal Army against British rule the War of 1857–58. The Mutiny exploded deep tensions stemming from heavy-handed British rule and the Indians' furious sense of disenfranchisement. When Britain ignored its commitments to the Nawab and annexed Oudh in 1856, it "undermined the Bengal Army's faith in the Raj it served." The British Raj imposed unwelcome social reforms, such as permitting widow remarriage in 1856; at the same time it required Bengali sepoys (soldiers) to serve in Burma. The last straw was the introduction of new cartridges for the sepoys' Enfield rifles. Rumors spread that the ammunition was greased with beef tallow and pig lard, which was important because the Hindu and Muslim sepoys were instructed to bite off the tips of the cartridges before inserting them into the breech of their guns to make the weapons fire more rapidly. The men in the Bengal Army now became convinced the British were plotting to subvert Hinduism and Islam.[32]

As the insurrection spread across northern India, both Delhi and Lucknow fell from British control. Order was eventually restored, but relations between the British and the Indians were never the same. The poisoned atmosphere in the wake of the Mutiny made the Baghdadis' identity as middlemen untenable. Gradually at first, after 1857, the Baghdadis distanced themselves from Indianness and embraced things British. Indian Jews, Baghdadis especially, instinctively supported the British during the Mutiny. In Calcutta, prayers for the British were conducted at Beth-El; in Bombay, David Sassoon asked the Jews to illuminate their homes and to recite prayers for the royal family.[33] No Bene Israel sepoys joined the insurrection, which in any case did not spread to the Bombay presidency. For the next fifty years, Calcutta's Baghdadis sought, gained, and enjoyed British status, only to have it rudely withdrawn in the early twentieth century.

After the Mutiny, the lines between British and Indian were drawn more starkly than ever. Whatever had been liberal about the British Raj was submerged, as the racist underbelly of imperialism emerged. University of California at Los Angeles historian Stanley Wolpert described the atmosphere of post-Mutiny India in his highly regarded *A New History of India:*

> As the first word of the murder of British men and women reached Lahore, Peshawar, Simla, and Calcutta, a terrible racial ferocity . . . erupted and inspired British vengeance. Wanton attacks on passive villagers and unarmed Indians, even faithful domestic servants, became common practice in the wake of the mutiny. Virtually all the bridges so painstakingly erected between British and Indian cultures were destroyed by fear and hatred. . . . [A British commander] went mad at the news of sepoys slaying English women and seriously proposed "flaying alive" any Indian guilty of such a crime. . . . Captured "mutineers" were, in fact, generally blown away from cannon to which they had been securely strapped. Entire villages were put to the torch.[34]

Such antipathy between the larger players profoundly disrupted the position of middleman groups such as the Baghdadis. As a result, Jews in Calcutta increasingly identified with the British. This transition entailed the gradual and uneven rejection of their "Arabian Jew of the British Raj" persona in favor of a new, British one that emerged in patterns of residence, language usage, clothes, choice of schools, and so on. Amid all this change, cuisine seemed to be the one cultural constant. In Bombay, the Baghdadi Jews did more than simply identify with British culture. They utterly rejected Indian culture, particularly as embodied by their coreligionists, the Bene Israel.

LANGUAGES

Obviously, as part of the Baghdadi Jews' process of identification with British culture, they adopted English as their mother tongue. This occurred very unevenly, because Arabic had been the Baghdadis' home language for generations. Judaeo-Arabic—Arabic written in the Hebrew alphabet—was their language of record in newspapers and in correspondence with Jewish communities elsewhere. Hebrew, of course, was the *lashon hakodesh,* holy speech, their ritual language. The Baghdadis' facility in conversational Hebrew was tested by shlichim from Israel, many of whom were Ashkenazim. Having no other language in common, they conversed in Hebrew. Considering the differences between Ashkenazim's and Baghdadis' pronunciation of Hebrew, it is a testimony to the fluency of each that they managed to understand each other at all.[35]

The Baghdadis used Hindusthani in the kitchen, on the street, and often when talking among themselves, especially during the last quarter of the nineteenth century. Occasionally, they used Indian vernacular tongues such as Bengali. Members of the Calcutta community understood enough to enjoy the Bengali theater.

Eventually, among Baghdadi families in Calcutta and Bombay, English replaced Arabic as the language of the home, the office, and culture. This shift in linguistic sensibilities followed an irregular process, influenced by a number of variables, particularly economic class. The rich Baghdadis came to English first, but it took time. For example, consider the man reputed to be Calcutta's richest Jew in the mid-to-late 1800s, fifty-year resident David Joseph Ezra. He signed his will in 1880 and a trust deed in 1882 in Hebrew, and his lawyer had to explain the contents of the English-language documents. "And if a man of his English contacts did not know English well enough to read and sign his name in it," wrote community historian Esmond D. Ezra, "it is a fairly safe assumption that most of his contemporaries knew even less English than he did." [36] In the home of Samuel Arakie, a leading merchant of the late nineteenth century, casual conversation was often in Hindusthani. [37] To facilitate this linguistic transition, in 1881 Calcutta's Jewish day schools adopted English as the medium of instruction for secular studies, although Arabic remained the language used for religious subjects until 1884 because so many of the religious teachers came directly from Baghdad. By 1885, the schools added Latin and French to the curriculum, which focused on English and Hebrew, but they no longer taught Arabic. [38]

During the twentieth century, English eclipsed Arabic as the mother language in most Baghdadi homes, led by the wealthy. By 1915 this transition had been effected among the elite, and by 1930 English was the language used for all community records, correspondence, and education. [39] Yet middle- and lower-class Jews still spoke Hindusthani and Bengali at home. "Anglicization was less complete further down the social structure," with English more widely used among the wealthy, who made up some 15 percent of the Baghdadi community, and Arabic and Hindusthani among the poor, who made up 50 percent; the remaining 35 percent made up the middle class. [40] The class-based use of English mirrored the class-based access to education. The community's literary life followed a similar linguistic transition. Calcutta obtained a Hebrew printing press in 1841. From then to 1890, all Hebrew books used Arabic for notes or translations. It was 1891 before a book was published in Arabic and English. [41]

The emotional embodiment of the shift from a Baghdadi to a British identity was the death in Baghdad of Chacham Joseph Hayyim (1833–1909), the last of the great leaders of Iraqi Jewry. Indian Baghdadis had looked to him for spiritual and legal advice for decades, but since he had no successor his death left a void. Subsequently, Baghdadis shifted their locus of religious authority from Baghdad to London and its two chief rabbis, Sephardi Dr. Moses Gaster and Ashkenazi Dr. Naftali Hertz.[42]

EDUCATION

The education a community provides for its children reveals a great deal about its identity, values, and orientations, as India's Baghdadi communities demonstrate. The earliest settlers hired tutors to teach children the Hebrew Bible and Hebrew prayers, but Bombay and Calcutta did not establish formal Jewish day schools until the middle of the nineteenth century.

In Bombay, David Sassoon built and endowed a number of Jewish educational institutions, including a Talmud Torah in 1861. To acculturate the children of his immigrant employees from Iraq, he built the David Sassoon Benevolent Institution, which taught languages, arithmetic, vocational skills, and *shechitah* (ritual slaughter of animals). He also built a reform school and a mechanics' institute, and his son Abdullah built Bombay's prestigious Elphinstone High School.[43] Other institutions followed, including the Sir Jacob Sassoon Free School in 1903, which taught indigent Baghdadi children in English. Bombay's wealthier Baghdadi families sent their children to Christian schools, as was done in Calcutta. The Israelite School for Bene Israel children was established in Bombay in 1892 and renamed after its Iraqi benefactor, Sir Elie Kadoorie, in 1932.[44] During the 1980s, Organization for Rehabilitation and Training (ORT) Schools have become focal points for the community. More recently, ORT's central role in the community has been eclipsed by the presence of the American Jewish Joint Distribution Committee (JDC).

The earliest Jewish school in Calcutta was an informal Talmud Torah that Eleazar Arakie led in his home from around 1843. Those who could afford it paid tuition, and the community subsidized the indigent. Both boys and girls attended, which was most unusual for the time, and they learned Hebrew, English, and religious subjects. As the number of pupils increased, Arakie hired additional teachers, but the school did not survive his death in 1864.[45]

In the meantime, Christians in Calcutta and Bombay established

British-style secular schools. These became very popular, especially among the middle- and upper-class Baghdadis who could afford the tuition. After Arakie's death, many of his pupils streamed into Calcutta's missionary schools, leaving the poorer Jews to get a traditional tutorial education if they got any at all. Throughout the 1870s, the community called for a proper Jewish day school that would emphasize Hebrew and English education, but as Rabbi Ezekiel N. Musleah charitably put it, "the school was experiencing a slow birth."[46] In 1874 a Christian missionary school was established in Calcutta's old Jewish neighborhood. By 1877, although the headmistress made no pretense about her goal of winning converts, it enrolled between fifty and sixty Jewish children. By 1881 the enrollment had climbed to one hundred, and a government grant kept the tuition as low as two rupees per month.[47] For most of the decade, the prevalent pattern was for elite Baghdadis to send their children to private, secular schools and for poorer ones to send them to the missionary school.

Spearheaded by a Tunisian émigré, Moses de Jacob Abeasis, in 1881 the Calcutta community established a Jewish day school, the Jewish Girls' and Infants' School (attended by both boys and girls, despite its name), which was staffed by two Hebrew and two English teachers. During the first year alone, enrollment rose from 18 to 108. By the end of the year, the Jewish Boys' School was established nearby. Soon, the schools merged as the Jewish Boys' and Girls' School, although boys and girls attended in different buildings with different faculties. Within a few years, the school curtailed Hebrew studies and expanded the curriculum to include English, geometry, algebra, physics, and Latin or French.[48]

Soon, free schools were established for children who could not afford even the Jewish Boys' and Girls' Schools' modest tuition. The school for indigent boys was established at Neveh Shalom Synagogue in 1882 under the direction of Chacham Solomon Abid Tweena, a recent immigrant from Baghdad. It excelled in Judaic studies and went through many changes of name, reflecting its many benefactors, until settling on the Elias Meyer Free School and Talmud Torah in 1907.[49] The Jeshurun Free School for Girls was not established until 1926 as an adjunct to the Jewish Girls' School. Government regulations prevented a tuition school from accepting more than a certain percentage of scholarship students, a technicality that blurred the demarcation between the two girls' institutions.[50]

The earlier pattern established in Bombay persisted in Calcutta: elite Baghdadi families continued to send their children to secular schools, while the Jewish schools educated lower- and middle-class children. This is somewhat surprising, because Calcutta's Jewish schools earned "European" classification several times. Being classified as European was more than a matter of pride. The designation carried government funding and provided access to the British-style examinations upon which admission to universities was based. On the other hand, the classification compelled the school to adhere to a government curriculum, which meant less instruction about Judaism and Hebrew and more about secular subjects.

The European classification, like accreditation in contemporary America, depended as much upon the school's financial base as on its academic standards, so the Calcutta community's erratic support for the school caused the periodic revocation and reinstatement of its European status. The Jewish Boys' and Girls' School remained on a shaky basis, although for most of the period from 1882 to 1927 it was headed by one of Calcutta's most competent educators, the Rev. E. M. D. Cohen. During periods when the school was not classified as European, its students were generally considered "Asiatic." Thus, they were subjected to strict government quotas that limited Asiatic children to 15 percent of the student body in Calcutta's prestigious European schools and colleges. Nevertheless, students at the Jewish school performed well on standardized tests, a testimony both to the institutions and to the individual students.[51]

Despite the availability of Jewish education, Mavis Hyman noted, "The majority of boys who came from middle income, and even poorer families, went to Christian schools, either Church of England or Catholic schools run by Jesuits, where the standard of education was superior to that in the Elias Meyer Free School for Boys. Many girls like myself also went to Christian schools, in spite of the fact that the education in the Jewish Girls' School, which was mainly fee-paying, was creditable."[52]

In both Christian and Jewish schools, "In the early years of the twentieth century there was an expansion in formal education in our community, and our model was largely based on the British system. Pupils studied in English as their first language, and they began to prepare for the overseas Cambridge School Certificate examinations. This was a far cry from home tuition, common in the nineteenth century, which concentrated on Hebrew and *Torah,* and where Arabic was the main language of instruction, since most of the *estads* [Arabic, teacher] would have come from Iraq."[53]

CLOTHING AND CUISINE

Clothing and cuisine are two bedrocks of culture, and both were expressions of identity among the Baghdadis in the late nineteenth and early twentieth centuries.

Baghdadi cuisine has been hailed as one of the world's finest, blending the tastes of the Middle East and India.[54] Community authors Flower Elias and Judith Elias Cooper summarized Calcutta's culinary staples:

> Like their ancestors in Aleppo and Baghdad, the Calcutta Jews lived mainly on chicken. This might occasionally be supplemented by fish [a Bengali staple]. They had four meals a day—breakfast, lunch, tea and dinner. For both lunch and dinner there was chicken generally in a wet dish with rice at lunch and dry, with vegetables, at dinner. Because of this basic sameness of ingredients, much ingenuity was used to vary the taste of the dishes and a wide selection was built up. Most of the recipes were of Arabian origin, but the menus of the community also included Indian dishes, such as curries, *bhajis* (mixed vegetables fried in oil), lentils and so on.
>
> One dish in particular [was popular], namely *aloo makala* . . . [or] "Jumping potatoes," because the whole potato, after being peeled, would be fried slowly until golden brown outside and soft, white and fluffy inside and when served, the crust would be so crisp that it tended to jump off the plate if not carefully pierced. . . . Another very popular dish among the community was *murug* (a chicken soup). . . . Another Hebrew word given to a dish was *hameen* (meaning 'hot'). Hameen was chicken, cooked with either barley or rice, carrots or other alternatives, on a slow fire all night, to be eaten for lunch on the Sabbath. Other dishes much favored by the community were *khutta* with *koobas* (sweet-sour chicken . . .); *mahashas* (. . . stuffed onions, tomatoes, cabbage leaves, etc.); *meeta* (Hindustani word for "sweet"—chicken generally cooked with carrots or green peas); *chutunny* (chicken with vinegar and sugar); *anjuli* (shredded chicken or fried fish, floating in coconut milk and lemon); *pilay matabak* (pilaw . . . cooked with fish and *lembo basra*—lemons dried and ground with special spices); *hulba* (fenugreek) . . .[55]

No discussion of Calcutta Baghdadi cuisine would be complete without considering Nahoum and Sons, bakers and confectioners extraordinaire, of New Market. Around the turn of the century, Baghdadi émigré Nahoum Ibn Israel eked out a living peddling door to door his products such as *makhbuz,* sweet and savory baked goods; *hulwaie,* sweets such as Turkish delight; and cheeses. In 1912, he opened a shop at New Market, near the Jewish community, and soon expanded his culinary repertoire to include western patisserie treats. In 1916, he rented larger quarters where his bakery shop cum community center has been ever since. During the 1920s, his confections were sold as far away as Burma and Ceylon, and his package business reached Jews wherever they lived in India.[56]

His grandson, Norman Nahoum, says the fact that his store is Jewish adds prestige to his products. He jokes that if his samosas are not selling well, he puts up a placard identifying them as "*Jewish* samosas." With such exotic appeal, they then sell briskly.[57] To this day, Nahoum's remains "*the* hub of the community." [58]

The cultural boundaries that came to separate European and native were more strictly maintained in matters of clothing than in culinary tastes, which allowed for curries on the same table with the roasted chicken. In the broadest terms, the Baghdadis wore Arabic/Turkish dress during the nineteenth century and switched to British clothing during the twentieth. Predictably, the men made the transition from Middle Eastern to western dress before the women. Reports conflict about Indian clothing: Elias and Cooper report that men wore the north Indian kurta-pyjama and women wore "wrappers," [59] while Hyman writes that Indian clothing was not worn—except for comfort in the home.[60]

One of Elias and Cooper's informants reported a remarkable anecdote. If it accurately reflects community mores, clothing was considered a more significant identity marker than ethnicity, because the story depicts Calcutta's Baghdadis not as having any objection to marrying Bene Israels as such but as objecting to marrying someone who wore Indian clothing. "There was the case of a boy in our community," the informant said, "marrying a Bene-Israel girl—this was when I was much older (1940s). The secretary of our synagogue in Calcutta objected to the marriage taking place there, because she was a Bene-Israel and was going to be married in a sari. I argued with him and said English clothes were not Jewish clothes and we accept them as Jewish; what difference if she wears a sari, so long as she is a Jewish girl—then he allowed the marriage to take place." [61]

Ezra summarized the Baghdadi approach to such cultural expressions as food, language, names, and clothing: " . . . they picked up the vernacular and spoke it fluently, though not elegantly, and Indian dishes, such as curries, became part of their diet. But unlike the Bene Israel Jews of the west coast of India, they neither adopted local dress nor local names . . . when they did give up their Arabic or Turkish dress and adopt non-Arabic first names, it was to copy the British model. Their general outlook and the education and upbringing of their children, too, had a very strong British bias."[62]

Economic historian Thomas A. Timberg described the gradual shift in residency patterns of Calcutta's Baghdadis from the greytown of the middlemen to more Anglicized neighborhoods, and Ezra analyzed the city's Jewish demographics in detail.[63] Following Shalom Obadiah Hakohen, for their first fifty years in Calcutta the Jews settled exclusively in an Armenian and Portuguese neighborhood known as Burrabazar, north of Fort William. Calcutta's first census in 1866 counted 558 Jews in Burrabazar and 121 in Kolutola, the next district to the east. All lived within a few hundred yards of a synagogue. A gradual migration to the south followed, to Bow Bazar and Fenwick Bazar. By the 1921 census, more Jews lived in Bow Bazar than in any of the city's other districts (645 in Bow Bazar and 271 in Fenwick Bazar compared with 133 in Burrabazar and 471 in Kolutola), and most Calcuttans, Jews and Gentiles alike, remember Bow Bazar as the city's Jewish neighborhood. Between the wars, elite Jews moved farther south into the whitetown districts such as Park Street (the unofficial dividing line between the greytown and the whitetown), Victoria Terrace, and even Ballygunge, even though Bow Bazar remained the hub of Jewish life. So complete was the Jews' abandonment of their original home that by 1931 only thirteen still lived in Burrabazar.[64]

Bombay's Baghdadis never clustered into a neighborhood like their cousins in Calcutta. Although Bene Israel congregated at first in Israel Mohalla in Mandvi and then spread out in clusters to Dongri, Mazgaon, Byculla, Jacob Circle, Parel, Dadar, and Kurla, the Baghdadis did not seem to settle in groups except in Byculla around Maghen David Synagogue and the downtown fort close to Kenesseth Eliyahoo.[65] Rather, they settled wherever they could afford housing, from Byculla to Colaba to posh Malabar Hill.

IN BOMBAY AND RANGOON: CLASHES WITH BENE ISRAEL

Unfortunately, Bombay's pre–World War I Baghdadis will be remembered primarily for their condescending and libelous attacks on the Bene Israel. But relations between the two groups of Jews started out amicably enough, as Roland describes:

When the Baghdadis first arrived in Bombay. they were welcomed by the Bene Israel, who invited them to attend services in their synagogues and to bury their dead in the Bene Israel cemetery. The Bene Israel had just recently learned of many of the *halachic* (Jewish legal) rules and Jewish traditions [from their Cochini teachers]. They were urbanized, some were educated and westernized, but they were less affluent than the Baghdadis. Those who were poor could not afford the two sets of eating and cooking utensils needed to keep kosher food regulations. If they had only one pot, they would kosher it by boiling water in it. If they could afford to eat meat at all, they ate only kosher meat. But the *hazans* (readers or cantors) from Cochin and the Baghdadi *Cohens* (descendants of priestly families) who officiated in Bene Israel synagogues would not eat in Bene Israel homes because they feared these households were not thoroughly kosher. This reluctance, although common to ultra-orthodox Jews the world over, seems to have had caste overtones in India. Nevertheless, the Baghdadis tried to help the Bene Israel in their efforts to return to orthodoxy.[66]

As early as 1836, however, the harmony between the Baghdadis and Bene Israel began to unravel. For reasons unknown, "David Sassoon and nine other Arab Jews sent a petition to the Bombay authorities requesting that a partition wall be erected in the cemetery to divide the two groups. They pointed out that there were two distinct tribes of Jews in Bombay, 'one having the customs of the natives of India and the other faithful to their Arabian fathers.'"[67] Relations deteriorated, and the Jewish traveler Israel Joseph Benjamin noted during his visit of 1849–50 that the "Babylonian" Jews of Bombay did not recognize that the Bene Israel even shared their religion, although Benjamin himself felt confident that they did and that they were one of the lost tribes.[68]

In all of this, Bombay's Baghdadis reflected long-standing Indian cultural patterns: the fairer, more recently arrived groups deemed themselves socially superior to the darker groups with long-standing residency. To go back to the paradigm, by the middle of the second millennium B.C.E., the Aryans were dominant over the Dravidians; later the Muslims over the Hindus; then the British over the Indians. So, too, it became the Baghdadis over the Bene Israel.[69] In another sense, the relationship between the Baghdadis and the Bene Israel resembled that between the British and the Anglo-Indians, the latter a source of tension and embarrassment to the former.

The decline in relations between the two groups was gradual and uneven, but the 1857 Mutiny had an indelible, deleterious impact. Just as in Calcutta, the Mutiny was a watershed event in Bombay and led to strict, British-mandated demarcations allying themselves with other

groups classified as "European" against the "natives." These barriers
were every bit as much a matter of attitude as of law. Marginal groups
were caught in the bind, and the Baghdadis were marginal even though
some of them were very wealthy. As Roland aptly put it, "The struggle
to escape their marginal status and to be considered fully European constitutes a main theme of the Baghdadis' sojourn in India; their relationships with government and their political affiliations and attitudes must
be examined in this context."[70]

In Calcutta during this pre–World War I period, the Baghdadi community was so much larger that it simply absorbed the few resident Bene
Israel and Cochinites. For them, the natives were the Hindus and Muslims. But in Bombay, where the Bene Israel outnumbered the Baghdadis,
the former group became the native shadow self of the latter, and as such
were subjected to a series of humiliations that eventually called into question their very Jewishness.

A direct relationship existed between the Bombay Baghdadis' degree
of Anglicization and their level of animus toward the Bene Israel. Initially
the groups had gotten along, but the Mutiny made the Baghdadis feel
more British, and so they began to distance themselves from the Bene Israel. Then, in the third of the four periods marking the evolution of India's Baghdadi communities, the British fought a war against the Otto-
mans—World War I. The Baghdadis were considered Turkish or, strictly
speaking, Ottoman subjects. To avoid being considered enemy aliens,
the Baghdadis accelerated their drive for acceptance as Europeans. This,
in turn, led to greater hostility between them and the Bene Israel. Finally,
during the nationalistic fourth step of the community's evolution, Indian
nationalism propelled the Baghdadis into an even more Anglicized sense
of self. In the Baghdadis' view, the Bene Israel thus became even greater
pariahs because they remained dangerously ambivalent about the triple
tugs of Anglicization, Indian nationalism, and Zionism.

Harking back to the period before World War I, then, the cemetery
was the first battleground between the Baghdadis and the Bene Israel.
Beginning with David Sassoon's 1836 attempt to have a dividing wall
erected, the cemetery remained an arena of strife until the turn of the century, when the struggle moved into the synagogue itself. Before 1900, the
Sassoons acquired a new cemetery for use by Baghdadis and Cochinis
only. Bene Israel continued to be buried in the older cemetery, which
soon filled up. The Baghdadis did not allow Bene Israel to use their new
cemetery during the interval until they had established a second new
burial ground of their own.[71] In Calcutta, where Bene Israel were always

welcomed and even honored in the synagogues, the cemetery was divided into four sections: Baghdadis, Bene Israel, Cochinis, and western Jews.[72]

During this period, most of the Sassoons' charitable trusts expressly excluded Bene Israel as beneficiaries. The Sir Jacob Sassoon Bombay Charity Fund, the Bombay Jewish Burial Ground, and the Lady Rachel Sassoon Dispensary all provided services to poor Jews "except Bene Israelites."[73]

This galled, but the most painful dimension of the dispute played out in the synagogues, where sometime soon after the turn of the century Bene Israel came to be denied ordinary ritual honors. Baghdadis refused to eat meat slaughtered by Bene Israel shochetim, and even refused to count their men as part of a minyan (the ten-member prayer quorum). Not counting someone toward a minyan is tantamount to denying his Jewishness. The community's discussion had fallen to just such a nadir. Sir Jacob Sassoon, the leader of the Baghdadis, was interviewed in the London *Jewish Chronicle* at the height (or depth) of the dispute. In the interview, "Sir Jacob accused the Bene Israel of having drifted away from Judaism and having assimilated with the Hindus, claiming that his grandfather, David Sassoon, had facilitated their return to Judaism. The white Jews [Baghdadis] regard themselves as a superior 'caste' to the Bene Israel, he noted. Bene Israel responded by asking Sir Jacob how many English Jews had managed to 'keep themselves free' from English ways and habits. Once again they defended Bene Israel orthodoxy and tried to clarify the difference between *Gora* and *Kala* Jews."[74]

The Bene Israel vigorously defended themselves in their newspapers, and they did have some outside support. Rabbi Shmuel Abe, a shaliach from Tsfat, commented in 1859 that the Bene Israel observed all the mitsvot of written and oral law. Eleven years later, shlichim from Tiberias and Tsfat, Sephardic and Ashkenazic respectively, said that being close to the Bene Israel was a great mitsvah. They warned against efforts to set the Bene Israel apart, an allusion to the Baghdadis.[75] The chief rabbi of Great Britain, a Romanian Sephardi, Dr. Moses Gaster, wrote, "I know the Bene Israel very well, and I know they are very religious and good Jews. I have often taken up their cause, and I have personally declared them to be identical with the rest of the House of Israel."[76] But the Baghdadis no more heeded the foreign rabbis than the Paradesi Cochinim adhered to repeated rabbinic admonitions not to discriminate against the meshuchrarim.

While Calcutta Baghdadis did not discriminate against the Bene Israel to such an extent, their satellite community in Rangoon did. At the turn of the century, some sixty Bene Israel lived among the city's 1,300 Baghdadis. In 1913 the trustees of Musmeah Yeshua Synagogue barred the Bene Israel from reciting the blessings over the Torah, except for occasional additional readings. When some Bene Israel members protested, the trustees first claimed that the Bene Israel did not observe Shabbat properly (being mainly civil servants, Saturday was a working day for them), and later raised a question about Bene Israel traditions regarding marriage, divorce, and levirate marriage. In 1926, the Rangoon synagogue authorities offered to permit one Bene Israel man to have synagogue honors if he would sign a pledge not to work on the Sabbath. The Bene Israel refused on the reasonable grounds that such a pledge was not required of other Jews.[77] The matter was taken to the civil courts. As the case was pending, a new synagogue, Beth-El, opened in Rangoon in 1932; Bene Israel enjoyed full participation in services. In 1936 the high court referred the matter to the London rabbinical court and ruled in accord with its finding: that the Bene Israel did not differ from other Jews and therefore had to be treated equally. The Musmeah Yeshua Synagogue trustees filed an appeal, which was dismissed.[78]

The Rangoon case set a precedent. In Bombay, a ward at the Jamsetji Jijibhoy Hospital was set aside for indigent Jews, and the ward's Baghdadi trustee insisted on excluding Bene Israel. The hospital referred the issue to the government, which ruled in favor of the Bene Israel on two grounds. First, the census and all official statistics counted the Bene Israel as Jews, and second, the Rangoon case had set the precedent. "There is therefore no ground for Government to introduce an invidious distinction between sections of the general Jewish community or to treat the Bene Israel community as not coming under the generic term 'Jews,'" the government report concluded.[79]

THE POST–WORLD WAR I PERIOD (1919–1935):
COMPETING NATIONALISMS AND
A "EUROPEAN" CLASSIFICATION

With the outbreak of World War I, the British government faced a dilemma. At the time, 3,197 Turkish subjects lived in India, the majority of whom were Bombay's 2,600 Baghdadis, so classified because Baghdad was part of the Ottoman Empire. The British wanted to keep all "enemy aliens" under surveillance, but they knew that certain minority groups in the Empire—the Jews and the Shiites in particular—were probably anti-Turkish. Their dilemma was basically semantic: in some contexts, the Baghdadis were considered Asiatic, in others European, and in still others, Turkish. Only the latter posed a wartime security risk, so the government incarcerated only "Turks proper," while "European Jewish Turks" and "Asiatic Turks"—meaning Baghdadi Jews and Arabs—remained at liberty.[80] Freedom to travel around India was another matter. As merchants, the Baghdadis needed this liberty, which was granted to other non-Muslim "Turkish" groups—namely, Calcutta's Armenians and Greeks. But the Bengal government refused, citing the Baghdadis' greater numbers, and preferring to move more cautiously, offering case-by-case permits.

After the war, many Baghdadis sought naturalization as British subjects, but the government stuck by its policy of not granting blanket naturalization to enemy alien subjects for ten years after a conflict, despite the Baghdadis' well-known passionate loyalty to the British.[81] This classification dilemma fueled the Baghdadis' quest for European status. They wanted an unambiguous resolution to the quandary of Turkish, Asiatic, and European classification. Indeed, the British found no ready classification for the Baghdadis. In 1885, Baghdadis—but not Parsis—were classified as European. In 1877, and from 1910 to 1930, Baghdadis and Bene Israel alike were welcome in the British Volunteer Corps. But Baghdadis who entered the British military or the civil service were paid on the scale of Anglo-Indians, not on the higher British scale; the Bene Israel, on the other hand, were remunerated on the lowest scale, that for native Indians. Finally, ambivalence prevailed, as reflected in the European Code of 1917, which read, "all Jews, Armenians and Parsees living European lives, or approximating their ways of living, [are to] be considered as European for the purposes of the Education Code."[82]

Musleah describes his community's attitude at the time: "the Jewish community came to accept its politically nebulous position because for the most part, the discriminatory measure existed only on paper. There was free social intercourse between statutory Europeans and Jews who were admitted to membership in the exclusive European institutions such as the fashionable clubs, a privilege to which prominent Indians could not aspire."[83]

In Bombay, the situation was less agreeable. Unlike Indian and Parsi firms, Baghdadi businesses were permitted to join the Chamber of Commerce, but like Indians and Parsis, they were often barred from the exclusive European clubs.[84] To some extent, this was a matter of pride and identity, but it was also a practical concern. Only European-classified schools offered scholarships for English universities. In 1908, one Home

Department official ruled that only Jews of European extraction could be eligible, while another bureaucrat held, as Roland put it, that "some Jews were native of England by statute, and some served the government of India and were practically European as the term was used in connection with the scholarship scheme." [85]

The stress of such ambiguity further damaged the Baghdadis' already deteriorating relationship with the Bene Israel and added more frustration to their quest for acceptance from those who would never grant it. These stresses multiplied as the competing Indian and Jewish nationalisms, Swaraj and Zionism, laid claim to India's Jews. The Baghdadis faced historic choices that splintered their community and their sense of self: they had to choose between Indian, Jewish-Zionist, and British identities. What had been seamless unraveled quickly.

The Government of India Act of 1919 mandated representation in the legislatures for India's myriad ethnic groups, a policy known as communalism. Representation was to be granted to four constituencies: Europeans (all whites domiciled in India); Anglo-Indians (descendants of mixed unions between European males and Asian females); "Mohammedans" (a religio-racial term offensive to Muslims as it implies worship of Muhammad rather than God; the British used it anyway); and non-Mohammedans, the largest group, comprised mostly of Hindus but including Jews.

Ten years later, Calcutta's Baghdadis petitioned the government to extend the definition of the term *European* to include "the British section of the Jewish community of Bengal." [86] At this time, the Baghdadis began to call themselves Sephardim, a designation indicating European origin. The term *Sephardim* derives from the Hebrew *Sepharad* (Spain). In this sense it reflects European background, but the designation has two overlapping nuances. In its more restrictive sense, *Sephardim* specifies descendants of Jews expelled from Spain and Portugal during the 1490s. The term also has a more expansive sense. When the Jews were expelled from the Iberian Peninsula, they went to North Africa, the Balkans, Turkey, and India, among other places. In each place, they encountered long-established Jewish communities that they came to dominate in matters of religious custom and law. Thus, in its second sense *Sephardim* broadly describes those who follow Sephardic religious law and customs.

Even while the Baghdadis in Calcutta and Bombay struggled with the British over categorization, Baghdadis in Shanghai declared themselves Sephardim. As University of London scholar Maisie Meyer wrote, "the

Shanghai Jews chose at about the same time and for similar reasons to be classified as Sephardim and so covertly as European. . . . The Shanghai Sephardim who had British passports could travel freely because of the effective and universal protection afforded by the British. They were governed by British law and their litigation was conducted in HM Supreme Court. By contrast the Jews who remained Turkish subjects had no extraterritorial protection outside the International Settlement." [87]

As it became increasingly clear that the British were planning to leave India, the Baghdadis' struggle for a European classification became all the more desperate. In 1933, they created a vague proposal that at least some of them be classified as European, namely "all natural-born British subjects of the Jewish community speaking the English language and dressed in European style." They argued that since the three Jewish schools in Calcutta were then classified as European, that courtesy should be extended to the community itself.[88]

The British equivocated. At first, they accepted wording suggested by the Calcutta Jews and supported by the Chamber of Commerce to include in the European designation "British subjects of the Sephardic Jewish community including British subjects of mixed European and Sephardic Jewish descent but excluding Bene-Israelites, Black Cochin Jews and persons of Indian or mixed Jewish and non-European descent." [89] The Jews were satisfied with this formula, but then the British backed off. By the time World War II broke out, British equivocation had leached into army policies, which distinguished between "Indian Jews," namely Bene Israel, and "Anglo-Indian Jews," Baghdadis. To muddy the waters more, the British Army also held:

> At present Indian Jews and Anglo-Indian Jews must be enrolled under the Indian Army Act as Indian soldiers. If, after enrollment, they are considered by their local military commanders to be habituated to a European or similar style of life and food, they may be granted British scales of rations. Anglo-Indian Jews, but not Indian Jews, get British courtesy ranks in certain units and in all cases, accommodation, clothing and medical treatment as for British soldiers. Indian Jews get these services as for Indian soldiers. . . .
>
> Anglo-Indians receive the same pay as Indians unless they are enlisted into British units when they receive British scales of pay.[90]

This farce of British classification soon became obsolete for two reasons. First, Indian independence was in the offing. Second, when several thousand Ashkenazi refugees from Nazism arrived in India, they had a sobering effect upon the debate. Even the most pretentious Baghdadi got

the message that the Holocaust made clear: distinctions among Jews
were empty, a point of view that gave a certain clarity to Zionist ideol-
ogy as well.

INDEPENDENCE AND THE BIRTH OF NEW IDENTITIES

Even as World War II approached, it became obvious that Britain would
grant independence to India soon after the war's end. At the same time,
Indian Jews were acutely aware of the Zionist struggle. These two forces
offered competing identities to all of India's Jews, the Cochinites and
Bene Israel as well as the Baghdadis: they must become Indians or make
aliyah as Jews. While the two identities had been balanced in the past,
the modern period bifurcated them.

A third option, one that eluded them in India, became available to
some Baghdadis: they might become British. Most Baghdadis found this
possibility attractive. For years, leading Baghdadi families traveled to
England frequently. Some maintained residences there. Most Baghdadi
families in Bombay, Calcutta, or Rangoon had relatives in London. After the fall of the Ottoman Empire and the establishment of British rule
in Iraq (1921–33), life for Jews in Iraq, the home country, temporarily
improved. (Iraq sympathized with Nazi Germany and after the war
helped lead Arab rejection of coexistence with Israel.) India's Baghdadis
simultaneously increased their business dealings with relatives both in
Iraq and in England, and developed an even greater attachment for the
British. By the mid-twentieth century, they were fluent in English and accustomed to British culture, clothing, and even cuisine; a half century of
Anglicization in India made Britain a natural home. Many moved there
in anticipation of Indian independence in 1947, or soon thereafter. Many
other Baghdadis settled elsewhere in the English-speaking world—Aus-
tralia, Canada, South Africa, and the United States. Those who moved
to Israel became Israeli; they participate easily in that nation's economic,
social, and cultural life and seem pleased to be living in the Middle East
again.[91]

Those who remained in India have embraced India as none of their
community ever did before. The few remaining Baghdadis carry their Indianness well. Their pride in "the most hospitable country in the world
toward the Jews" is mirrored by the feelings of the last Jews of Cochin,
as well as those Bene Israel who chose to remain in India.[92] Norman Nahoum, a leader of Calcutta's Baghdadis and proprietor of the famous con-
fectionery, perceives deep cultural similarities between Indic and Judaic

civilizations. "We are taught to abhor idolatry to prevent its assimilation into Abraham's family of religions," he said. "We don't want to profess too much all these similarities because Judaism will not accept, but if you look at it closely you will see that Judaism and Hinduism have so much in common." In India, "We are accepted totally, at the same time we are treated with kid gloves, like special guests." Referring to Hindus, he defiantly maintains, "*These* people are civilized; the others are barbarians, bent on proselytization. If you ask any Jew who has lived in India, from Cochin to Calcutta," he concludes, "you will find that although the Hindus are called idolaters, they are more accepting of Jews than those so-called new religions that grew out of Judaism."

Nahoum recognizes that his new, proud Indian-Jewish identity is "an absolute reversal of the thought that has been inculcated in our minds for years." Regarding the issue of idolatry, he wonders only, "What happens when you start loving people your own religion teaches you to abhor?" [93]

Conclusion

This introductory study of three Indian Jewish communities helps us understand both Judaic and Indic civilizations, and the nature of communal continuity.

Thinking about the three communities' history, social organization, and religious life deepens our understanding of both India and Israel. The Cochin Jews achieved a synthesis of their Jewish and Indian identities. Crude, superimposed categories of "east" and "west" vanish in a seamless persona. In the spice trade, the Cochinis crossed cultural boundaries with regularity. Their amicable relations with their neighbors, particularly the local nobility, obviated the defensive identity barriers often found among Jews who live under Christian or Muslim rule. The unique Hindu polity that insists each group in society should maintain its own cultural and religious distinctiveness enabled Jewish acculturation without assimilation.

That the Cochin Jews abandoned India for Israel in no way diminishes the quality of their life on the Malabar Coast. They lived as all Jews should have been permitted to: free, pious, creative, and prosperous, contributors to both their host culture and their own Jewish world. When conditions permitted, they returned to the ancestral home of their dreams and prayers. The story of their community reads like an idealized script about Jewish dignity and survival.

The Bene Israel and the Baghdadis have very different stories. The years of Bene Israel history before their "First Awakening" are irretrievably lost, save for legend and current DNA research. The sole remaining reconstructions of that history reveal more about the eras when they were articulated than about the lost centuries whose meanings they purport to convey. The Bene Israel survived without Halachah, the rudder of normative Judaism. Seemingly, they did not actively construct their own identity, but rather responded to identity-forming events. On the other hand, their very reactions show Bene Israel creativity as they responded to their Cochini and Baghdadi coreligionists, Christian missionaries and British bureaucrats, and Zionists and Swarajists.

Certainly, the first, most significant distinction between the ways in which the Cochin Jews and the Bene Israel formed their identities is that the Cochin Jews had a historical consciousness of themselves throughout most of their sojourn in India. Their continuity with mainstream Jewish history and norms equipped them to balance the cultural worlds of Judaism and Hinduism. The Bene Israel, on the other hand, lost all of that intellectual equipment in their legendary shipwreck, and as a result tumbled more deeply into assimilation. The story of their recovery to the Jewish world is as unlikely as it is inspiring.

Viewing the Baghdadis as the actors and the Bene Israel as the acted upon is all too easy. Both struggled for an identity and a niche in British India. True, the Baghdadis were powerful and the Bene Israel were not. But the Baghdadis' nineteenth-century arrival in India was, in the first place, a reaction to dangerous persecutions in Iraq, Iran, and elsewhere. They arrived as disenfranchised refugees, outcasts from their ancestral homes, only to find themselves pioneers on several cultural frontiers simultaneously: the British culture of the elite, the Anglo-Indian culture of the greytowns of Calcutta, and the Hindu and Muslim cultures of Bengal and Maharashtra. The Baghdadis' snubs of the Bene Israel echoed the snubs they themselves received. Given the highly charged racial climate of British India, especially after the Mutiny of 1857, the Baghdadis may have had few options other than social climbing upon the backs of their Bene Israel coreligionists, as was the sorry case in Bombay. The Baghdadis maintained a tenacious grasp on foreign, especially Iraqi, Jewish institutions, as part of their need to be seen as anything except Indian. Their maintenance of family and other ties outside of India, in Singapore, Hong Kong, and London, seemed to rely upon keeping this nonnative identity.

Viewing the three communities together also demonstrates that communal identity is not fixed but is, instead, a creative response to dynamic, outside events. In this sense, it is a response to an external demand implicit in the social, historical, and economic conditions surrounding the community. For example, when de Paiva came to Cochin in 1686 looking for lost tribes, he reported that the Cochin Jews told him they were the lost tribe of Menasseh. Even a cursory familiarity with their history, however, shows they were never lost but had maintained steady contact with other Jewish communities and knowledge of events in world Jewry for centuries before de Paiva's visit. In 1968, when the Cochin Synagogue celebrated its four-hundredth anniversary, the Cochin Jews proudly proclaimed their origin in Second Temple–era Jerusalem. During recent years, they sought status and approval from world Jewry, for whom a Jerusalemite origin bespeaks good yichus. Seventeenth-century Amsterdam Jews, on the other hand, wanted to honor lost tribes and cast the Cochin Jews in that role. In each case, the Cochin Jews gave their assumed interlocutors what they wanted, or so their interlocutors reported. Clearly, the Cochinim could have reported other versions of their story, depending upon which foreign group was being addressed.

Jewish communities in Calcutta and Bombay developed and changed more rapidly than the one in Cochin. Consequently, the identities of the Bene Israel and the Baghdadis evolved more rapidly and within the purview of relatively modern history. Thus, we can trace the continuity of these two communities' identities more closely than we can that of the Cochin Jews, for whom change seems to have occurred at a more leisurely pace.

In just two and a half centuries, the Bene Israel matured from an anonymous oil-pressing caste of the Konkan to urban, modern Jews of Bombay. Thanks in part to the pioneering analysis by Benjamin J. Israel, we can trace their religious evolution rather closely.[1] The Baghdadis' religious development is even clearer, because their sojourn in India, after all, lasted barely two centuries. The maturation of Baghdadi identity is clearly connected to specific historical events, including the 1857 uprising, the war against the Axis including the Ottoman Empire, World War II and the Holocaust, and Indian and Israeli independence. Indeed, the Bene Israel and the Baghdadis generated and articulated their identities in response to parallel and sometimes identical external events. Faced with the overwhelming force of such world-shaking events, these two tiny, marginal Jewish communities responded as best they could.

The three very different communities of Jews in India had one determining factor in common: the absence of indigenous anti-Semitism. All three testify that maintaining Jewish identity is not merely a defense mechanism against a hostile world. On the contrary, the Jews of India demonstrate how Jewish communities flourish in an atmosphere of amity. Save for isolated incidents—Portuguese rule in Cochin, for example, or the pro-German faction of the Swaraj movement—Jews in India have always enjoyed the respect and affection of their Hindu, Christian, Muslim, and other neighbors. Indeed, today Jews play a significant role in Indian political discourse, in which Hindu tolerance is a major theme. The so-called Hindu nationalist Bharatiya Janatha Party (BJP) government in New Delhi recently appointed a Jew, General Frederick Jacob, as governor of Goa and recently promoted him to the demanding position of governor of the Punjab.[2] This is but the latest instance in the modern Indian political discourse of tolerance toward Jews that dates to former Prime Minister Indira Gandhi's talk at the Cochin Synagogue in 1968.

Jewish identity in India is significant in contemporary discussions about continuity within the Jewish world. Identifying aspects of both Judaic and Indic cultures that enabled Jews to live so long in India, fully as Indians if they wished, while at the same time preserving their religious and cultural life provides new ways for other Diaspora Jews to meet the challenge of preserving religion while participating fully in the modern world. Case studies from India may cast light upon the perplexing question of how to acculturate without assimilation. As Deen Khandelwal, president of the Hindu University of America, put it, "An understanding of the dynamics and mechanisms of Jewish acculturation in India is our most effective tool for addressing contemporary Jewish issues; indeed, it can help any diasporized culture."[3]

Today, of the three communities discussed here, only the Bene Israel community of Bombay remains vital. Its satellite communities in Ahmedabad and Pune have active synagogues but little else. New Delhi has diplomats, businessmen, and a handful of Bene Israel Jews. But elsewhere—in Calcutta, Cochin, Rangoon—Jewish life is no longer possible, and the few remaining, elderly Jews bitterly endure Shabbats without prayers, holy days without joy. In Cochin, there is some small solace in visits from dignitaries, whether the president of Israel or the queen of England, but footsteps echo through the cavernous Maghen David in Calcutta, and the Jews of Cochin are overwhelmed in their own street by tourist shops and curiosity seekers.

The remaining Indian Jews' loss, generally, is Israel's gain. Although most Jews have relocated from India, they have not vanished. In Israel, efforts are under way to preserve elements of Indian Jewish heritage, and a recent exhibition at the Israel Museum focused on the transplanted community.[4] Still, mother languages are forgotten, close community ties dissolve in the melting pot of Israel, and memories fade. Perhaps this book may stem that tide just a little. At the same time, it may shed light on Jewry's contemporary issues by viewing them from the perspective of the historic dynamics of establishing a community identity.

Notes

INTRODUCTION

1. Karp, "Seeking Lost Tribes of Israel in India, Using DNA Testing."

2. For the Cochin Jews, the most significant reference groups were the local dominant caste, the Nayars, and the Perumpadappu royal family of Cochin, in particular, the Nambudiri priests, the Nazaranee Māpilla Christian community, and colonialists from Portugal, Holland, and Britain. For the Bene Israel, the most significant such groups were their rural neighbors in the Konkan, the Cochin Jews, Christian missionaries, Baghdadi Jews, and the British. For the Baghdadis, they were Armenians in Calcutta, Parsis (Indian Zoroastrians) in Bombay, the Bene Israel, and the British.

3. Dutt, ed. and trans., *The Dharma Shastra,* 287–88.

4. Whiting, *You Gotta Have Wa.*

5. Thanks to my FIU colleague Dr. Steven Heine for this analogy.

6. Perlmann, "The History of the Jews in China," 182–83.

7. It is not surprising, then, that the past decade's fecundity for the study of Indian Jewish communities has also been evident in important comparative studies of Hindu and Judaic thought: the edited volume by Hananya Goodman (*Between Jerusalem and Benares*) and the studies by Barbara Holdrege (*Veda and Torah*) and Margaret Chatterjee (*Studies in Modern Hindu and Jewish Thought*). The ongoing vitality of this sort of intellectual exercise is confirmed by the recent establishment of an American Academy of Religion study group (the AAR's Comparative Studies in Hinduisms and Judaisms Group, established in 1995 and chaired by Barbara Holdrege) and an academic journal (the *Journal of Indo-Judaic Studies,* edited by this author and Braj Mohan Sinha).

Compared with the earlier record, the 1990s were a veritable whirlwind of academic activity, a frenzy attributable to the synergy of disciplinary and cultural expertise that comprised Indo-Judaic studies and to the engagement of talented, inquisitive scholars.

Like other area studies, Indo-Judaic studies is interdisciplinary and rooted in languages. The disciplines that are brought to bear include religious studies and its many subspecialties, such as ritual studies, liturgics, and phenomenology of religion; anthropology and sociology, including ethnography and physical anthropology; history and its subfields, paleography, archaeology, and epigraphy; political science; comparative literature; population studies and human geography; women's studies; and so on. Also like area studies, Indo-Judaic studies is rooted in languages, especially Hebrew and Sanskrit, but also India's regional languages (Malayalam, Marathi, Bengali) and Jewish creoles (Ladino, Judaeo-Arabic, Judaeo-Persian, Judaeo-Malayalam). Readers in the field also encounter works in Arabic, Yiddish, German, Portuguese, and the like.

Of necessity, Indo-Judaic studies includes relevant data from biblical, ancient, and classical studies. It is as concerned with medieval economic history as with contemporary diplomacy. It looks for images of India and Indians in Jewish literature and for images of Jews and Judaism in Indian literature. It deals with contemporary religio-nationalist movements in the context of secular governments.

Indo-Judaic studies takes seriously the contemporary dialogue between Hindus and Jews. These dialogues may be philosophical or religious, or they may be ethnic, as in the United States, where no two identifiable ethnic groups so closely resemble one another as do Jewish Americans and Indian Americans in terms of economics, education, professions, and entrepreneurship. Indian Americans may see Jews as their predecessors in the role of a religious minority that seeks a balance between traditional values and modern achievements. Other Asian Americans may look to Jews as models for preserving a culture in a Diaspora, or they may wish to emulate American Jews' perceived success in influencing American foreign policy to favor a "special relationship" with their country of origin. On the other hand, many Jews look to Hinduism and Buddhism for spiritual riches, the phenomenon Rodger Kamenetz describes in *The Jew in the Lotus* as "JuBus."

The emergence of Indo-Judaic studies provides the context for recent studies of Indian Jewish communities. In the past they have been approached only as exotic appendages to Jewish studies by individuals trained in Jewish cultures and languages. On rare occasions, someone expert in Indology wrote on an aspect of Indian Jewish life, usually in deciphering an inscription or drawing folkloric comparisons. But today this area of scholarship demands facility in both classical cultures (languages, history, and so on) and an academic focus.

CHAPTER 1. A BALANCED IDENTITY: THE JEWS OF COCHIN

1. On their Malayalam folk songs, see Jussay, "The Song of Evarayi," in *Jews in India,* 145–60. For their Hebrew liturgical songs (*shirot*), see Roby, *Shirot Tefilah l'Moshe.* Among their historical writings are Roby, *Divrei Y'mei HaYehudim b'Cogin* and *Toldot Beit Rahabi b'Cogin;* Koder, "Kerala and Her Jews," in *Jews in India;* and Hallegua, "The Paradesi Synagogue." An example of their guidebooks is Salem, *Eternal Light or Jewtown Synagogue.*

2. Local customs of observance are known in Hebrew as *minhagim* (pl.; sing. *minhag*).

3. Koder, *Commemoration Volume.*

4. Gandhi, "Great Heritage," 5–8.

5. The significance of these paintings was first discussed by Johnson, "Shingli or Jewish Cranganore."

6. Narayanan, *Cultural Symbiosis,* 23–30.

7. Johnson, "Emperor's Welcome," in *Jews in India,* 161–76.

8. It was not only foreign communities that evolved tales of welcome from a benevolent ruler upon whom they became dependent. The Kurumba community of sorcerers relied upon the dominant Badaga farmers of the Nilgiri Hills, just beyond the Western Ghat Mountains from Kerala. According to the Kurumbas' story, because of a drought they migrated to the Badaga-dominated region, were hospitably received, and settled there. See Beck, Claus, and Handoo, eds., *Folktales of India,* 125–29.

9. Goitein, "Yahudut teman u-shar hodu ha-yehudi," in *Yahudat Teman,* 47.

10. Koder, "Jews of Malabar," 34.

11. Ibid., 35.

12. For the history of the Cochin Jews, see Katz and Goldberg, *Last Jews of Cochin,* 25–160, and Segal, *History of the Jews of Cochin.*

13. James, "Acts of Thomas," 364.

14. Ibid., 365.

15. Weil, "Symmetry," 185.

16. James, "Acts of Thomas," 367–68.

17. Logan, *Malabar,* 225.

18. Swiderski, *Blood Weddings,* 51.

19. Ibid., 52.

20. Ibid.

21. Ayyar, *Anthropology of the Syrian Christians,* x–xii.

22. Ibid., 2–3.

23. Swiderski, *Blood Weddings,* 37–50.

24. Vellian, "Jewish Christian Community of India," 104–5.

25. Weil, "Symmetry," 186–88. On the unique South India cry known as the *kurava,* see Tarabout, *Sacrificier et Donner,* 112 n6: "The cry *kurava* . . . , shrill and high pitched, is raised by women at the time of auspicious events, of which a typical example is the birth of a boy . . . in the inverse case of the birth of a girl, the ground is beaten with the branches of coconut palms."

26. Vellian, "Jewish Christian Community," 105.

27. Weil, "Symmetry," 194.

28. Thomas, "South Indian Tradition," 214; Ayyar, *Anthropology of the Syrian Christians,* 2–3; Puthiakunnel, "Jewish Colonies," 189–90.

29. Segal, "Jews of Cochin," in *Essays,* 386.

30. Wheeler, *Indus Civilization,* 81, 134–37.

31. Lamotte, "Les premières relations entre l'Inde et l'Occident," 95f.

32. Narayanan, *Cultural Symbiosis in Kerala,* 39.

33. Rowlandson, trans., *Tohfut-ul-mujahideen.*

34. Ibid., 5.

35. The *Keralolpatti* version is discussed by Logan, *Malabar*, 265. The conversion there is taken up by Narayanan, *Cultural Symbiosis in Kerala*, ix. Much as with the Muslim legend, Knani Christians narrate how the "Cheraman Perumal" king who welcomed Thomas of Cana in 345 C.E. converted to Christianity and made pilgrimage to the tomb of St. Thomas the Apostle in Mylapore. There he died and was buried alongside the apostle. "It seems that Cheraman Perumal is a good empty name to fill with whatever events satisfy the audience of the faithful. He legitimates one or another foreign religion in India by welcoming its proselytes and himself becoming a convert in the end" (Swiderski, *Blood Weddings*, 64).

36. Logan, *Malabar*, 269.

37. Narayanan, *Cultural Symbiosis in Kerala*, 38–42.

38. Muslim purists such as Shaikh Abdul Qadir strongly rebuked them for this practice. See Bayly, *Saints, Goddesses and Kings*, 113.

39. Narayanan, *Cultural Symbiosis in Kerala*, 1–8.

40. Logan, *Malabar*, 1. A more plausible etymology, however, would connect *mala* with *vâram*, slope (J. Richardson and Sumathi Freeman, personal communication, 9 September 1989).

41. Menon, *Survey of Kerala History*, 10.

42. Ibid., 9.

43. Goldman, *Gods, Priests, and Warriors*, 85. On Parasurama, see also Gail, *Parasurama, Brahmane und Krieger*, 35–39, and Logan, *Malabar*, 258–60.

44. *Keralolpatti*, quoted by Menon, *Survey of Kerala History*, 8.

45. Dennis Hudson, personal communication, 1991.

46. Logan, *Malabar*, 274.

47. Narayanan, *Cultural Symbiosis in Kerala*, 5.

48. Ibid.

49. Segal, "Jews of Cochin," 384.

50. Daniélou, trans., *Shilappadikaram*, 6.

51. Johnson, "Shingli or Jewish Cranganore," 166–69.

52. Lévi-Strauss, "Structural Study of Myth," 85.

53. Wheeler, *Indus Civilization*, 122, 134.

54. Oppenheim, "The Seafaring Merchants of Ur," 8. Oppenheim argues on this basis for "the well-established links between Southern Mesopotamia—especially Ur itself—and the civilization of the Indus valley. . . . The discovery of Indian seals . . . and of specially treated carneol beads . . . in Mesopotamian excavations has proven beyond doubt the existence of such trade missions" (12). Beyond Mesopotamia, Wheeler suggests links with Anatolia (Asia Minor), Egypt, and the Aegean as well (*Indus Civilization*, 111). This commercial and cultural intercourse was well established as early as the pre-Sargonid era in Ur, around 2350 B.C.E. (*Indus Civilization*, 117)—five hundred years before Abraham—thus providing our earliest, unequivocal evidence that "the twain" did indeed meet.

55. Rabin, "Loanword Evidence," 433, 437.

56. Rawlinson, *Intercourse between India and the Western World*, 4. Cf. Cowell and Rouse, eds. and trans., *Jataka*, 83.

57. Rawlinson, *Intercourse between India and the Western World*, 5. Emphasis in original.

58. Rhys Davids, ed. and trans, *Buddhist Birth Stories*, xxii–xxvi.

59. *B'pelpul hatalmeideim*, "sharp discussion with students," *Pirqei Avot*, 58.

60. Rejwan, *Jews of Iraq*, 125–26; *Encyclopedia Judaica*, s.v. "India," 1350.

61. Lamotte, "Les premières relations," 84.

62. Ibid., 95.

63. Rawlinson, *Intercourse between India and the Western World*, 109.

64. Thomas, "Roman Trade Centers in Malabar," 259.

65. Pliny, quoted by Thomas, "Roman Trade Centers in Malabar," 259.

66. Scott, ed. and trans., *Periplus of the Erythrean Sea*, 44.

67. Menon, *Survey of Kerala History*, 19–20.

68. Johnson makes this point in "Shingli or Jewish Cranganore," 13; the quote is from Thomas, "Roman Trade Centers in Malabar," 260.

69. Schmidt, "Between Jews and Greeks," 47–48.

70. Josephus, *Works*, 338–39.

71. Schmidt, "Between Jews and Greeks," 41–54.

72. Isenberg, *India's Bene Israel*, 19. Cf. Stillman, *Jews of Arab Lands*, 163–64.

73. Isenberg, *India's Bene Israel*, 20.

74. Levanon, *Jewish Travellers*, 20.

75. Bridgeman, "Jews in China," 172.

76. Levanon, *Jewish Travellers*, 16–17.

77. Asher, ed. and trans., *Itinerary of Benjamin of Tudela*, 138–40.

78. Ibid., 64.

79. Asher, *Itinerary of Benjamin of Tudela*, 140–41.

80. Levanon, *Jewish Travellers*, 335.

81. Ibid., 336.

82. Lord, *Jews of India*, appendix 12. The Rambam's letter poses more difficulties than it answers: the basic problem is determining to whom Maimonides was referring. Some believe Maimonides was referring to the Bene Israel, the subject of chapter 2 of this work. Isenberg, *India's Bene Israel*, 23–24.

83. Polo, *Travels of Ser Marco Polo*, 301.

84. Sternbach, "India as Described," 15.

85. Roby, *Shirot Tefilah l'Moshe*, 51; Koder, trans., *History of the Jews*, 6.

86. Gibb, trans., *Travels in Asia and Africa*, 238–39.

87. Lesley, "Shingly in Cochin Jewish Memory and in Eyewitness Accounts," 7–19.

88. Adler, *Jewish Travellers: A Treasury*, 299; quoted by Johnson, "Shingli or Jewish Cranganore," 24.

89. Cited by Johnson, "Shingli or Jewish Cranganore," 24. The reference to the Code of Maimonides, another name for the *Mishneh Torah*, tends to corroborate the Rambam's claim, discussed above, that Indian Jews during the twelfth century knew his work.

90. Burkitt, "Hebrew Signatures," 323.

91. Narayanan, *Cultural Symbiosis in Kerala*, 92–93.

92. Burnell, "On Some Pahlavi Inscriptions," 310.

93. Joseph, "Date of Bhaskara Ravi Varman," 21–22.

94. Dirks, *Hollow Crown,* 94–96.

95. Narayanan, *Cultural Symbiosis in Kerala,* 81.

96. Daniélou, trans., *Shilappadikaram,* 13, 22.

97. Narayanan, *Cultural Symbiosis in Kerala,* 81–82.

98. Simon, "Songs of the Jews of Cochin," 22–23.

99. Jussay, "Song of Evarayi," 157 n3. Cf. Simon, "Songs."

100. Narayanan, *Cultural Symbiosis in Kerala,* 84–85.

101. Cohen, trans., in "Shingli or Jewish Cranganore," 127.

102. Johnson, "Shingli or Jewish Cranganore," 138–40. In a curious parallel, Nambudiri brahmins may not reside in Cranganore, although they may visit for brief periods (Induchudan, *The Secret Chamber,* 173–74).

103. Mandelbaum, "Social Stratification," 176.

104. Moens, *Memorandum,* 197.

105. Jacob Cohen, conversation with author, 31 March 1987.

106. Fischel, "Cochin in Jewish History," 39.

107. Elazar, *The Other Jews,* 72–73.

108. Menon, *Survey of Kerala History,* 147.

109. Logan, *Malabar,* 348 n1.

110. Bayly, *Saints, Goddesses and Kings,* 248.

111. Roby, *Divrei Y'mei HaYehudim b'Cogin,* 5; Johnson, "Shingli or Jewish Cranganore," 99.

112. Gladys Koder, conversation with author, 17 March 1987.

113. Bar-Giora, "Toldot Beth Keneseth b'Kogin," 44.

114. *Sotah* 41b; cited by Greenbaum, "Cochin Jewish Community," 88.

115. Bar-Giora, "Toldot Beth-Hakeneseth b'Kogin," 44.

116. Greenbaum, "Cochin Jewish Community," 87. Cf. Bar-Giora, "Toldot Beth Keneseth b'Kogin," 44.

117. Jacob Cohen, conversation with author, 2 April 1987.

118. Jackie Cohen, conversation with author, 28 March 1987.

119. Sassoon Cohen, conversation with author, 1 March 1987.

120. Bayly, *Saints, Goddesses and Kings,* 135.

121. Koder, "Saga," 134–35.

122. Fischel, "Exploration of Jewish Antiquities," 237.

123. Fischel, "Cochin," 623.

124. Whiteway, *Rise of Portuguese Power,* 57.

125. Fischel, "Cochin in Jewish History," 41.

126. Ibid., 42.

127. Fischel, "Exploration of Jewish Antiquities," 234 n28.

128. Koder, "Saga," 123.

129. Ibid.

130. Ibid.

131. Ibid., 124.

132. Ibid., 129–31.

133. Parasuram, *India's Jewish Heritage,* 45; Fischel, "Literary Creativity," 26.

134. Parasuram, *India's Jewish Heritage*, 40.

135. Ibid., 41, 43.

136. Das Gupta, *Malabar in Asian Trade*, 108; Parasuram, *India's Jewish Heritage*, 42.

137. Fischel, "Literary Creativity," 27.

138. Sassoon, *Ohel Dawid*, 262–65.

139. Ibid., 967.

140. Ibid., 547.

141. Rabinowitz, *Far East Mission*, 128.

142. "Cochin," 137.

143. Sassoon, *Ohel Dawid*, 547; Rabinowitz, *Far East Mission*, 125. See also I. S. Hallegua, letter to author, 12 June 1989.

144. Samuel Hallegua, conversation with author, 16 January 1987; Sattu Koder, conversation with author, 17 January 1987.

145. P. M. Jussay, conversation with author, 3 January 1987.

146. Whitehead, *Village Gods*, 20.

147. Ibid., 30.

148. Gamliel Salem, conversation with author, 10 January 1987.

149. Whitehead, *Village Gods*, 110–11.

150. Gold, *Fruitful Journeys*, 142–43. What Gold wrote about pledges made by Rajasthani women is also true about Cochini women's vows: "Pledges are often made at home when some distress or problem is at hand. . . . The pattern of pledge and fulfillment involves explicit bargaining. . . . Such negotiations and deals are appropriately entered into with lesser gods and goddesses. They would not be suitable in approaching the Lord in temples."

151. It is not uncommon in India for "women [to] fast to ensure the continued good health of their husbands" (Beck, *Folktales of India*, 26; cf. 48–49).

152. Reynolds, "Auspicious Married Woman," 50, 52, 55.

153. Bayly, *Saints, Goddesses and Kings*, 34.

154. Ibid., 41; cf. Whitehead, *Village Gods*, 89–91.

155. Sattu Koder, conversation with author, 25 October 1986.

156. Katz and Goldberg, "Leaving Mother India," 35–53.

157. Gandhi, "Great Heritage," 6–8.

158. Koder, *Commemoration Volume*, vi.

159. Elijah, "Cochin, India Synagogue," 539.

160. Raymond Salem, conversation with author, 25 January 1987.

161. Dumont, *Homo Hierarchicus*, 191.

162. Edgerton, *Buddhist Hybrid Sanskrit Dictionary*, 240.

163. Dumont, *Homo Hierarchicus*, 21.

164. Daniel, *Fluid Signs*, 179–81.

165. Johnson, "'Our Community' in Two Worlds," 109–10.

166. Segal, "White and Blacks Jews at Cochin," 230–31. Cf. Marx, "Contributions à l'histoire," 293–96.

167. Mandelbaum, "Social Stratification," 173.

168. Ibid., 200.

169. Mandelbaum, "Jewish Way of Life in Cochin," 446.

170. Mandelbaum, "Social Stratification," 177.

171. Fischel, *Unknown Jews in Unknown Lands*, 114.
172. Reinman, "Masa'oth Shlomo b'Kogin," 38.
173. Ibid., 58.
174. Johnson, "'Our Community,'" 61.
175. Salem, *Eternal Light or Jewtown Synagogue*, 41.
176. Gandhi, *Non-Violent Resistance*, 177–203.
177. Menon, "The Namboodiris: Traumatic Decline," 92.
178. Gandhi, *Non-Violent Resistance*, 185.
179. Mandelbaum, "Jewish Way of Life in Cochin," 449.
180. The A. B. Salem diaries are in the library of the Judah L. Magnes Museum and are cited with permission of Johnson, "'Our Community,'" 85–86.
181. Such was the case for the Jews in Cochin, but the same phenomenon can be observed among smaller immigrant Indian communities in America. See Katz, *Tampa Bay's Asian-Origin Religious Communities*.
182. Raymond Salem, conversation with author, 15 April 1987.
183. Dumont, *Homo Hierarchicus*, 43.
184. *Encyclopedia of Asian History*, s.v. "Caste," 3–4.
185. Mandelbaum, "Case History of Judaism," 226.
186. Johnson, "Emperor's Welcome," 162–65.
187. Chill, *Minhagim*, xx.
188. Kaelber, "Asceticism," 441; Rader, "Fasting," 286.
189. Kaelber, "Asceticism," 442.
190. Rader, "Fasting," 289.
191. Turner, *Ritual Process*.
192. Zalman, *Shulchan 'Arukh Orech Chayyim*, III, 1. Cf. Fredman, *Passover Seder*, 12–13; Berman, *Popular Halacha*, 148.
193. Jacob Cohen, conversation with author, n.d.
194. Sarah Cohen, conversation with author, n.d.
195. Ganzfried, *Kitzur Shulchan 'Arukh*, vol. 3, 43.
196. Johnson, "'Our Community.'"
197. Zalman, *Shulchan 'Arukh Orech Chayyim*, vol. 2, 53–107, 504ff.; cf. Cohen, *Royal Table*, 128.
198. Johnson, "'Our Community,'" 237.
199. Zalman, *Shulchan 'Arukh Orech Chayyim*, vols. 3–4, 1025.
200. Schneerson, *Haggadah for Pesach*, 43 n a.
201. Johnson, "'Our Community,'" 163.
202. In Morocco, too, Jews ended the semi-fast of Passover in a party hosted by their Gentile, in this case Muslim, neighbors. See Deshen, *Mellah Society*.
203. In his influential book *The Ritual Process*, anthropologist Victor Turner analyzed African coming-of-age rituals in terms of the marginalization of the group (corresponding to Pesah work) and a period of liminal separation (Pesah itself), followed by a ritualized reaggregation (the "hamas party").
204. Dumont, *Homo Hierarchicus*, 139.
205. Ibid., 56.
206. Dumont's approach to caste ranking, with its emphasis on purity, has been called attributional, meaning that a caste's social superiority or inferiority is based on certain inherent attributes that the group may or may not possess.

Marriott augmented Dumont's theory by suggesting an interactional approach to caste ranking, in which castes are ranked according to the structure of their transactions with other castes, especially those involved in the ritualized giving and taking of food. In this system, the emphasis is on transactions more than on qualities (Marriott, "Interactional and Attributional Theories," 96–97).

207. Chill, *Minhagim*, 236.

208. Hallegua, "Simchat Torah in Cochin," 6.

209. Mandelbaum, "Jewish Way of Life in Cochin," 458.

210. Ibid., 457–58.

211. Lesley, "Shingly in Cochin Jewish Memory and in Eyewitness Accounts," 13.

212. *Seder Mincha Simchat Torah*, 13f, 15f, 25f, and 35–40.

CHAPTER 2. AN IDENTITY TRANSFORMED: THE BENE ISRAEL

1. Yechezkel Rahabi, "Letter of 25 Tishri 5528," in *Hameassef* (1790), vol. 2, 129–60, 257–76; Koder, trans., "A Hebrew Letter of 1768," 1–6.

2. Cited by J. Henry Lord, *Jews of India*, appendix 12. The Rambam's comment has been the subject of extensive discussion, both in scholarly circles and among Indian Jews themselves (see Katz and Goldberg, *Last Jews of Cochin*, 303 n28).

3. Fischel, "A Hitherto Unknown Jewish Traveler in India," 174, as quoted by Isenberg, *India's Bene Israel*, 49–50.

4. On the Surat community, see Fischel, "Immigration of 'Arabian' Jews to India in the Eighteenth Century," 1–20, and the discussion about this community in chapter 3. How isolated the Bene Israel actually were is a controversy. Strizower, "Jews as an Indian Caste," 33, offers evidence that "suggests that the Bene Israel were not as isolated from Jewry or as ignorant of Judaism as their historical memories imply," namely a 1715 Hebrew tombstone inscription. However, Israel has strongly challenged Strizower's contention—I believe successfully (see his *Bene Israel*, 55).

5. Lord, *Jews in India*, 10–15. A monument to these ancestors was erected on this site during the 1970s.

6. Preliminary results of contemporary DNA research being conducted by Parfitt and Bradman have "confirmed that there is a genetic link between Lemba tribesmen in southern Africa, Jews from Yemen and now the Bene Israel. The finding, says Mr. Parfitt, validates Islamic sources about the Jews' path into Africa and could revise the history of ancient Jewish commerce across the Indian Ocean." (Karp, "Seeking Lost Tribes," 1, 5). This finding might eventually corroborate the Bene Israel origin story.

7. Isenberg surveys the numerous debates about the origin of the Bene Israel (*India's Bene Israel*, 3–18).

8. Like anyone who studies the Bene Israel, I am deeply indebted to Haeem Samuel Kehimkar's descriptions of turn-of-the-century religious life (*History of the Bene Israel*, written in 1897 but not published until 1937 by Immanuel Olsvanger). His ethnographic observations are updated in work by Strizower (1971), Gussin (1972), Weil (1977), Roland (1989), and especially Isenberg

(1988), as well as by my own observations. Throughout this chapter, descriptions of religious life prior to the mid-twentieth century are based on Kehimkar and on Isenberg's summaries of his work. Their religious life in Bombay was described in Gussin's dissertation and Roland's book, and their acculturation in Israel was first analyzed by Weil, and more recently by Isenberg and Roland.

9. Israel, *Bene Israel*, 53–87.

10. Isenberg discusses the many unanswered questions regarding "David Rahabi" and his "discovery" of the Bene Israel, in *India's Bene Israel*, 43–44.

11. Roland, "Indian-Jewish Identity," 119.

12. See Isenberg, "Paradoxical Outcome," 348–60.

13. Isenberg, *India's Bene Israel*, 65–80.

14. Roland, *Jews in British India*.

15. Ahad Ha'am, "Sabbath and Zionism," 286–87.

16. "Shabbath Observance" in Gadkar, ed., *Religious and Cultural Heritage*, 81.

17. Isenberg, *India's Bene Israel*, 100.

18. "Miracle," in Gadkar, ed., *Religious and Cultural Heritage*, 81.

19. Kehimkar, *History of the Bene Israel*, 41.

20. Dumont, *Homo Hierarchicus*, 21.

21. Among the scholars who view the Bene Israel as a caste are Newman ("Caste and the Indian Jews"), Jain ("Review of Strizower [1971]"), and Tinker ("Review of Strizower [1971]"). Katz and Goldberg have argued similarly that the Cochin Jews formed a caste within Malabari society ("Asceticism," 53–82).

22. Among those who consider the Bene Israel's social organization "caste-like" rather than caste behavior proper are Strizower ("Jews as an Indian Caste") and Isenberg (*India's Bene Israel*).

23. Strizower, "Jews as an Indian Caste," 44.

24. Tinker, "Review of Strizower (1971)," 98.

25. Ibid., 98–99.

26. Isenberg, *India's Bene Israel*, 104–7.

27. On a parallel subdivision of the Cochin Jewish community, see Katz and Goldberg, "Jewish 'Apartheid,'" 147–76.

28. This sort of concubinage, wherein a higher-caste man keeps a lower-caste woman, was fairly common in India. On an analog from Cochin, see Katz and Goldberg, *Last Jews of Cochin*, 148–51.

29. Strizower, "Jews as an Indian Caste," 49.

30. Kehimkar, *History of the Bene Israel*, 32.

31. Srinivas, *Religion and Society*.

32. So reported Yakobeth Warulkar in the recent video *The Bene Israel: A Family Portrait* (Brandeis University, The National Center for Jewish Film, 1994).

33. Israel suggests that the Kala/Gora distinction was not an emulation of the Indian caste system so much as an "imitation of misunderstood Cochini practice" (*Bene Israel*, 86). As Gussin notes, "The difference between the Bene Israel, and Indians involved in Sanskritization, is simply that there are differences in reference points" ("Bene Israel of India," 134 n4).

34. Roland, *Jews in British India*, 65–85.

35. Gussin, "Bene Israel of India," 162.

36. Weil, "Bene Israel Indian Jews," 316.

37. "Shevat 15—New Year for Trees: Why the Bene-Israels Adore This Festival the Most," in Gadkar, ed., *Religious and Cultural Heritage,* 83.

38. See the theoretical discussion and example from Cochin in Katz and Goldberg, *Last Jews of Cochin,* 103–8.

39. Sachar, *A History of the Jews,* 50–51.

40. Isenberg, *India's Bene Israel,* 112.

41. "Shevat 15—New Year for Trees," in Gadkar, ed., *Religious and Cultural Heritage,* 82.

42. Quoted by Isenberg, *India's Bene Israel,* 112.

43. Weil, "Bene Israel Indian Jews," 319. This author has not observed liver at any Malida rites he has attended, even at a 1987 vow-fulfillment Malida that was the climax of a Bombay family's pilgrimage to Khandala; the myrtle sprigs and flowers are retained as a protection against various evils. Isenberg outlines the Malida rite liturgy in *India's Bene Israel,* 113.

44. Kehimkar, *History of the Bene Israel,* 25.

45. Weil, "Bene Israel Indian Jews," 320.

46. Reynolds, "Auspicious Married Woman," 50.

47. Among Cochin's Jewish women, the Qabbalist Nehemia Mota is the object of these vow exchanges (see Katz and Goldberg, *Last Jews of Cochin,* 107–8).

48. "Shevat 15—New Year for Trees," in Gadkar, ed., *Religious and Cultural Heritage,* 83.

49. Weil, "Bene Israel Indian Jews," 333.

50. Ibid., 326.

51. Ibid., 334.

52. Ibid., 321.

53. Kehimkar, *History of the Bene-Israel,* 16–17. Cf. Isenberg, *India's Bene Israel,* 118–19.

54. Gussin, "Bene Israel of India," 122.

55. Ibid., 122 n18.

56. Kehimkar, *History of the Bene Israel,* 17–18.

57. Ibid., 18.

58. "Observance of 'Yom Kippur' and 'Shabbath' by the Ancient Bene-Israels," in Gadkar, ed., *Religious and Cultural Heritage,* 80.

59. On Simchat Cohen in Cochin, see Katz and Goldberg, *Last Jews of Cochin,* 177–78.

60. Isenberg, *India's Bene Israel,* 120.

61. Ibid., 120.

62. "Shevat 15—New Year for Trees," in Gadkar, ed., *Religious and Cultural Heritage,* 82.

63. Kehimkar, *History of the Bene Israel,* 20. *Subja,* or basil, is known to Hindus as a *tulasi,* a sacred plant associated with the god Krishna (Isenberg, *India's Bene Israel,* 123–24 n12).

64. Kehimkar, *History of the Bene Israel,* 20.

65. Ibid., 65. Some Cochin Jews continue to criticize this type of devotion to

religious personalities, whether in the form of the Bene Israel reverence for Eliahu Hanabi on Tu B'Shevat or in the Cochinim's reverence for Nehemia Mota on the first night of Chanukkah or for Shimon bar Yochai on Lag B'Omer (see Katz and Goldberg, *Last Jews of Cochin,* 316–17). Some contemporary Jews view the veneration of Rabbi Menachem Mendel Schneerson, the late Lubavitcher Rebbe, with similar disdain.

66. Weil, "Bene Israel Indian Jews," 321–22.
67. Kehimkar, *History of the Bene Israel,* 21.
68. Isenberg, *India's Bene Israel,* 121.
69. Fischel, "Introduction" to *Haggadah.*
70. Kollet, "Bene Israel Tisha B'Ab," 12.
71. According to Kehimkar, the occasional performances of the Malida rite correspond to the sacrifices performed in the Temple of Jerusalem:

> The first of the Temple sacrifices so replicated is the Thanks-offering, *Sebah Toda,* performed on occasions when the Gomel prayer would be recited in synagogues elsewhere: when one "has recovered from a severe illness, or has returned safe from a long journey either by land or sea, or has been rescued from a gale or storm," is performed as described by Weil above, and must be consumed in its entirety in one day. The Peace-offering, *Sebah Shelamim,* is "made when a dispute is settled among the Bene-Israel, or when a person buys a house, a field or a garden" and is eaten for two days. The Free Will-offering, *Korban Nedaba,* "is made by a Bene-Israel when a new house is built, or when his residence has changed," differs slightly from the Thanks-offering in ways Kehimkar does not specify, and is eaten in two days. Bene Israel also performed the Nazarite offering, *Korban Neser.* When a Bene Israel woman has no male child for ten years or more, she vows that if a son is granted her, she will follow aspects of the Biblical *nazir* pledge (Num. 6:14–21) for six or seven years, in that the boy's hair will not be cut. When the time comes for the hair to be cut, he is taken by the door of a synagogue, his head is shaved, and the hair is weighed against gold or silver, depending on the woman's vow, the value given to charity. After the hair is thrown into the sea, goats are slaughtered and a feast prepared—although the boy's parents observe the day as a fast. That evening, an extensive Malida rite is performed. When the officiant gives the woman the sprig of myrtle, he asks her reasons for undertaking her vow. After responding, she is declared free of her obligations, and is presented with the Malida foodstuff—a share retained by the officiant as a hallah was retained by the Temple priests—which is then distributed. The offering must be consumed within two days. An abbreviated Malida is also performed to mark the end of a woman's impurity after childbirth. Called the Purification-offering, *Korban Tahara,* it will be discussed below in conjunction with birth rituals. Kehimkar notes that several offerings were not performed by Bene Israel, the Guilt-offering or *Sebah Asham,* the Sin-offering or *Sebah Hatath,* and the Burnt-offering or *Olah,* as it is believed that these could have been performed only by kohanim at the Temple. Thus, out of eleven offerings, eight have been shown to have existed amongst the Bene-Israel from time immemorial (*History of the Bene Israel,* 25–29).

72. Isenberg, *India's Bene Israel,* 127.
73. Kehimkar, *History of the Bene Israel,* 111.
74. Ibid., 111–12.
75. Isenberg, *India's Bene Israel.* 128.
76. Ibid., 143 n1, 128.
77. Ibid., 128. Cf. Kehimkar, *History of the Bene Israel,* 112.
78. Kehimkar, *History of the Bene Israel,* 112–13.
79. Isenberg, *India's Bene Israel,* 128.

80. Kehimkar, *History of the Bene Israel*, 113–14.

81. Ibid., 115.

82. Ibid., 118.

83. Samuel, "Bene Israel Cradle Ceremony," 43–44.

84. Kehimkar, *History of the Bene Israel*, 113–20.

85. Isenberg observes that this is clearly a borrowing from the local Hindu tradition of exposing a child to the sun for the first time on the twelfth day. Isenberg concludes her discussion of Bene Israel postnatal rituals with the contention that "practically every . . . element of 19th century Bene Israel post-natal ritual (except for circumcision) was also a part of Hindu custom or a variant thereof" (*India's Bene Israel*, 130).

86. Olsvanger suggested that this was the song sung on this occasion. See Kehimkar, *History of the Bene Israel*, 120–21.

87. Kehimkar, *History of the Bene Israel*, 122–24.

88. Ibid., 26.

89. Isenberg, *India's Bene Israel*, 132.

90. Kehimkar, *History of the Bene Israel*, 126.

91. Ibid., 126–28.

92. Isenberg, *India's Bene Israel*, 137.

93. Ibid., 133.

94. Ibid.

95. Katz and Goldberg, *Last Jews of Cochin*, 233.

96. Isenberg, *India's Bene Israel*, 134. Isenberg notes that *ud* is burned at the tombs of Muslim saints, the likely source for this Bene Israel custom.

97. Kehimkar, *History of the Bene Israel*, 134–35.

98. Isenberg, *India's Bene Israel*, 134.

99. Ibid.

100. Ibid., 135.

101. "A Bene Israel Marriage Custom," 17. Najara was a Sephardi born in Damascus who became a member of Rabbi Isaac Luria's mystical circle in Tsfat, according to Musleah (*Kol Zimra*, 208).

102. Cochin Jews also submerge the wedding ring in the goblet of wine (Katz and Goldberg, *Last Jews of Cochin*, 233).

103. Isenberg, *India's Bene Israel*, 135–36.

104. On the use and meaning of the *tali* among the Cochin Jews, see Katz and Goldberg, *Last Jews of Cochin*, 231–32.

105. Isenberg, *India's Bene Israel*, 135–36.

106. Ibid., 136.

107. Israel, *Bene Israel of India*, 62.

108. Ibid.

109. Joseph, "Samaji's Synagogue," 361–66.

110. Ibid., 365.

111. Kehimkar, *History of the Bene Israel*, 181.

112. Information about Bene Israel synagogues in Bombay is largely adapted from Kolet and Benjamin, *List of Synagogues,* and from field observations made during 1984 and 1987. As recently as 1987 Sha'ar Ha-Rahamim, Sha'ar Ratzon, Beth El of Revdanda, Beth El of Panvel, Beth Ha-Elohim, Sha'ar HaShamaim,

Tifereth Israel, Etz Hayim, Rodeph Shalom, and Maghen Hassidim were active. The Bene Israel synagogues in Pune, Ahmedabad, and New Delhi remain vibrant.

113. See Isenberg, *India's Bene Israel,* 61.

114. Israel, *Bene Israel of India,* 64.

115. On the Christian reference group, see Isenberg, "Paradoxical Outcome."

116. Isenberg, *India's Bene Israel,* 148.

117. Lord, *Jews of India,* 30.

118. See ibid.; cf. Modi, "The Kiss of Peace," 84–95.

119. Isenberg, *India's Bene Israel,* 150.

120. Gourgey, "Indian Jews," 85.

121. Goodrick-Clarke, *Hitler's Priestess.* Goodrick-Clarke overestimates the influence of sympathy for Hitler, which was confined to the extreme fringes of the Swaraj movement and of Indian intellectual history in general.

122. Werblowsky, "Bene Israel Battle," 25, 40.

123. Nissim, ed., *B'nei Yisrael: Piskei Halakhah,* quoted in Werblowsky, "Bene Israel Battle," 25.

124. Werblowsky, "Bene Israel Battle," 40.

125. Sommer, "Indian Jews Fight for Recognition," 14.

CHAPTER 3. AN IDENTITY ALOOF: BAGHDADI JEWS OF THE RAJ

1. Actually, the Middle Eastern Jews were the third group of Jews to establish a trading center at Surat, where Portuguese, Dutch, and British traders had settled since the sixteenth century. Portuguese-Dutch Jews from Amsterdam arrived late in the seventeenth century, and Ashkenazim from London, Amsterdam, and Hamburg came during the second quarter of the eighteenth century (Fischel, "Immigration of 'Arabian' Jews," 1–2).

2. Silliman, "Crossing Borders, Maintaining Boundaries," 57.

3. Calcutta was the capital of British India between 1784 and 1912, when the British moved the government to newly created New Delhi.

4. Roland, *Jews in British India,* 15.

5. Ezra, *Turning Back the Pages,* 80.

6. Musleah, *Banks of the Ganga,* 19.

7. Timberg, "Indigenous and Non-indigenous Jews," 146.

8. Timberg, "The Jews of Calcutta," 39 n1.

9. Musleah, *Banks of the Ganga,* 533–36.

10. Ibid., 47.

11. Ezra, *Turning Back the Pages,* 135.

12. Ibid., 138–41.

13. Musleah, *Banks of the Ganga,* 200.

14. Elias and Cooper, *Jews of Calcutta,* 80; Hyman, *Jews of the Raj.*

15. Musleah, *Banks of the Ganga,* 188.

16. Ibid., 255.

17. Ibid., 116, 197.

18. Ibid., 199–200. This custom is similar to that practiced in Cochin, with

the significant difference that the Cochini parochets had been a woman's skirt (*mundu*), which was converted into a parochet after her death (Katz and Goldberg, *Last Jews of Cochin*, 77). Baghdadis, too, expressed their strong connection to home by using special cloth from Baghdad for their funeral shrouds (Elias and Cooper, *The Jews of Calcutta*, 135).

19. Musleah, *Banks of the Ganga*, 199.
20. Ibid., 189–91.
21. Ibid., 192.
22. Ibid., 189.
23. Ibid., 85.
24. On the attitudes of Mizrachi Jews toward the British during the mid-nineteenth century, see Fischel, "Mulla Ibrahim Nathan," 336.
25. Fischel, "Garcia de Orta," 407–32.
26. Gadkar, *Religious and Cultural Heritage*, 1–10.
27. Kelly, *Kenesseth Eliyahoo Synagogue Centenary Souvenir*, 41.
28. Roland, *Jews in British India*, 17.
29. Roth, *Sassoon Dynasty*, 48.
30. Kelly, *Kenesseth Eliyahoo Synagogue Centenary Souvenir*, 49–50.
31. Roland, *Jews in British India*, 19.
32. Wolpert, *New History of India*, 232–33.
33. Roland, *Jews in British India*, 22–23.
34. Wolpert, *New History of India*, 238.
35. Musleah, *Banks of the Ganga*, 411.
36. Ezra, *Turning Back the Pages*, xix.
37. Ibid., 232.
38. Musleah, *Banks of the Ganga*, 81, 299, 278.
39. Timberg, "The Jews of Calcutta," 34, 39.
40. Silliman, "Crossing Borders, Maintaining Boundaries," 59.
41. Musleah, *Banks of the Ganga*, 522–31.
42. Meyer, "Sephardic Jewish Community," 4.
43. Roland, *Jews in British India*, 17–18.
44. Ibid., 129.
45. Musleah, *Banks of the Ganga*, 271–72.
46. Ibid., 275.
47. Ibid., 275–76.
48. Ibid., 276–78.
49. Ibid., 299, 280.
50. Ibid., 294.
51. Ibid., 283–95.
52. Hyman, *Jews of the Raj*, 139.
53. Ibid., 138.
54. On Calcutta's Baghdadi cuisine, see Marks, "The Jewish Kitchen (Cooking of the Jews of Calcutta)," in *The Varied Kitchens of India*.
55. Elias and Cooper, *Jews of Calcutta*, 148–49, as corrected by J. E. Cooper.
56. Hyman, *Jews of the Raj*, 17–26.
57. Norman Nahoum, conversation with author, February 1987.

58. Hyman, *Jews of the Raj*, 25.
59. Elias and Cooper, *Jews of Calcutta*, 163.
60. Hyman, *Jews of the Raj*, 90.
61. Elias and Cooper, *Jews of Calcutta*, 49.
62. Ezra, *Turning Back the Pages*, 9.
63. Timberg, "Jews of Calcutta," 34; Ezra, *Turning Back the Pages,* 441–49.
64. Ezra, *Turning Back the Pages*, 446.
65. Isenberg, *India's Bene Israel*, 224–25.
66. Roland, *Jews in British India*, 20.
67. Ibid.
68. Ibid., 20–21.
69. Ibid., 20.
70. Ibid., 57.
71. Ibid., 71.
72. Ibid., 72.
73. Ibid.
74. Ibid., 73; see also the previous chapter. *Gora*, or "white," Bene Israel were said to be descendants of the original shipwrecked couples, and *Kala*, or "black," Bene Israel were descendants of converts or irregular marriages. The two subcastes did not intermarry, and the former group was much larger than the latter, which no longer exists (or so it is held). There are close analogies, and also important distinctions, among the animosities between the Baghdadi and Bene Israel in Bombay, the *Gora* and *Kala* Bene Israel of the Konkan, the Paradesi and Malabari, and the *Meyuchasim* and *Meshuchrarim* in Cochin.
75. Roland, *Jews in British India*, 21.
76. Ibid., 74.
77. Ibid., 139–40.
78. Ibid., 141.
79. While it is generally true that the British census did not distinguish Baghdadis from Bene Israel, the 1881 census had separate categories for "Jews proper" (2,264) and Bene Israel (1,057) (Roland, *Jews in British India*, 65–66, 143).
80. Roland, *Jews in British India*, 62.
81. Ibid., 63.
82. Ibid., 58, 39, 40–41, 61.
83. Musleah, *Banks of the Ganga*, 346.
84. Roland, *Jews in British India*, 61.
85. Ibid., 60.
86. Musleah, *Banks of the Ganga*, 347.
87. Meyer, "Sephardi Jewish Community," 2–3.
88. Musleah, *Banks of the Ganga*, 348.
89. Ibid., 350.
90. Ibid., 351.
91. Unfortunately there have been no studies about India's Baghdadis in Israel.

92. Norman Nahoum, conversation with author, February 1987.
93. Ibid.

CONCLUSION

1. Israel, *Bene Israel of India,* chap. 1.
2. "D'Souza Installed as Goa Chief Minister."
3. Khandelwal, Introduction.
4. Slapak, ed., *Jews of India.*

Glossary

The following abbreviations are used: Heb., *Hebrew;* Skt., *Sanskrit;* Tam., *Tamil;* Hind., *Hindu/Hindustani;* Mar., *Marathi;* Yid., *Yiddish;* Mal., *Malayalam.*

aliyah (Heb., sing.; *aliyot,* pl.) Literally "to ascend." (1) To ascend the *bimah* for a synagogal honor. (2) To make pilgrimage to Jerusalem. (3) To migrate to Israel.

Aron Hakodesh (Heb.) Holy Ark where Torah scrolls are stored in synagogues. See also *heichal.*

Arvit (Heb.) The evening prayer service.

asarah (Heb.) A prayer quorum. See also *minyan.*

ayin hara (Heb.) The evil eye.

ayshet chayil (Heb.) Woman of valor. Cf. *cumankali* (Tam.).

azarah (Heb.) A synagogue vestibule.

Bhagavatism (Hind.) The religion of the Lord, viz., Vishnu. Also known as Vaishnavism.

bimah (Heb.) The altar where synagogal prayer services are conducted. Known to Sephardim as *tebah.*

brahmins (Skt.) The hereditary priests of Hinduism.

brit milah (Heb.) The covenant (*brit*) of circumcision (*milah*). See also *milah* and *mohel.*

chacham (Heb., sing.; *chachamim,* pl.) "Wise man." A Sephardic rabbi.

chamets (Heb.) Leavening, which is scrupulously avoided during Passover.

chanukiyah (Heb.) A Chanukkah lamp.

chazzan (Heb., sing.; *chazzanim,* pl.) A cantor or prayer leader.

Chitpavans The leading brahmin caste of Maharashtra.

Chumash (Heb., sing.; *Chumashim,* pl.) Five, viz., the Five Books of Moses.
chuppah (Heb.) Marriage canopy.
cumankali (Tam.) A virtuous woman. See also *ayshet chayil.*
dargah (Hind.) A (usually Muslim) saint's shrine/tomb.
dewan (Hind.) The British advisor to the local king.
duchan (Heb.) (1) The platform before the Aron Hakodesh upon which koha-
    nim stand while reciting the priestly benediction. (2) The rite of giving the
    priestly benediction.
Eliahu Hanabicha Oorus (Mar.) The festival of Elijah the Prophet, as Tu B'She-
    vat (the new year for trees) is known among the Bene Israel.
etrog (Heb.) A species of citron, used ritually during Sukkot.
ezrat nashim (Heb.) The women's section in a traditional synagogue.
grama-devata (Hind.) Hinduism's "village gods."
gymnosophists (Greek) The term used by Greek authors to refer to Indian holy
    men.
Haftarah (Heb.) The section from the Prophets read in synagogues on *Shabba-
    tot* and holy days.
Halachah (Heb.) Highway, Judaic law. Adj. *halachic.*
hamische (Yid.) Homely, familiar, comfortable.
haqafot (Heb.) Circumnambulations or rodeamentos.
Hashkavah (Heb.) The Sephardic memorial rite. Cf. the Ashkenazic *Yizkor.*
Hebrewization The process by which the Bene Israel adopted characteristics of
    upper-caste Jews, namely, the Cochin Jews and the Baghdadis, thereby ele-
    vating their caste status. See also Sanskritization.
heichal (Heb.) The cabinet in which Torah scrolls are stored. See also *Aron
    Hakodesh.*
hiddur mitsvot (Heb.) Embellishments of mitsvot.
Hodu (Heb.) India.
Holi (Hind.) A springtime Hindu festival associated with both the goddess Ho-
    lika and the god Krishna.
Jainism An Indian religion based on the teachings of the sixth-century B.C.E.
    saint Mahavira. Noun and adj. *Jaina.*
janta (Mar.) An exorcist.
jati (Skt., Hind.) (1) Literally "birth." (2) A caste.
Judaeo-Arabic The language of commerce among Mizrahi Jews. Essentially,
    Hebrew written in the Arabic alphabet.
kaji (Heb.) The religious leadership of the Bene Israel trained by David Yechez-
    kel Rahabi.
kehunah (Heb.) Priesthood, the status of being a kohen.
keter Torah (Heb.) Crown of Torah. The decorative metal work atop Torah
    scrolls.
ketubah (Heb.) A marriage contract, called by Bene Israel *akhtama* (Mar.).
kiddush (Heb.) Sanctification, in particular the blessing over wine used on all
    joyous occasions: Shabbat, festivals, weddings, etc.
kiddushin (Heb.) The consecration or preliminary part of the wedding service.
    See also *nissuin.*

kohen (Heb., sing.; *kohanim,* pl.) The hereditary priests of Judaism. Adj. *kohenite.* See also *kehunah.*

Krishna The eighth *avatara* of the great god Vishnu.

kshatriyas (Skt.) The nobles, warriors, and large-scale landowners of traditional India.

laccha (Mar.) A wedding pendant. See also *tali* and *mangal-sutra.*

Ladino A creole of Spanish and Hebrew spoken by many Sephardic Jews.

Machazor (Heb., sing.; *Machazorim,* pl.) Festival prayer books.

Malayalam The language of Kerala, derived from Old Tamil.

malchut (Heb.) Kingship. God's kingship is the liturgical leitmotif of the High Holy Day liturgy.

Malida (Mar.) A Bene Israel thanksgiving prayer associated with Eliahu Hanabi, involving parched rice, fruits, flowers, and incense.

mangal-sutra (Skt., Hind.) A "blessing thread" or wedding pendant. See also *laccha* and *tali.*

Manushastra (Skt.) A fourth-century C.E. Sanskrit text attributed to Manu that outlines Hindu law and social policy. Also known as *Dharmashastra.*

Marathi The language spoken in Maharashtra, derived from Sanskrit.

matsah (Heb.) The unleavened bread eaten by Jews during Passover.

mechitsah (Heb.) The barrier that separates the men's and women's sections in a synagogue.

mehndi (Hind.) The henna ceremony prior to a wedding.

meshuchrar (Heb., sing.; *meshuchrarim,* pl.) Manumitted slaves. Literally, "one in possession of a *shichrur,* a writ of manumission." See also *shichrur.*

milah (Heb.) Circumcision. See also *brit milah* and *mohel.*

Minchah (Heb.) The afternoon prayer service.

minhag (Heb., sing.; *minhagim,* pl.) Local customs associated with the observance of Halachah.

minyan (Heb.) A quorum of ten adult males required for complete prayer services. See also *asarah.*

miqveh (Heb.) A ritual bath.

Mishneh Torah (Heb.) A twelfth-century Torah commentary by Maimonides.

mitsvah (Heb. sing.; *mitsvot,* pl.) Commandments, both ethical and ritual, given in the Torah. According to rabbinical calculations, there are 613 mitsvot in the Torah. Any good deed.

mohel (Heb.) A ritual circumciser. See also *brit milah* and *milah.*

mudaliar (Mal. and Tamil) A "headman," the title given by the Dutch to the leaders of the Cochin Jews.

mundu (Mal.) A cloth used by men and women to cover the lower half of their bodies. Also known as a *lunghi* (Tamil) or a sarong.

Musaf (Heb.) The "Additional" prayer service that commemorates the Temple sacrifices on Shabbat and festivals.

Nambudiri (Mal.) The highest brahmin caste in Kerala.

Nayar (Mal.) The dominant caste that rules Kerala, even though it belongs to the shudra (artisan) and not the kshatriya (nobility) grouping.

Nazaranee Māpilla (Mal.) The oldest Christian community in India.

Ne'ilah (Heb.) The "closing of the gate" service that concludes the Yom Kippur liturgy.

ner tamid (Heb.) The "eternal light" that hangs before the *Aron Hakodesh* in synagogues.

nissuin (Heb.) The "elevation" or concluding part of the wedding service. See also *kiddushin*.

olam haba (Heb.) "The world to come," paradise.

orumakar (Mal.) The term used by Malabari Jews to refer to their manumitted slaves. See also *meshuchrar*.

Parasurama (Skt.) Rama Who Wields a Battle-Ax, regarded as the sixth *avatara* of Vishnu.

parochet (Heb.) The curtain that hangs before the *Aron Hakodesh*.

Parsis Indian Zoroastrians.

Pidyon Haben (Heb.) The ransoming of the firstborn, a rite performed by *kohanim* for all firstborn males who are neither *kohanim* nor *leviim* (descendents of nonpriestly Temple servants).

pilpul (Heb.), from *pilpeil* (Skt.) Pepper.

prasadam (Skt.) Grace. The remains of food offered at a Hindu temple.

Rama The seventh *avatara* of Vishnu.

Rosh Hashanah (Heb.) The Hebrew new year.

Sanskritization The process by which a lower caste emulates high-caste behaviors, especially the brahmin use of Sanskrit, in order to rise in the caste hierarchy. See also Hebrewization.

satyagraha (Skt., Hind.) Grasping truth, a term coined by Mahatma Gandhi for civil disobedience.

Sefer Torah (Heb., sing.; *Sifrei Torah*, pl.) Torah scroll.

Shacharit (Heb.) The morning prayer service.

shaikh (Arabic) In Sufism, a spiritual master; in exoteric Islam, a secular leader.

shakti (Skt.) Power, the spiritual energy associated with the goddess and with virtuous women.

shaliach (Heb., sing.; *shlichim*, pl.) An emissary. A shaliach is often sent by charitable institutions in Israel to raise funds in the Diaspora.

shamash (Heb.) The caretaker of a synagogue.

Shanwar Teli (Mar.) "Saturday Oil Pressers." The caste name of the Bene Israel.

Shema (Heb.) The central creedal formula of Judaism: "Hear, O Israel! The Lord Is Your God, the Lord Is One."

shichrur (Heb.) A legal document of manumission from slavery. See also *meshuchrar* (sing.; *meshuchrarim*, pl.), "those with a *shichrur*," or manumitted slaves.

Shilappadikaram (Tam.) A second-century C.E. Tamil epic poem.

Shimini Chag Atseret (Heb.) The festival of the "eighth day of the assembly," immediately following Sukkot.

shmittah (Heb.) The sabbatical year.

shochet (Heb., sing.; *shochetim*, pl.) A ritual slaughterer. The rules for kosher slaughter are known as *shechitah*.

shofar (Heb. sing.; *shofarot*, pl.) A ceremonial horn.

Simchat Torah (Heb.) The festival of "rejoicing in the Torah" when the annual cycle of Torah reading is completed and begun anew. It falls on the twenty-third day of the Hebrew year.

Sitali Devi (Skt.) The Cool One, the goddess who protects/infects from/with smallpox.

S'lichot (Heb.) Penitential prayers.

sukkah (Heb. sing.; *sukkot* pl.) "Tabernacle." The temporary dwellings in which traditional Jews take meals and perhaps sleep during the *Sukkot* festival.

Sukkot (Heb.) The week-long autumn harvest festival. It takes its name from *sukkah*.

tali (Tam.) A wedding pendant. See also *laccha* and *mangal-sutra*.

tallit (Heb. sing.; *tallitot* pl.) A fringed prayer shawl.

Talmud Torah (Heb.) A Jewish elementary school.

Tashlich (Heb.) The rite of casting off one's sins, performed between Rosh Hashanah and Yom Kippur at a lake, ocean, or other body of water.

taskira (Urdu) A Muslim saint's biography.

tevah (Heb.) The Sephardic term for the altar from which prayer services are led. See also *bimah*.

tevilah (Heb.) Ritual immersion in a miqveh.

tsedaqah (Heb.) Charity.

Tu B'Shevat (Heb.) A minor Jewish festival known as the new year for trees. Bene Israel highlight this festival, which they associate with Eliahu Hanabi. See also Eliahu Hanabicha Oorus.

Vishnu One of the great gods of Hinduism, preserver of the cosmic order.

yichus (Heb.) Lineage or ancestry. A *meyuchas* (pl. *meyuchasim*) is one who has attestable Jewish ancestry.

Yom Kippur (Heb.) The Day of Atonement, the tenth day of the Hebrew year.

Zoroastrian, -ism The dominant religion of pre-Islamic Persia, based on the teachings of the Prophet Zoroaster, believed to have lived during the eighth century B.C.E. Followers of this religion in India are called Parsis, "Persians."

References

Adler, Elkan N. *Jewish Travellers: A Treasury of Travelogues from Nine Centuries*. London: George Routledge, 1930; reprint, New York: Hermon Press, 1966.

Adler, Marcus Nathan, ed. and trans. *The Itinerary of Benjamin of Tudela: Critical Text, Translation and Commentary*. New York: Philipp Feldheim, 1907.

Asher, A., ed. and trans. *The Itinerary of Benjamin of Tudela*. New York: Hakesheth, n.d.

Ayyar, Rao Bahadur L. K. Anantakrishna. *Anthropology of the Syrian Christians*. Ernakulam: Cochin Government Press, 1926.

Bar-Giora, Naphtali. "Toldoth Beth-Hakeneseth b'Kogin" [History of the synagogues of Kerala]. In *Mi Kotsin l'Ertez Yisrael,* edited by Shalva Weil. Jerusalem: Kumu Brinah, 1984, 40–59.

Bayly, Susan. *Saints, Goddesses and Kings: Muslims and Christians in South Indian Society, 1700–1900*. Cambridge: Cambridge University Press, 1989.

Beck, Brenda E. F., Peter J. Claus, Praphulladatta Goswami, and Jawaharlal Handoo, eds. *Folktales of India*. Chicago: University of Chicago Press, 1987.

"A Bene Israel Marriage Custom." *Ohr* 25 (1988): 15–17.

Berman, Jacob. *Popular Halacha: A Guide to Jewish Living*. 2 vols. Jerusalem: World Zionist Organization, 1976, 1982.

Bridgeman, E. C. "Jews in China: Notices of Those in the East by Josephus, Peritsol, Benjamin of Tudela, Manasseh, and the Jesuits." *Chinese Repository* 3 (1834): 172–75.

Burkitt, F. C. "Hebrew Signatures on the Copper-Plate." *Kerala Society Papers* 6 (1930): 323.

Burnell, A. C. "On Some Pahlavi Inscriptions in South India." *Indian Antiquary* 3 (1874): 308–16.

Chatterjee, Margaret. *Studies in Modern Jewish and Hindu Thought.* Hounds-mill, England: Macmillan Press; New York: St. Martin's Press, 1997.

Chill, Abraham. *The Minhagim: The Customs and Ceremonies of Judaism, Their Origins and Rationale.* New York: Sepher-Hermon Press, 1979.

Cohen, Jacob. *The Royal Table: An Outline of the Dietary Laws of Israel.* Jerusalem: Feldheim, 1970.

Cohen, Yaacov Daniel, trans. *Seder Mincha Simchat Torah.* Cochin, India: Cohen, 1877.

Courter, Gay. *Flowers in the Blood.* New York: Dutton, 1990.

Cowell, E. B., and W. H. D. Rouse, eds. and trans. *The Jataka: or, Stories of the Buddha's Former Births.* 6 vols. Cambridge: Cambridge University Press, 1907.

Daniel, E. Valentine. *Fluid Signs: Being a Person the Tamil Way.* Berkeley: University of California Press, 1984.

Daniel, Ruby, with Barbara C. Johnson. *Ruby of Cochin: An Indian Jewish Woman Remembers.* Philadelphia: Jewish Publication Society, 5755/1995.

Daniélou, Alain, trans. *Shilappadikaram (The Ankle Bracelet), by Prince Ilango Adigal.* New York: New Directions, 1989.

Das Gupta, Ashin. *Malabar in Asian Trade, 1740–1800.* London: Cambridge University Press, 1967.

David, Esther. *The Walled City.* Chennai, India: East-West Books, 1997.

Desai, Anita. *Baumgartner's Bombay.* London: Penguin Books, 1988.

Deshen, Shlomo. *The Mellah Society: Jewish Community Life in Sherifian Morocco.* Chicago: University of Chicago Press, 1989.

Dirks, Nicholas B. *The Hollow Crown: Ethnohistory of an Indian Kingdom.* Cambridge: Cambridge University Press, 1987.

"D'Souza Installed as Goa Chief Minister." *News India-Times,* 7 August 1998.

Dumont, Louis. *Homo Hierarchicus: The Caste System and Its Implications.* Chicago: University of Chicago Press, 1980.

Dutt, Manmatha Nath. *The Dharma Shastra, or the Hindu Law Codes.* Varanasi: Chaukhamba Amarbharati Prakashan, 1977.

Edgerton, Franklin. *Buddhist Hybrid Sanskrit Dictionary.* New Haven, Conn.: American Oriental Society, 1953; reprint, Delhi: Motilal Banarsidass, 1977.

Elazar, Daniel Judah. *The Other Jews: The Sephardim Today.* New York: Basic Books, 1989.

Elias, Flower, and Judith Elias Cooper. *The Jews of Calcutta: The Autobiography of a Community, 1798–1982.* Calcutta: Jewish Association of Calcutta, 1974.

Elijah, Samuel H. "Cochin, India Synagogue." *Philatelic Judaica Journal* 17/4 (1968): 539–46.

Encyclopedia of Asian History: A Selection of Sample Articles. Edited by Ainslee Embree. s.v. "Caste." New York: Charles Scribner's Sons, 1987.

Encyclopaedia Judaica. s.v. "Cochin." Jerusalem: Keter Publishing House, 1971, 3: 621–28.

The Encyclopaedia of Religion. Edited by Mircea Eliade. New York: Macmillan, 1987.

Ezra, Esmond D. *Turning Back the Pages: A Chronicle of Calcutta Jewry.* 2 vols. London: Brookside Press, 1986.

Fischel, Walter J. "Mullah Ibrahim Nathan: Jewish Agent of the British during the First Anglo-Afghan War." *Hebrew Union College Annual* 29 (1958): 331–75.

———. "Cochin in Jewish History: Prolegomena to a History of the Jews in India." *Proceedings of the American Academy for Jewish Research* 30 (1962): 37–59.

———. "A Hitherto Unknown Jewish Traveler to India: The Travels of Rabbi David D'Beth Hillel to India, 1828–1832." In *Time of Harvest: Essays in Honor of Abba Hillel Silver on the Occasion of His 70th Birthday,* edited by Daniel Jeremy Silver. New York: Macmillan, 1963, 170–85.

———. "The Immigration of 'Arabian Jews' to India in the Eighteenth Century." *Proceedings of the American Academy for Jewish Research* 38/9 (1965): 1–20.

———. "The Exploration of Jewish Antiquities of Cochin on the Malabar Coast." *Journal of the American Oriental Society* 87 (1967): 230–48.

———. Introduction to *The Haggadah shel Pesach in Marathi of the Bene Israel.* New York: Orphan Hospital Ward of Israel, 1968.

———. "The Literary Creativity of the Jews of Cochin on the Malabar Coast." *Jewish Book Annual* 28 (1970/71): 25–31.

———. *Unknown Jews in Unknown Lands: The Travels of Rabbi David D'Beth Hillel, 1824–1832.* New York: Ktav, 1973.

———. "Garcia de Orta—A Militant Marrano in Portuguese India in the 16th Century." In *Salo Wittmayer Baron Jubilee Volume on the Occasion of His Eightieth Birthday.* English section. Jerusalem: American Academy for Jewish Research, 1974, 1: 407–32.

Fredman, Ruth Gerber (Cernea). *The Passover Seder.* New York: New American Library, 1981.

Gadkar, Ezekiel Moses Jacob, ed. *The Religious and Cultural History of the Bene Israels of India, "Gate of Mercy" Synagogue.* 2 vols. Bombay: E. M. Jacob Gadkar for "Gate of Mercy" Synagogue, 1984.

Gail, Adalbert. *Parasurama, Brahmane und Krieger: Untersuchung über Ursprung und Entwicklung eines Avatara Vishnus und Bhakta Sivas in der indischen Literatur.* In German. Wiesbaden: Otto Harrassowitz, 1977.

Gandhi, Indira. "Great Heritage." In Koder et al., eds., *Commemoration Volume: Cochin Synagogue Quatercentenary Celebrations.* Cochin: Kerala History Association and Cochin Synagogue Quatercentenary Celebration Committee, 1971, 5–8.

Gandhi, Mohandas K. *Non-Violent Resistance (Satyagraha).* Edited by Bharatan Kumarappa. New York: Schocken Books, 1961.

Ganzfried, Solomon. *Kitzur Shulchan 'Arukh: Code of Jewish Law.* Translated by Hyman E. Goldin. New York: Hebrew Publishing, 1961.

Ghosh, Amitav. *In an Antique Land.* Delhi: Ravi Dayal Publisher, 1992.

Gibb, H. A. R., trans. *Travels in Asia and Africa, 1325–1354,* by Ibn-Battuta. 1929. New York: Augustus M. Kelley, 1969.

Goitein, Solomon D. F. "Yahudut teman u-shar hodu ha-yehudi" [Yemenite Jewry and the India Trade]. In *Yahudat teman,* edited by Yisrael Yeshayahu and Yosef Tobi. Jerusalem: Yad Itzhak Ben-Zvi, 1975, 47–69.

Gold, Ann Grodzins. *Fruitful Journeys: The Ways of Rajasthani Pilgrims.* Berkeley: University of California Press, 1988.

Goldman, Robert P. *Gods, Priests, and Warriors: The Bhrgus of the Mahabharata.* New York: Columbia University Press, 1977.

Goodman, Hananya, ed. *Between Jerusalem and Benares: Comparative Studies in Judaism and Hinduism.* Albany: State University of New York Press, 1994.

Goodrick-Clarke, Nicholas. *Hitler's Priestess: Savitri Devi, the Hindu-Aryan Myth, and Neo-Nazism.* New York: New York University Press, 1998.

Gourgey, Percy. "Indian Jews and the Freedom Struggle." *India Weekly,* 31 May– 6 June 1991.

Greenbaum, Aaron. "The Cochin Jewish Community: Impressions from a Mission to India, 1955." *Midrashia: A Journal Devoted to Halacha, Jewish Thought and Education* (1970): 82–94.

Gussin, Carl Mark. "The Bene Israel of India: Politics, Religion, and Systematic Change." Ph.D. dissertation, Syracuse University, 1972.

Ha'am, Ahad. *Kol kitve Ahad Ha'am.* Tel Aviv: Hotsa'at 'Ivrit, 1947.

Hallegua, I. S. "The Paradesi Synagogue of Cochin and its Dying Community of Jews." Manuscript. Cochin,1988.

Hallegua, S. H. "Simchat Torah in Cochin." *Kol Bina* 6/1 (1986): 6.

Holdrege, Barbara A. *Veda and Torah: Transcending the Textuality of Scripture.* Albany: State University of New York Press, 1996.

Hyman, Mavis. *Jews of the Raj.* London: Hyman Publishers, 1995.

Induchudan, V. T. *The Secret Chamber: A Historical, Anthropological, and Philosophical Study of the Kodungallur Temple.* Trichur, India: Cochin Devaswom Board, 1969.

Isenberg, Shirley Berry. "Paradoxical Outcome of a Meeting of Bene Israel and Christian Missionaries in Nineteenth Century India." In *Jews in India,* edited by Thomas A. Timberg. New Delhi: Vikas, 1986, 348–60.

———. *India's Bene Israel: A Comprehensive Inquiry and Sourcebook.* Bombay: Popular Prakashan; Berkeley: Judah L. Magnes Museum, 1988.

Israel, Benjamin J. *The Bene Israel of India: Some Studies.* Hyderabad, India: Orient Longman, 1984.

Jain, Ravindra K. "Review of Strizower, 1981." *Jewish Journal of Sociology* 15 (1973): 126–27.

James, Montague Rhodes, trans. "The Acts of Thomas." In *The Apocryphal New Testament. Being the Apocryphal Gospels, Acts, Epistles and Apocalypses.* Oxford: Clarendon Press, 1924, 364–438.

Jerusalem Bible. In Hebrew and English. Jerusalem: Koren Publishers, 1971.

Johnson, Barbara C. "Shingli or Jewish Cranganore in the Traditions of the Cochin Jews of India." Master's thesis, Smith College, 1975.

———. "'Our Community' in Two Worlds: The Cochin Paradesi Jews in India and Israel." Ph.D. dissertation, University of Massachusetts, 1985.

———. "The Emperor's Welcome: Reconsiderations of an Origin Theme in Cochin Jewish Folklore." In *Jews in India,* edited by Thomas A. Timberg. New Delhi: Vikas, 1986, 161–76.

Joseph, Brenda. "Samaji's Synagogue: Tales and Traditions." In *Jews in India,* edited by Thomas A. Timberg. New Delhi: Vikas, 1986, 361–66.

Joseph, T. K. "The Date of Bhaskara Ravi Varman: A Rejoinder." *Indian Antiquary* (1929): 21–27.

Josephus. *The Works of Josephus, with a Life Written by Himself.* Translated by William Whiston. Standard edition. New York: A. C. Armstrong, 1888.

Jussay, P. M. "The Song of Evarayi." In *Jews of India,* edited by Thomas A. Timberg. New Delhi: Vikas, 1986, 145–60.

Kaelber, Walter O. "Asceticism." In *The Encyclopaedia of Religion,* edited by Mircea Eliade. New York: Macmillan, 1987, 1: 441–45.

Kamenetz, Rodger. *The Jew in the Lotus: A Poet's Rediscovery of His Jewish Roots in Buddhist India.* San Francisco: Harper San Francisco, 1995.

Karp, Jonathan. "Seeking Lost Tribes of Israel in India, Using DNA Testing." *Wall Street Journal,* 11 May 1998.

Katz, Nathan. *Tampa Bay's Asian-Origin Religious Communities.* Tampa, Fla.: National Conference of Christians and Jews, 1991.

———. "Reconnecting East and West: Judaism and Eastern Religions." Largo, Fla.: Summit Productions, 1997. Videocassette series.

———, ed. *Studies of Indian Jewish Identity.* New Delhi: Manohar, 1995.

Katz, Nathan, and Ellen S. Goldberg. "Asceticism and Caste in the Passover Observances of the Cochin Jews." *Journal of the American Academy of Religion* 57/1 (1989): 52–83.

———. "Jewish 'Apartheid' and a Jewish Gandhi." *Jewish Social Studies* 50/3–4 (1988/1993): 147–76.

———. *The Last Jews of Cochin: Jewish Identity in Hindu India.* Columbia: University of South Carolina Press, 1993.

———. "Leaving Mother India: Reasons for the Cochin Jews' Immigration to Israel." *Population Review* 39/1–2 (1995): 35–53.

Kehimkar, Haeem Samuel. *History of the Bene-Israel of India.* 1897. Tel Aviv: Dayag Press, 1937.

Kelly, Sophy, ed. *The Keneseth Eliyahoo Synagogue Centenary Souvenir.* Bombay: Keneseth Eliyahoo, 1985.

Khandelwal, Deen. Introduction to "Maharajas, Mughals and Mystics—Two Thousand Years of Jewish Experience in India," by Nathan Katz. Vol. 1, "Reconnecting East and West: Judaism and Eastern Religions." Largo, Fla.: Summit Productions, 1997. Videocassette series.

Koder, Sattu S., trans. "A Hebrew Letter of 1768," by Yechezkel Rahabi. *Journal of the Rama Varma Archaeological Society* 15 (1949): 1–6.

———. "The Jews of Malabar." *India and Israel* (1951): 31–35.

———. "Kerala and Her Jews." In *Jews in India '64 with Who Is Who,* edited by E. Elias and E. Isaac. Ernakulam, India: Indo-Israel Publications, 1965. 21–34.

———. "Saga of the Jews of Cochin." In *Jews in India,* edited by Thomas A. Timberg. New Delhi: Vikas, 1986, 121–42

———, trans. *History of the Jews of Kerala.* Cochin: privately published, 1974.

Koder, Sattu S., et. al., eds. *Commemoration Volume: Cochin Synagogue Quatercentenary Celebrations.* Cochin: Kerala History Association and Cochin Synagogue Quatercentenary Celebration Committee, 1971.

Kolet, Ezra, and Daniel Elijah Benjamin Gadkar. *List of Synagogues and Prayer*

Halls in South Asia (India, Burma and Pakistan). Bulletin 11. New Delhi: Jewish Welfare Association and Centre for Jewish and Inter-Faith Studies, 1983.

Kollet, Shimeon. "The Bene Israel Tisha B'Ab." *Kol Bina* 6/1 (1986): 10–12.

Lamotte, Étienne. "Les premières relations entre l'Inde et l'Occident." *Nouvelle Clio* 5 (1953): 83–118.

Lesley, Arthur M. "Shingly in Cochin Jewish Memory and in Eyewitness Accounts." *Journal of Indo-Judaic Studies* 3 (2000): 7–19.

Levanon, Yosef. *The Jewish Travellers in the Twelfth Century.* Lanham, Md.: University Press of America, 1980.

Lévi-Strauss, Claude. "The Structural Study of Myth." In *Myth: A Symposium,* edited by Thomas A. Sedeok. Bloomington: Indiana University Press, 1955, 81–106.

Logan, William. *Malabar.* Vol. 1. Trivandrum: Charithram Publications, 1981.

Lord, J. Henry. *The Jews of India and the Far East.* Kohlapur, India: Mission Press, 1907; reprint, Westport, Conn.: Greenwood Press, 1976.

Mandelbaum, David G. "The Jewish Way of Life in Cochin." *Jewish Social Studies* 1/4 (1939): 423–60.

———. "Social Stratification among the Jews of Cochin in India and Israel." *Jewish Journal of Sociology* 17/2 (1975): 165–210.

———. "A Case History of Judaism: The Jews of Cochin in India and in Israel." In *Jewish Tradition in the Diaspora: Studies in Memory of Walter J. Fischel,* edited by Maswari Caspi. Berkeley: Judah L. Magnes Museum, 1981, 211–30.

Marks, Copeland. *The Varied Kitchens of India.* New York: M. Evans & Co., 1986.

Marriott, McKim. "Interactional and Attributional Theories of Caste Ranking." *Man in India* 39/2 (1959): 92–107.

Marx, Alexander. "Contributions à l'histoire des Juifs de Cochin." *Révue des Études Juivres* 89 (1930): 293–304.

Menon, A. Sreedhara. *A Survey of Kerala History.* Madras: S. Viswanathan, 1984.

Menon, Ramesh. "The Namboodries: Traumatic Decline." *India Today,* 15 July 1991, 90–92.

Meyer, Maisie. "The Sephardic Jewish Community of Shanghai and the Question of Identity." Paper presented at conference on "The Jews of China: From Kaifeng to Shanghai," Sankt-Augustin, Germany, September 1997.

Modi, Shams ul-ulma Jivanji Jamshadi. "Kiss of Peace among the Bene Israels of Bombay and the Hamazor among the Parsees." *Journal of the Anthropological Society of Bombay* 8/2 (1907/8): 84–95.

Moens, Adriaan. *Memorandum on the Administration of the Coast of Malabar, Dated 18th April 1781 a.d.* Translated by Rev. P. Groot and A. Galletti. New Delhi: Usha Publications, 1984.

Musleah, Ezekiel N. *On the Banks of the Ganga: The Sojourn of Jews in Calcutta.* North Quincy, Mass.: Christopher Publishing House, 1975.

———. *Kol Zimra—The Sound of Song.* In Hebrew and English. Brooklyn: Israel Shelanu, 1983.

Narayanan, M. G. S. *Cultural Symbiosis in Kerala*. Trivandrum, India: Kerala Historical Society, 1972.

Nathanson, Karen, and Jean-François Fernandez. *The Bene-Israel: A Family Portrait*. In Marathi with English subtitles. Waltham, Mass.: Brandeis University, National Center for Jewish Film, 1994. Videocassette.

Newman, Robert S. "Caste and the Indian Jews." *Eastern Anthropologist* 28/3 (1975): 195–213.

Nissim, Itzhak. *Benei Yisrael: Piskei Halakhah* [Bene Israel: Halakhic Decision]. Yerushalayim: Chief Rabbinate of Israel, 1962.

Oppenheim, A. L. "The Seafaring Merchants of Ur." *Journal of the American Oriental Society* 74 (1954): 6–17.

Parasuram, T. V. *India's Jewish Heritage*. New Delhi: Sagar Publications, 1982.

Perlman, S. M. "The History of the Jews in China." In *Jews in Old China: Some Western Views*. Edited by Hyman Kublin, 1912. New York: Paragon Book Reprint Corp., 1971, 119–211.

Polo, Marco. *The Travels of Ser Marco Polo*. New York: Orion Press, n.d.

Puthiakunnel, Thomas. "Jewish Colonies Paved the Way for St. Thomas." In *Orientalia Christiana Analecta*, edited by Jacob Vellian. N.p., 1970, 187–191.

———. "The Malabar Church." In *Orientalia Christiana Analecta*, edited by Jacob Vellian. N.p., 1970, 186.

Rabin, Chaim. "Loanword Evidence in Biblical Hebrew for Trade between Tamilnad and Palestine in the First Millennium B.C." In *Proceedings of the Second International Seminar of Tamil Studies*. Madras: International Association of Tamil Research, 1971, 432–40.

Rabinowitz, Louis. *Far East Mission*. Johannesburg: Eagle Press, 1952.

———. "A Note on the Origin of the Jews of Cochin." *Jewish Quarterly Review* 47 (1958): 376–79.

Rader, Rosemary. "Fasting." In *The Encyclopaedia of Religion*, edited by Mircea Eliade. Vol. 5. New York: Macmillan, 1987, 286–90.

Rahabi, Yechezkel. "Letter of 1768." *Ha-Meassef* 2/6 (1790): 129–60, 257–76.

Rawlinson, Hugh George. *Intercourse between India and the Western World: From the Earliest Times to the Fall of Rome*. Cambridge: Cambridge University Press, 1926.

Reinman, Shlomo. "Masa'oth Shlomo b'Kogin." In *Mi Kotsin l'Ertez Yisrael*, edited by Shalva Weil. Jerusalem: Kumu Brinah, 1984, 31–39.

Rejwan, Nissim. *The Jews of Iraq: 3000 Years of History and Culture*. Boulder, Colo.: Westview Press, 1985.

Reynolds, Holly Baker. "The Auspicious Married Woman." In *The Powers of Tamil Women*, edited by Susan S. Wadley. Syracuse, N.Y.: Syracuse University Maxwell School of Citizenship and Public Affairs, 1980, 35–50.

Rhys-Davids, Thomas William, ed. and trans. *Buddhist Birth Stories; or, Jataka Tales*. London: Trübner, 1880.

Roby [Rahabi], Naphtali Elijah. "Divrei Y'mei HaYehudim b'Cogin," 1911. Manuscript, Sassoon catalogue no. 268, Cochin.

———, ed. *Shirot Tefilah l'Moshe*. N.d. Manuscript, Cochin.

Roland, Joan G. *Jews in British India: Identity in a Colonial Era*. Hanover, N.H.: University Press of New England, 1989.

———. "Indian-Jewish Identity of the Bene Israel during the British Raj." In *Studies of Indian Jewish Identity,* edited by Nathan Katz. New Delhi: Manohar, 1995, 117–131.

Roth, Cecil. *The Sassoon Dynasty.* London: Robert Hale, 1941; reprint New York: Arno Press, 1977.

Rowlandson, M. J., trans. *Tohfut-ul-mujahideen: An Historical Work in the Arabic Language, by Zain al-Din (Zeen-ul-Deen).* London: Oriental Translation Fund, 1833.

Rushdie, Salman. *The Moor's Last Sigh.* New York: Pantheon Books, 1997.

Sachar, Abraham Louis. *A History of the Jews.* 5th ed. New York: Knopf, 1963.

Salem, Avraham Barak. *Eternal Light or Jewtown Synagogue.* Ernakulam, India: Printing Works, 1929. Reprinted as *Cochin Jew Town Synagogue,* Haifa: Eliahu Publishers, 1972.

Samuel, Flora. "The Bene Israel Cradle Ceremony: An Indian Jewish Ritual for the Birth of a Girl." *Bridges* 7/1 (1997/98): 43–44.

Sassoon, David. *Ohel Dawid: Descriptive Catalogue of the Hebrew and Samaritan Manuscripts in the Sassoon Library, London.* 2 vols. London: Humphrey Milford, 1932.

Schmidt, Frances. "Between Jews and Greeks: The Indian Model." In *From Jerusalem to Benares: Comparative Studies in Judaism and Hinduism,* edited by Hananya Goodman. Albany: State University of New York Press, 1994, 41–53.

Schneerson, Menachem Mendel. *Haggadah for Pesach, with an Anthology of Reasons and Customs.* Translated by Jacob Immanuel Schochet. Brooklyn: Qehot, 1985.

Scott, Wilfried, ed. and trans. *The Periplus of the Erythrean Sea.* London: Green, 1912.

Segal, J. B. "The Jews of Cochin and their Neighbors." In *Essays Presented to Chief Rabbi Israel Brodie on the Occasion of His Seventieth Birthday,* edited by H. J. Zimmels, J. Rabinowitz, and I. Feinstein. Jews' College Publications n.s., no. 3. London: Soncino Press, 1967, 381–91.

———. "White and Black Jews at Cochin: The Story of a Controversy." *Journal of the Royal Asiatic Society* 2 (1983): 228ff.

———. *A History of the Jews of Cochin.* London: Vallentine Mitchell, 1993.

Silliman, Jael. "Crossing Borders, Maintaining Boundaries: The Life and Times of Farha, a Woman of the Baghdadi Jewish Diaspora, 1870–1958." *Journal of Indo-Judaic Studies* 1 (1999): 57–79.

Simon, A. I. "The Songs of the Jews of Cochin and Their Historical Significance." *Bulletin of the Rama Varma Research Institute* 13 (1947).

Slapak, Orpa, ed. *The Jews of India: A Story of Three Communities.* Jerusalem: Israel Museum, 1995.

Solomon, Sally. *Hooghly Tales: Stories of Growing Up in Calcutta under the Raj.* London: David Ashley Publishing, 1998.

Sommer, Allison Kaplan. "Indian Jews Fight for Recognition." *Jerusalem Post International,* 6 December 1997.

Srinivas, M. N. *Religion and Society among the Coorgs of South India.* Bombay: Asia Publishing House, 1965.

Sternbach, Ludwik. "India as Described by Medieval European Travellers: Jewish Dwelling Places." *Bharatiya Vidya,* n.s. 7/1–2 (1946): 10–28.

Stillman, Norman A. *The Jews of Arab Lands: A History and Source Book.* Philadelphia: Jewish Publication Society, 1979.

Strizower, Schifra. "Jews as an Indian Caste." *Jewish Journal of Sociology* 1/1 (1959): 43–57.

———. *The Bene Israel of Bombay: A Study of a Jewish Community.* New York: Schocken Books, 1971.

Swiderski, Richard Michael. *Blood Weddings: The Knanaya Christians of Kerala.* Madras: New Era Publications, 1988.

Tarabout, Gilles. *Sacrificier et donner à voir en pays Malabar.* Paris: École Française d'Extrême Orient, 1986.

Thomas, P. J. "The South Indian Tradition of the Apostle Thomas." *Journal of the Royal Asiatic Society of Great Britain and Ireland* (1924): 213–23.

———. "Roman Trade Centers in Malabar." *Kerala Society Papers* 2/10 (1932): 259–70.

Timberg, Thomas A. "The Jews of Calcutta." In *Jews of India,* edited by Thomas A. Timberg. New Delhi: Vikas, 1986, 28–47.

———. "Indigenous and Non-Indigenous Jews." In *Studies of Indian Jewish Identity,* edited by Nathan Katz. New Delhi: Manohar, 1995. 135–52.

———, ed. *Jews in India.* New Delhi, Vikas, 1986.

Tinker, Hugh. "Review of Strizower." *Race* 13 (1971): 81–84.

Turner, Victor W. *The Ritual Process: Structure and Anti-Structure.* Ithaca, N.Y.: Cornell University Press, 1977.

Vellian, Jakob. "The Jewish Christian Community of India." *Judaism* 20/1 (1971): 104–7.

Wadley, Susan S., ed. *The Powers of Tamil Women.* Syracuse, N.Y.: Syracuse University Maxwell School of Citizenship and Public Affairs, 1980.

Weil, Shalva. "Bene Israel Indian Jews in Lod, Israel: A Study of the Persistence of Ethnicity and Ethnic Identity." D.Phil. thesis, University of Sussex, 1977.

———. "Symmetry between Christians and Jews in Kerala: The Cnanite Christians and the Cochin Jews of Kerala." In *Jews in India,* edited by Thomas A Timberg. New Delihi: Vikas,1986, 177–204.

———, ed. *Mi Kotsin l'Ertez Yisrael* [From Cochin to the Land of Israel]. Jerusalem: Kumu Brinah, 1984.

Werblowsky, Zwi. "Bene Israel Battle." *Jewish Chronicle,* 16 March 1962, 1, 40.

Wheeler, Sir Mortimer. *The Indus Civilization.* 3rd ed. Cambridge: Cambridge University Press, 1968.

Whitehead, Henry. *The Village Gods of South India.* Calcutta: Association Press (YMCA), 1921.

Whiteway, R. S. *The Rise of Portuguese Power in India, 1497–1550.* New York: Augustus M. Kelley, 1899.

Whiting, Robert. *You Gotta Have Wa.* New York: Vintage Books, 1990.

Wolpert, Stanley. *A New History of India.* 4th ed. New York: Oxford University Press, 1993.

Zalman, Schneur, comp. *Shulchan 'Arukh Orech Chayyim.* 4 vols. Brooklyn: Quhot, 1985.

Index

acculturation, 3, 9–10, 87–88, 91, 106, 161, 164; distinguished from assimilation, 3, 10, 91, 161
Acts of Thomas, 17, 19
Adeni, Eliahu, 52
Ahmedabad, 121, 164
al-Din, Shaikh al-Mabari Zain, 20–21
Alibag, 93, 102, 121
Amsterdam, 26, 49, 63, 139, 163
ancient world, 20, 26, 27–30
Anglo-Indians, 129, 130, 131, 151, 155, 156, 157, 162
Anjuvannam (Ancuvannam), 13, 33, 34–35
anti-Semitism, 4, 16, 26, 57, 163
Arakie, Eleazar, 145–146
Aristotle, 29
Armenians, 129, 130, 131, 132, 140, 150, 155, 167n2
Ashkenazi, Isaac, 78
assimilation, 3, 9–10, 26, 91, 153, 161, 162, 164
Azar, Joseph, 15, 38–39, 50

Bar-Giora, Naphtali, 45
Bene Israel: origin legend, 2, 93, 124, 162; Jewishness of, 99, 100, 124, 151, 152, 153
Benjamin, Israel Joseph, 151
Benjamin of Tudela, 30–31
Beta Yisrael Jews (of Ethiopia), 75, 124

Beth-El Synagogue (Calcutta), 133, 142; photograph, 134
Beth-El Synagogue (Rangoon), 154
Bhaskara Ravi Varman, 21, 25, 34, 35, 64
British, 15, 26, 54, 55, 57, 64, 66–67, 90, 91, 95, 100, 101, 120, 123, 124, 126, 129, 130, 131, 133, 136, 137, 139, 141, 142, 143, 144–145, 146, 147, 149–150, 151, 152, 155, 156, 157, 158, 162, 167n2
Burnell, A. C., 33

Cairo *geniza,* 31–32
Calicut, 21, 32, 55; zamorin of, 21, 37, 39, 50, 51, 52
caste system, 59–69, 70, 71, 73, 87, 98–99; Jews and, 59–69, 70–71, 72, 73–81, 88, 98–99, 100, 101, 151, 153
Castro, Rabbi Jacob de, 61–62
Chatterjee, Margaret, 167n7
Chendamangalam, 32, 37; photograph, 66
Cheraman Perumal, 13, 14, 16, 18, 19, 21, 22, 23, 33–35, 39, 50, 71, 72, 88, 170n35
Chinese Jews, 3, 5, 31, 157
Chitpavan (brahmin caste of Maharashtra), 93
Christian missionaries, 91, 93, 95, 122, 146, 162

Christians (Indian), 3, 7, 11, 13, 17, 22, 23, 25, 33, 47, 53, 54–55, 63, 78, 164, 167n2; origin legend, 11, 16–20; relations with Jews, 10, 33, 38, 78. *See also* Nazaranee Mapillas
Cochangadi, 38
Cochin, Maharaja of, 13, 14, 15, 16, 21, 37, 39, 40, 48, 50, 51, 55, 57, 66, 72; photograph, 16
Cochin Synagogue, 9, 13, 15, 33, 36, 40–42, 46, 47, 49, 53, 56–58, 60, 65, 66, 68, 72, 82, 87, 128, 163, 164; construction of, 14, 38, 39–40, 72; photographs of, 16, 38, 39, 41, 43, 44, 58, 83; quartercentenary celebrations, 11, 12, 16, 56–58, 163
Cohen, Rev. E. M. D., 147
Cohen, Jackie, 47
Cohen, Jacob, 36, 46, 77, 80–81
Cohen, Sarah, 9, 10, 74, 75, 77, 78, 79, 91
Cohen, Sassoon "Sunny," 47
Cohen, Shalom: photograph, 43
Cohen, Yaakob Daniel, 46, 86
communist government (of Kerala), 71
Cooper, Judith Elias, 133, 148, 149
copper plates, 13, 16, 19, 21, 22–23, 33–35, 37, 45; photograph of, 34; translation of, 34–35
Courter, Gay, 6
Cranganore (Kodungallur, Muziris), 11, 13, 14, 17, 18, 20, 21, 29, 30, 32, 33, 35, 37, 38, 47, 49, 50, 64, 71, 72, 84, 85, 88. *See also* Shingly

Daniel, Ruby, 6
David, Esther, 6
Desai, Anita, 6
Divekar, Samuel Ezekiel (Samaji Hassaji), 120
Dumont, Louis, 80
Dutch, 21, 26, 38, 48, 49, 50–51, 55, 167n2
Dutch East India Company, 48, 50, 52
Dwek, Moses, 132–133, 135

Eliahu Hanabi (Elijah the Prophet), 101–105, 107–108, 109, 110, 112–113, 122, 135
Elias, Flower, 133, 148, 149
Ernakulam, 49, 55, 67, 81, 84
Ezra, Abraham Meir ibn, 30
Ezra, Esmond D., 6, 144, 149, 150
Ezra Hasopher (Ezra the Scribe), 135; shrine of (El-Ozeir, Iraq), 135

Fischel, Walter J., 48, 49

Gadkar, E. M. Jacob, 107
Gama, Vasco da, 38
Gandhi, Indira, 12, 45, 57, 164; photograph, 58
Gandhi, Mohandas K. ("Mahatma"), 67, 123, 124
Gaster, Rabbi Dr. Moses, 145, 153
Ghosh, Amitav, 6
Goa, 26, 50, 164
Goitein, Solomon D., 32
Goldberg, Ellen S., 6
Goodman, Hananya, 167n7
Gora/Kala subcastes, 99–100, 153, 176n33, 182n74
Greenbaum, Rabbi Aaron, 46

Ha'am, Ahad, 96
Hakohen, Shalom Obadiah, 130–136, 150
Halachah (Judaic law), 5, 10, 32, 38, 59, 60, 61, 62, 64, 66, 70, 71, 73, 74, 75, 88, 91, 96, 123, 124, 128, 151, 162
Hallegua, I. C., 80
Hallegua, Queenie, 76
Hallegua, Samuel, 80–81
Hallegua, Yosef, 77; photograph, 83
Hayyim, Chacham Joseph, 145
"Hebrewization," 100, 121, 122
Hertz, Rabbi Dr. Naphtali, 145
Hillel, David D'Beth, 63, 121
Hindu-Jewish parallels: dietary codes, 72, 73–81, 98; family purity, 72, 124; philosophy, 90–91; ritual behavior, 40, 42, 54, 69–88, 101, 103, 104, 106, 108, 110–111, 112, 115, 118, 119; ritual language, 72, 100; "saint" veneration, 54; women's religious life, 54–55, 103, 110–111, 112, 115, 118
Hindu-Jewish relations: in Cochin, 9–10, 14, 23, 32, 35, 36, 38, 40, 57, 91; in Bombay and Calcutta, 90–91, 96, 106, 109, 153, 158–159, 162
Hindus, 11, 13, 17, 40, 42, 47, 48, 53, 54, 58, 78, 101, 103, 105, 116, 126, 129, 142, 152, 156, 164; origin legend, 11, 23–25, 91; relations with Muslims, 20, 21, 23, 53, 121, 151; tolerance, 9, 10, 24–25, 55, 57–58, 60, 88, 161, 164
Holdrege, Barbara A., 167n7
Holi festival, 75, 85, 108
Hyman, Mavis, 6, 133, 147, 149

Ibn Battuta, 32
Indian independence, 12, 56, 129, 158, 163
Indo-Judaic Studies, 6, 167–168n7; *Journal of Indo-Judaic Studies,* 167
Indus Valley Civilization, 20, 27
Inquisition, 26
Isenberg, Shirley Berry, 6, 109
Israel, Benjamin J., 94, 120, 163
Israel Museum, 6, 165
Israeli independence, 56–57, 129, 163

Jacob, Gen. Frederick, 164
Jain, Jainism, 77, 78, 79, 80, 81
JDC (Joint Distribution Committee), 145
Johnson, Barbara C., 6, 75
Josephus, 26, 29–30
Jussay, P. M., 80

Kadoorie, Sir Elie, 145
kaji, 97, 118, 121
Kamenetz, Rodger, 168n7
Karachi, 117, 121
Karaites, 124
kashrut, 70, 71, 72, 73, 77, 96, 98, 132, 141, 151
Kehimkar, Haeem Samuel, 98, 107, 108, 109–110, 115–116, 121, 123
Kenesseth Eliyahoo Synagogue (Bombay), 139, 150; photograph, 140
Keralolpatti, 21, 24, 170n35
Khandala, 102, 104, 107; photograph, 104
Khona, D. B. "Bapusait," 78, 80, 81
Knayi Thomen, 18
Koder, Cecil, 85
Koder, Elias, 80
Koder, Sattu, 15–16, 45, 46, 47, 86; and Gladys, 78; photographs, 16, 58
Krishna, 14, 40, 69, 87, 108, 112

Lévi-Strauss, Claude, 25–26
Lord, Rev. J. Henry, 93, 122–123

Maghen David Synagogue (Bombay), 139, 150
Maghen David Synagogue (Calcutta), 133, 164
Maghen Hassidim Synagogue (Bombay), 90
Maimonides (the Rambam), 31, 33, 92, 95, 117
Mala, 37

Malabari Jews, 14, 65; rivalry with Paradesis, 14, 63, 65
malida rite, 101–105, 107, 108, 109, 110, 114, 118, 178n71; photograph, 104
Mandelbaum, David, 62, 68, 71, 85
Manu, 69
Manushastra, 3–4
Marco Polo, 32
Marwaris, 129, 130, 132
Mattancheri, 13, 14, 37, 39
meshuchrarim, 14, 65–69, 71–72, 153
Meyer, Maisie, 156–157
miqveh (ritual bath), 19, 36, 47, 118, 122, 129, 139
Mishneh Torah (Code of Maimonides), 31, 33, 92
Moens, Gov. Adriaan, 38
Mori, Moshe ben Abba, 85–86
Mota, Nehemia, 52–54, 135
Mountbatten, Lord, 45
mudaliar, 38, 47–55
Musleah, Rabbi Ezekiel N., 6, 146, 155
Muslims, 7, 11, 13, 17, 22, 23, 25, 37, 39, 42, 47, 48, 53, 54–55, 63, 78, 92, 101, 102, 103, 104–105, 107, 119, 121, 123, 126, 142, 152, 156, 164; origin legend, 11, 20–22; relations with Hindus, 20, 21, 23, 151; relations with Jews, 10, 38, 78, 92, 109, 162
Musmeah Yeshua Synagogue (Rangoon), 154
Mutiny of 1857, 129, 130, 136, 142–143, 151, 152, 162

Nahoum family, 148–149, 158–159
Nambudiris (brahmin caste in Kerala), 10, 19, 42, 69, 72, 73, 167n2
Navgaon (Nawgaon), 93
Narayanan, M. G. S., 23, 25, 34–35
Nayars, 10, 13, 16, 22, 24, 35, 69–70, 72, 73, 81–88, 167n2
Nazaranee Mapillas, 18–20, 167n2
Nazism, 129, 157–158
Neveh Shalom Synagogue (Calcutta), 133, 146
New Delhi, 12, 121, 142, 164
Nissim ben Reuben, Rabbi, 21, 32
North Parur (Parur), 15, 20, 33, 37, 40

Ohel David Synagogue (Pune), 126, 139; photograph, 127
opium, 132, 139, 140
ORT (Organization for Rehabilitation and Training), 145
Orta, Garcia de, 139

Paiva, Moses Perreira de, 49–50, 63, 163
Panvel, 121
Parashurama, 24–25
Parasuram, T. V., 51
Pen, 100, 121
Perumpadappu Swarupam, 39, 87, 167n2
Portuguese, 13, 14, 15, 20, 21, 25, 26, 32, 37, 38, 48, 49, 130, 131, 139, 150, 164, 167n2
priesthood (Jewish; *kohen, kohanim*), 1–2, 18, 42, 70, 76, 77, 106–107, 114, 126–128, 151; and DNA, 2, 175n6; parallels with Hindu priesthood, 42, 70, 76
Pune, 121, 126, 127, 128, 139, 164

Quilon (Chulam, Kollan), 21, 30, 33

Rabban, Joseph, 13, 14, 15, 21, 25, 33–35, 36–37, 47, 50, 64, 88
Rabin, Chaim, 27
Radanites, 30
Rahabi (Raby), House of, 50, 72; David, 49, 50, 94, 96, 98, 102, 107, 120; Naphtali, 50; portrait, 51; Yechezkel, 46, 50, 51–52, 91, 97
reference groups, 3, 10, 11, 94–96, 100, 122, 129, 130, 139, 167n2
Reuben, Rebecca, 102
Reubeni, David, 32
Revdanda, 94, 121
Roland, Joan G., 6, 95, 150–151, 152, 156
Rushdie, Salman, 6

Salem, Avraham Barak, 67–69
Salem, Gamliel, 54, 77
Salem, Raymond, 59, 69
Salem, Reema, 78
Samuel, Flora, 112
Sanskritization, 100, 124
Sartorius, Rev. J. A., 92–93, 97
Sassoon, House of, 56, 132, 139, 140, 152, 153; Abdullah (Albert), 140–141, 145; David, Shaikh, 126, 130, 139, 140, 142, 145, 151, 152, 153 (statue of, 138); Elias David, 141; Flora, 141; Jacob, 139, 145, 153; Solomon, 141
Segal, J. B., 6

Selaisse, Haile, 45
Semah, Jacob, 132, 136–137
Sephardic Jews, 14, 38, 42, 52, 53, 62, 63, 105, 124, 126, 135, 156–157; rites of, 45, 52, 53, 105, 122
Sha'ar Harahamim (Samaji Hassaji Synagogue), 107, 120–121
Shilappadikaram, 35
Shingli Machazor, 49, 53
Shingly, 11, 12–13, 14, 16, 22, 26, 29, 30, 32, 35, 36, 38, 84, 85–86; parallels with Jerusalem, 14, 17, 22, 36–37, 88. *See also* Cranganore
Sitali (Devi), 100, 115
Slapak, Orpa, 6
Solomon, King, 13, 17, 27, 28, 46
Solomon, Solly, 6
Sri Lanka (Ceylon), 21, 31, 149
Srinivas, M. N., 100
Succath Shelomo Synagogue (Pune), 126
Surat, 55, 93, 128, 131, 132, 137
Swaraj, 27, 95, 123–124, 156, 162, 164

Talmud, 26, 28, 31
Tashlich: among Bene Israel, 105–106
ten lost tribes, 31, 93, 151, 163
Thane, 121
Thomas, Apostle, 17–20, 22
Tibetans, 3, 31, 45
Tifereth Israel Synagogue (Bombay), 97
Timberg, Thomas A., 6, 150
Tinker, Hugh, 99
Tohfut-ul-Mujahideen, 20
Travancore, 15, 18, 38, 55, 67; maharajah of, 15, 21, 45, 51

Upanishads, 90

Vishnu, 24
Vishu (Kerala Hindu festival), 77

Warulkar, Yakobeth, 100
Weil, Shalva, 19, 101, 102
Whitehead, Rev. Henry, 53–54
Wolpert, Stanley, 142–143
women, role of: among Baghdadis, 135; in Bene Israel Judaism, 102–103, 106, 109–120, 122; in Cochin Judaism, 42, 45–46, 53–54, 72–73, 75, 76, 78, 82, 84, 85, 173n150

Yemen (Aden), Yemenite Jews, 2, 15, 31,
    37, 52, 53, 63, 64, 75, 108, 129, 130,
    133, 135
yichus: twofold, 11, 16, 17, 33, 35, 59,
    64, 88; from ancient Israel (meyucha-
    sim), 14, 60, 61, 72, 163; and me-
    shuchrarim, 14, 59–69

Zimra, Rabbi David ben Solomon ibn,
    32, 61–62
Zionism, 27, 57, 95, 100, 122, 123–124,
    129, 152, 156, 158, 162
Zoroastrians (Parsis), 3, 7, 78, 123, 129–
    130, 139–140, 155, 167n2

Text: 10/13 Sabon
Display: Sabon
Composition: G&S Typesetters
Printing and binding: Edwards Brothers